THE GLOBAL LEADER

LEADER

Critical Factors for Creating the World Class Organization

THE GLOBAL LEADER

Critical Factors for Creating the World Class Organization

TERENCE BRAKE

IRWIN
Professional Publishing®
Chicago • London • Singapore

**Times Mirror
Higher Education Group**

Library of Congress Cataloging-in-Publication Data

Brake, Terence
    The global leader : critical factors for creating the world class
organization/ Terence Brake.
        p.   cm.
    Includes index.
    ISBN 0-7863-0821-4
    1. Leadership.   2. International business enterprises--Management.
I. Title.
HD57.7.B727   1997
658'.049--dc20   96–34765

Printed in the United States of America
1 2 3 4 5 6 7 8 9 0 DOC 3 2 1 0 9 8 7 6

FOREWORD

I was making a presentation to a leading U.S. corporation which was paying a visit to the INSEAD business school and in particular to its research and executive education resource for the Asia Pacific region, the Euro-Asia Centre. The corporation was having a tough time trying to negotiate a joint venture in Japan. My next slide contained the words, "The Yes which means Yes and the Yes which means No."

At that moment, the CEO leaped to his feet and exclaimed: "Godammit, that's the . . . problem! So how do you know?"

I think he was a little disappointed that I could not give him a pocket guide to negotiating with the Japanese, but we have worked together since as this company has moved from a domestic U.S. corporation to a global firm,, involved across Europe, in China, India, and Southeast Asia.

Had this book been available at that time, I am sure I would have recommended it. Let me explain a little why.

Every day, we experience, hear about, or read about another example of greater and greater links between the countries of the world. Whether it is the cars we drive, the TV we watch, the internet we surf, or the business we pursue, more and more we mix, match, and compete on a global scale.

In the business environment, change is constantly under discussion. Why? Is this just the latest theory, that organizations have got to keep shuffling the deck all the time? Not a bit. If you were a smalltown grocer competing with a guy across the street, you could keep tabs on what he was doing, and you know your customers by firstname. Global business means competing with anyone, anywhere—and often you can't even pronounce your customers' names.

To say that this kind of business leadership requires new sets of skills is a gross understatement. It requires the ability to constantly acquire new skills. It requires the openness to say "what worked yesterday, won't work today and probably won't work tomorrow." It requires managing and communicating that attitude at the human level right through to even the largest corporations. That's what change means.

I like this book by Terence Brake because it reaches from the broad organizational issues right down to the personal skills of individual executives. This book is very much about people for people. There are things to do for each reader personally in each chapter. It's the theory and the practice which you normally only get sitting in class working on case studies.

I like this book, too, because it is as relevant to the guy sitting in head office wondering what is happening to the China joint venture as it is to the poor devils trying to manage that operation! An, finally, I like this book because it addresses leadership not just as something the people at the top ought to do, but really stresses how success is built on competent people, in responsive organizations, who are prepared to take leadership as part of their own daily working responsibility.

I hope some of you reading the book will say to yourselves, "Why, this is obvious . . . of course . . ." Then you'll know that the message is getting across. I have a presentation on international management titled "Principles So Obvious They Are Usually Overlooked." It's so easy to fall into the trap of thinking you know it all and then ignoring it.

My last words of introduction concern how much richer global leadership makes working life. Companies and executives that are successful either in working with, or actually in, different cultures from their own origins, normally are more successful at the domestic level too. Why? Because they develop that most important characteristic in business: sensitivity. They accept less at face value and search out more for the deeper truth. They start to understand market like never before. They work in teams which become much greater than the sum of the parts. They respond through knowledge and understanding, rather than through gut reaction. In leading, they earn respect.

But don't just take my word for it. It's all here in this excellent book.

Kenneth Smith
Executive Committee, INSEAD, Fontainebleau, France

PREFACE

You'd better get your passports up to date if you want to keep up with us.

Edward E. Hagenlocker, president of Ford Automotive Operations

THE FOCUS

Global competitiveness may have become a cliché, but that doesn't make it any the less real or easier to achieve and sustain. *The Global Leader* addresses one of the critical success factors for winning in this new business environment: a company's ability to build global leadership bench strength in its organization, that is, the development of leaders at multiple levels in the company who

- Grasp the challenges and opportunities of the global marketplace.
- Generate and channel the personal and organizational energies needed to attack global challenges and opportunities.
- Transform those energies into world-class performance.

This book is not about the specifics of preparing to go on an international assignment or learning the do's and taboos of particular cultures, although references to these issues are scattered throughout the book. Those issues are important, but numerous other texts can better meet your needs in those areas. Above all else, this book addresses three major questions:

- In what kind of environment do global leaders need to operate?
- What are the key competencies global leaders need to be successful in this new environment?
- How do we build companies that develop global leadership resources to their fullest potential?

THE NEED

Despite the cries from some political quarters for "an American economy for Americans," the global economy continues to put down roots. A growing world middle-class with heavy buying power and a taste for consumerism is increasing demand for quality goods and services, particularly in the 10 biggest emerging markets of China, Indonesia, India, South Korea, Turkey, South Africa, Poland, Argentina, Brazil, and Mexico. Government policies of deregulation, privatization, and open trade, combined with the reach of communications technologies into homes across the globe, have raised material expectations and sparked a revolutionary demand for everything from banking services and razors to cognac and TVs. Personal consumption is now *the raison d'être* of a large portion of the world's population. The graffiti artist who left the following message on a remnant of the Berlin Wall in 1989 says it all: "We came, we saw, and we shopped a while." The voracious global genie is truly out of the bottle.

To move into high competitive gear, American business needs men and women who have the vision and capabilities to lead companies that have traditionally focused on the large and increasingly saturated domestic marketplace. This new breed of men and women will thrive on the adventure of change, and their curiosity and spirit will lead them to seek out and overcome challenges on the new frontiers of global business. Chrysler CEO Robert Eaton knows these people are hard to find. He can't find enough people to expand as fast as he wants into global markets. In an interview with *Fortune,* he said, "For the first time in Chrysler's recent history we have the capital available, but we don't have enough engineers and managers to grow any faster abroad than we currently are, which is about 20 percent a year."[1]

Unfortunately, one of the disturbing practices of American business over the last decade or so has been its wasteful inability to capitalize on international learning and expertise. One example should be enough to capture an all too familiar occurrence. At the end of a visit to a client in Chicago, I stepped into a car to take me to O'Hare Airport. Being an off-the-scale introvert, I was somewhat dismayed to find I was sharing the ride. My companion turned out to be a very bright, young manager who had just returned from a three-year assignment in Belgium. I asked him what he was doing now. "Well, that's an interesting question," he said. "They've put me in a conference room with a PC and told me that I had better write my résumé because they don't have a position for me." The same old story! No planning ahead on the part of the organization. No concern with capturing the learning of those years in Europe. Just more bad feelings that no doubt spilled over to others considering an international assignment. Yet more dilution of global strengths.

---

[1]Marshall Loab, "Empowerment That Pays Off," *Fortune,* March 20, 1995, p. 145.

While the above situation has been all too familiar, it is changing rapidly. Increasingly, senior executives are recognizing the importance of developing core competencies that support both the formation and implementation of global strategies. Top management needs to clearly understand that defensive cost-cutting strategies, reengineering, and other realignment initiatives are only part of the successful business equation. Growth also needs to be integrated into the business puzzle, and increasingly that growth will come from either radical innovation, the international arena, or more likely both. A Conference Board survey of 1,250 manufacturers made it very clear that sustained growth and profitability are highly dependent on a broad base of international operations.[2] More specifically, "Corporations—in all size categories and industries—that had global activities grew at significantly faster rates; sales figures for those companies without foreign activities grew at *half* the survey average."

In this environment, nothing will slow down a globalizing company faster than individuals trapped in parochial mindsets and skill portfolios tested only in domestic waters. The race to develop global leaders is on.

As this realization hits home, many companies are looking to find and develop people who can transfer their skills across borders. Taking a global assignment is becoming the passport to higher levels within organizations. In 1995, 28 percent of the searches to fill senior-level positions at major corporations had *international experience* as a requirement.[3] This number was up from 4 percent in 1990.

Another Conference Board project surveyed 130 multinational companies from the United States, Asia, and Europe about their recruitment and selection of international managers.[4] While the recruitment of people is difficult (largely because of the skepticism and fear generated by the type of repatriation problems experienced by my expat friend in Chicago), those surveyed were actively promoting internationalism in their ranks. About half of the companies had more than 50 executives serving abroad, and 25 percent had between 200 and 2,000. But a word of warning: Sending a select few executives and managers abroad is only the tip of the global leadership iceberg. To maximize their potential collective intelligence, global

[2]Charles Taylor and Gail D. Fosler, "The Necessity of Being Global," *Across the Board,* February 1994, pp. 40–43.

[3]Joann S. Lublin, "An Overseas Stint Can Be a Ticket to the Top," *The Wall Street Journal,* January 29, 1996, p. B1.

[4]David A. Weeks, *Recruiting and Selecting International Managers,* Report Number 998, New York: The Conference Board, 1992.

companies need to grow and develop global leadership qualities at multiple levels within the organization. Global leadership is about more than having international experience; it is also about understanding how to operate successfully in a complex and dynamic global organization.

THE AUDIENCE

If you have picked up this book, you are probably on the cutting edge (or is it the "bleeding edge"?) of globalization. You may be a senior executive looking for ideas about how to become a better leader in your globalizing company. Or you might want thoughts from practitioners on how best to foster the development of global leaders throughout your organization to go head to head with your competitors. You might be a cosmopolitan manager browsing through books in an airport store, wondering if there is anything on the shelf that will help you extend the range of your global leadership skills. On the other hand, you might be a human resources professional looking for insights into the personal and professional capabilities global business leaders need in selecting and developing those men and women who will lead your company into the global century. Alternatively, you might be a student thinking about making a career in the challenging but rewarding field of international business. Then again, you could be a general reader who wants to find out more about the transformation of our planet into World Inc. If any of these issues are of interest, you will find material in this book that touches on your needs.

THE APPROACH

What is a global business leader, and what kind of company promotes his or her growth and development? In searching for answers, several approaches were taken.

First came a review of the extensive literature on global business issues. Out of this review came a framework for thinking about global competitiveness at the organizational level as well as insights into the factors that make for individual success when working across geographic, cultural, and functional borders.

Second, interviews were conducted with practitioners from a number of leading global companies, including Avon, Bechtel, Colgate-Palmolive, Hughes Electronics, International Flavors and Fragrances (IFF), and NYNEX. The purpose of these interviews was to gain practical insights from the front lines of globalization. What assumptions are being made? What questions are being asked? What decisions are being taken?

The overall result is a snapshot of what many minds think about the development of global business leaders in the late 20th century.

Chapter 1: Leading in the World-Class Organization

This chapter sets the stage by examining the key characteristics of world-class organizations and the critical role distributed global leadership plays in building and sustaining competitiveness. We are not talking about leadership as a position to be attained. Beyond position and title, leadership is mindset, a way of *being* in the world. Global leaders, whatever their level in the organization, take accountability for identifying global challenges and opportunities, energizing their circles of influence and forming collaborative networks, and driving toward performance that is better than the best in the world.

Chapter 2: Global Leadership Capabilities

This chapter presents a model of global leadership competencies called the Global Leadership Triad and explores how many of these competencies play out in the real world of global management. The model consists of three competency clusters: business acumen, relationship management, and personal effectiveness. Business acumen is the ability to pursue and apply appropriate professional knowledge and skills to achieve optimal results for the company's stakeholders. Relationship management is the ability to build and influence cooperative relationships in a complex and diverse global network to direct energy toward the achievement of business strategies. Personal effectiveness is the ability to attain increasing levels of maturity to perform at peak levels under the strenuous conditions of working in a global enterprise. A major challenge for global individuals is to commit to lifelong learning in all three competency clusters.

Chapter 3: Leadership in a Collaborative Global Enterprise

This chapter examines the collaborative nature of global organizations and highlights four factors senior managers need to address to make collaboration a reality: global role analysis and competency development, global context building, global value clarification, and global skill development.

The chapter presents a model, called the global leadership spectrum, that highlights global leadership competency needs within four bands: individual associate, first-line manager, middle manager, and senior manager. To help leaders perform their global roles within these bands and to facilitate collaboration, organizations need to help individuals understand the global and organizational contexts in which they work, clarify their values, and promote collaborative skill development.

Chapter 4: Building the Global Leadership System

This chapter overviews the approaches taken to developing global leaders in several major companies: Avon, Bechtel, Colgate-Palmolive, Hughes Electronics, and NYNEX. Maximizing the collective intelligence of the organization requires a commitment to systematic organizational change. A generic model of an organizational system is presented to frame the discussion. Items discussed include strategy, competencies, culture, architecture, and performance systems such as selection, education and training, compensation, and career development. Without the development of such systems, globalization is likely to remain an abstraction at best and a very tempting, easy target for cynicism at worst.

Chapter 5: Toward a Culture of Possibility

This chapter highlights the importance of building a competitive global leadership culture that expands the *zone of possibility* and is not simply a "glue" holding the scattered organization together or a zone of familiarity (habitual beliefs, norms, etc.). Such cultures aim to shift their *modus operandi* from command and control to committed engagement. In creating a leadership culture, we must plan an attack on those individual and organizational forces that inhibit engagement: denial, homeostasis, limiting beliefs, scattered energy, manipulation, and alienation. Within a global leadership culture, individuals engage in a process of facing reality, committing to growth, adopting transformational beliefs, focusing energies, relating to others, and engaging with purpose. In making our attack upon traditionally passive cultures, we move through a process of disturbing the present, surfacing obstacles, challenging obstacles, creating new expectations, and integrating new expectations.

WHAT MATTERS? A PERSONAL NOTE

On one level, this book is about what it takes for a company to be successful in a global business environment. On another level, this book is more personal and driven by beliefs about what matters in a global business environment.

First, *business matters*. Business at its best is a moral act. It is *the* vehicle for creating wealth, and only by creating and distributing wealth can we confront poverty and the social disintegration it fosters. Anyone who comes from a poor background knows there is nothing ennobling about poverty. It eats away at the spirit as well as the body. It frames the mind with artificial boundaries of what is real and possible.

While the creation of wealth undoubtedly causes other problems, particularly in relation to the environment, let us not forget that a large portion of the world's population is still struggling to emerge from a survival state of being, if that! By being leaders in global business organizations, we can contribute to enhancing the quality of life of numerous others. At its worst, globalization can degenerate into an extension of the old colonialist mindset that grabs opportunities for personal, corporate, and national gain at a tremendous cost to others. At its best, globalization is an opportunity to release ingenuity and imagination in the pursuit of prosperity, liberation, and world community. Seeing commerce in a wider context than just the next quarter's results or the latest reengineered process flows is perhaps the first step toward a more rewarding career in business. I hope that readers come away from the book with a deeper sense of purpose and meaning. When we reduce business to a technical rather than a human concern, we not only diminish the role of business, we also diminish ourselves.

Second, *leadership matters*—not just leadership at the top, but leadership throughout organizations and societies. Leaders are the men and women, from boardroom to basement, who take risks to redefine what they and others are capable of becoming. They are the women and men who engage when others disengage, who act when others remain passive, who speak when others are silent. They help us to define our realities and move us into new worlds of possibility and meaning. Above all, they embrace challenge and turn it into energy for further transformation into performance. In a highly competitive global marketplace, leadership needs to be thought of both in terms of assigned role or function (there will always be a need for leadership levels) and more important, in terms of every individual's potential to affect and expand his or her sphere of influence. Unfortunately, in many of our organizations and societies, individual associates often look to others to provide leadership. Operating in corporate bureaucracies and formal hierarchical structures, we can lose touch with our own leadership qualities; we lose our sense of responsibility for making things happen and our accountability for results. Too often, those who could be transforming challenge into performance retreat into learned helplessness and victimization. Leadership is too important to be left to our *formal* leaders. As Keshavan Nair says, "We are all leaders. Each one of us is setting an example for someone else, and each one of us has a responsibility to shape the future as we wish it to be."[5] Ideally, we will start to build corporate cultures that release leadership qualities rather than stifle them.

Third, *expectations matter.* Leaders emerge and thrive in a culture in which the expectation is for everyone to be a leader. When I first came to live and work in the States, I was disappointed at what I felt to be the lower expectation levels (not so much in sports but certainly in intellectual matters). This was particularly the case for my children in school. I can't count the number of times I heard, "We really can't expect them to . . ." I have heard the same in business when developing training programs for managers: "That's really too much of a stretch," "I'm not sure they'll be able to sustain that level of concentration," "Perhaps we should make it more 'idiot-proof,' " If we are to develop global leaders in our organizations, we must establish cultural expectations for global leadership. This means examining the mind barriers we create for our own self-entrapment and the impoverishment of others.

Finally, *action matters.* It is not enough to create models and neat conceptual systems, although these can offer superficial assistance. Only by a deep participation and engagement in all the messy and ambiguous realities of existence do we learn what will work in our given set of circumstances. Very few want to hear that message. The quick fix dominates our thinking. Guiding transformational change in thought and action, however, cannot be accomplished by applying a formula, although our culture drives us endlessly to create the next five-step model for success. Deep participation and engagement is the key.

---

[5]Keshavan Nair, *A Higher Standard of Leadership: Lessons from the Life of Gandhi,* San Francisco: Berrett-Koehler, 1994.

USING THIS BOOK

This book has been designed to help you compete, from an organizational and a personal perspective, in the race for developing global leadership talent. If you are approaching the book from an organizational perspective, you will learn how to think about developing a global leadership system. If you are reading from an individual perspective, you will learn a great deal about what you need to know and do to be an effective leader in our new world. *Some Action Ideas* at the end of each chapter suggest next steps from both the individual and organizational perspectives.

A key characteristic of the emerging organization is that it is built on dialogue rather than monologue. To make this book as useful as possible in promoting dialogue and the generation of ideas, the reader will find *Dialogue Boxes* within the text. Associates within a company may want to read the book at the same time and meet periodically to discuss the issues raised in one or more Dialogue Boxes. This could be done in "brown bag" meetings at lunchtime, during regular staff meetings or retreats, at a global forum, or within team meetings. The dialogue could even take place over e-mail or groupware. Imagination is the only limitation. Mysteriously, the time needed to do this is created when the need is articulated and the imagination engaged. Enjoy the adventure.

Terence Brake
Princeton, New Jersey

ACKNOWLEDGMENTS

This is a book of synthesis rather than raw creativity. I sometimes think there are enough ideas in the world and we just need to spend more time thinking about how to use them effectively.

In creating this synthesis, I have received the support of many people, both directly and indirectly. My grateful thanks go to the following:

♦ Those writers and thinkers who are bringing semicoherence to the chaos of our brave new world: Christopher Bartlett and Sumantra Ghoshal, Rosabeth Moss Kanter, Peter Drucker, Gary Hamel and C. K. Prahalad, Douglas A. Ready, Robert B. Reich, Charles Hampden-Turner, Alfons Trompenaars, Geert Hofstede, George Lodge, Peter Senge, Alvin Toffler, and many others too numerous to mention.

♦ The practitioners in the field who shared their time and numerous practical insights: Eric Campbell, International Flavors and Fragrances; Philip Evans, Avon Products, Inc.; Bettye Hill, Avon Products, Inc.; Paul Kurppe, NYNEX; Donna McNamara, Colgate-Palmolive; Michael Michl, Avon Products, Inc.; Pat Morgan, Bechtel; and Ted Westerman, Hughes Electronics.

♦ Dr. Stephen Rhinesmith for inspiration in the early days of my involvement in the global project.

♦ My good friends at Transnational Management Associates (TMA)—Chris Crosby, Hans van der Linden, and Steve Pritchard—for their interest in and encouragement of my work. Together we can really make a difference.

♦ My friends at Princeton Consultants Incorporated, especially Steve Sashihara, for helping me pay the bills during the writing of this book.

♦ Laurie Quinn for making sense of my pencil scribbles and turning them into graphic art.

♦ Rose Babau for her insightful comments on early drafts.

♦ My friends at Prudential Preferred Financial Services, especially Patricia O'Malley, Paul Cocco, and Dawn McCrea. Thanks for your patience and flexibility, but most of all for allowing me to participate in your efforts to build a new way of being in the workplace. Thanks also to Scotty O'Toole for pointing me in the direction of Margaret Mead.

♦   Michelle Erhlich for her great help in locating sources and materials.

♦ Cynthia Zigmund at Irwin Professional Publishing for her great forbearance.

♦ My father, Ronald Brake, for his hospitality and patience during my frequent trips back to the Old Country.

♦ My good friends and neighbors David Craig, Jocelyn Sisson, and Claudia Eve for the loan of books on ethics. Yes, they will be returned!

♦   My children: Morgan, Sam, and Benjamin. Thank you, Morgan, for leading me into exciting new worlds. Thank you, Sam, for your gift of new beginnings. And thank you, Ben, for your quiet wisdom and humor.

♦   And last, but never least, my beautiful wife (and partner at the movies), Dianne, for her patience and love during long, tedious months when I was lost behind piles of books and papers. I love you.

CONTENTS

CHAPTER 1

Leading in the World-Class Organization

Excellence is all about extending a chain of leadership throughout the organization, from the top to the smallest department and the most junior job. Our objective is to ensure that the company works as a team, integrating our vision and mission with our goals and strategies. We will continue to lead to the extent that we continue to develop our leadership resources.

Sir Colin Marshall, British Airways[1]

Preview

- World-class competitiveness is highly dependent on responsiveness, speed, and adaptability. Only companies that foster leadership at all levels and locations can hope to win over time.

- Being "global" is not an end in itself. It is only one means to being a world-class competitor.

- A global organization pursues integrated organizational strategies to maximize the flow and leverage of resources worldwide to optimize results for the total organization.

- To build and sustain global competitiveness, an organization must develop the six capabilities of strategic focus, momentum, agility, relationships, technology, and spirit.

[1]D. A. Ready, *Champions of Change: A Global Report on Leading Business Transformation,* Lexington, MA: ICEDR/Gemini Consulting, 1994.

◆ To drive toward world-class performance, 10 management practices are recommended: goal stretching, inclusive leadership, proactive measures, best practices, efficiency and effectiveness, continuous innovation, building capabilities, paradox management, intelligence gathering, and acting out.

◆ To maximize effectiveness, companies must work to create a global leadership culture within the organization. The aims of this culture are to drive out leadership passivity in the organization and to promote the use of the collective intelligence of the organization's members.

◆ All global leaders, at whatever level or location, engage in (1) embracing the challenges of global competition, (2) generating organizational energy to meet those challenges, and (3) transforming organizational energy into world-class performance.

DISTRIBUTED GLOBAL LEADERSHIP RESOURCES

Most medium- to large-size companies around the world are going through a period of dramatic change. Ask today's businesspeople about *change* and, after they have rolled their eyes and sighed deeply, they will tell you that they live in "The Age of Re": restructuring, reengineering, reinventing, reframing, revitalizing, and so on. Intense global competition is at the heart of much of this change. Many companies are recognizing their high vulnerability to global competitors.

We are living in the first *global* revolution, and one thing is clear: Organizations that face operating in a world of such complexity and unpredictability need to encourage and support leadership at all levels if they are to be effective. Heavy control from the top is no longer a feasible option in an environment that forces you to run twice as fast just to keep up and be super-responsive to global and local customers and conditions.

This doesn't mean hierarchy has no role in our new organizations. There will always be a need to set overall strategic intent and assume final accountability for results, and someone must make decisions to allocate resources among conflicting demands. Randall Tobias, CEO of Eli Lilly, is right in warning of the dangers of "anarchic empowerment."[2] But one of the great challenges for global organizations is to develop leadership initiative at all levels and locations. Without distributed leadership resources, the global company will never maximize its adaptability, responsiveness, and speed.

Distributed leadership is central to today's military and is developed by use of mission tactics. A senior commander will prescribe the method of execution only to the point necessary for overall coordination of operations. Allowing leaders at local levels to develop their own means for conducting the mission promotes adaptability and speed. Senior business leaders who believe organizations must be run in a military fashion need to make sure they understand what "military" means. The new military is based on maneuverability through multiple levels of leadership with high levels of trust, harmonious initiative, and lateral coordination as keys to winning.[3]

To compete in a world characterized by permanent revolution, we must strip away the vestiges of a past based on traditional military/industrial structures and attitudes. More expansionist thinking patterns that encourage us to look at our companies as open systems, organisms, boundaryless organizations, networks, and energy fields will challenge us to redefine what leaders are, how we work together, and how we generate and sustain high performance.

DIALOGUE BOX

How vulnerable is your company to global competition? Where are your strengths and weaknesses relative to global competitors? Discuss your responses to the following questions:

- *Customers:* Are there factors in the environment that could cause our customers to look elsewhere, such as, deregulation, an influx of new competitors, patent expiration, or innovations developed by others?

- *Competition:* How easy is it for competitors to enter our markets? Are our products and services highly susceptible to replication and substitution?

Continued

---

[2]Ron Ashkenas et al., *The Boundaryless Organization: Breaking the Chains of Organizational Structure,* San Francisco: Jossey-Bass, 1995, p. 56.

[3]General A. M. Gray, *Warfighting,* New York: Doubleday, 1994, p. 92.

Concluded

+ *Competencies:* Do we have core competencies that others (competitors, customers, etc.) would define as world class? How focused is our company on leveraging its core competencies across the organization? To what extent is our company dedicated to continuous improvement of its existing core competencies? Is our company actively engaged in identifying and building those competencies it needs for *future* competitive advantage?

+ *Currency:* Are we sufficiently focused on maximizing efficiencies to generate resources to fund growth opportunities?

+ *Communication:* Are we maximizing the flow of information around the company to promote the transfer of knowledge, skills, and ideas that can generate added value?

+ *Collaboration:* How well do business units/teams in our company work together to create synergy?

+ *Creativity:* Are we doing all we can to release talent in the organization to develop those innovations that will alter the rules of the competitive game in our favor?

BEYOND GLOBAL TO WORLD CLASS

While many companies are looking to become "global," it is important to keep in mind that being global is not an end in itself. It is a means toward being a winning, world-class competitor. Before we discuss the type of leadership needed to build and sustain world-class organizations, we will explore what we mean by *global* and *world class*. This exploration will take us into the drivers of global businesses, the basic capabilities global organizations must nurture, and the management practices that drive an organization toward world-class competitiveness (see Figure 1–1).

Global Organizations: Four Drivers

At a very general level, we can offer the following working definition of a global business:

> Pursuing **integrated** organizational strategies to maximize the **flow** and **leverage** of resources worldwide to **optimize** results for the total organization.

Integrated While a global business organization is composed of many units operating across the world, it needs to be managed as a single entity.

The more traditional multinational organization operated with relatively autonomous units, each one focused on maximizing results within its territory. The problem with such a structure is that the business fragments, produces suboptimal results, and loses potential synergies. Today global companies seek to weave their units into more flexible, weblike structures with a dual focus: local and global. The winning formula at Asea Brown Boveri (ABB) is local presence with global vision.

Continuous dialogue rather than formal control becomes the integrative force in our new organizations. For this dialogue to take place, units need to operate with shared understandings of global business goals, strategies, vision, values, and so on, that is, with a psychological infrastructure.

During an interview, Bettye Hill, director of global education at Avon, pointed to a plastic box full of different-colored beads. "This was a gift from a global group we had been training," she said. "The colored beads represent all the different cultures and peoples in Avon.

FIGURE 1–1

From Global to World Class

Global Drivers	Global Capabilities	World-Class Actions*
Integration	Strategic focus	Goal stretching
Flow	Momentum	Inclusive leadership
Leverage	Agility	Proactive measures
Optimization	Relationships	Best practices
	Technology	Efficiency and effectiveness
	Spirit	Continuous innovation
		Building capabilities
		Paradox management
		Intelligence gathering
		Acting out

© Terence Brake, 1996.
*Adapted from "From Ugly Ducklings to Elegant Swans: Transforming Parochial Firms into World Leaders," in *Business Strategy Review*, Vol. 6, Number 2, Summer 1995.

The plastic box is Avon, the corporation. There can be all these differences in the way you do business, but there is an Avon philosophy, a value system. You can go to any Avon location anywhere in the world and you will notice something about the spirit of the place, something unique. There's a spirit about the people, a connect, a very strong culture that pulls the people together."

At Avon, time and effort are spent on making this happen. It would be easy, for example, to simply create a vision statement for the company and post it on walls around the world. The Avon vision is on the walls, but there is more to it than mere words. Moving beyond simple translation into the local language, Avon management works with local companies to interpret the vision and make it meaningful in terms of the local culture. Part of the vision relates to the self-fulfillment needs of women. But what does that mean in Asia or Latin America? Only through interpretive work in the field does the vision come alive and take on meaning. Only when the meaning is owned locally can people relate their decisions and daily communications to the overall vision of the company.

Flow   To maximize speed and responsiveness to opportunities anywhere in the world, resources (information, innovations, capital, expertise) must be able to flow throughout the organization to wherever they can add most value at any point in time. This means breaking down the "not invented here" syndrome that can put the brakes on product development. In designing the 1999 Escort for sale worldwide, Ford is pulling quality ideas from different parts of the company. The system for redesigning prototype parts was found to be better in the United States, while the procedure for monitoring engineering work arising from warranty claims was more effective in Europe.

Cross-boundary relationships and rapid mobilization are at the heart of new organizations. This requires developing what some call the "boundaryless organization," a concept first pioneered at General Electric. Ashkenas et al. identify four types of boundaries that need to be made permeable:[4]

---

[4]Ashkenas et al., *The Boundaryless Organization*, p. 3.

1. **Vertical:** the boundaries between levels and ranks of people.
2. **Horizontal:** the boundaries between functions and disciplines.
3. **External:** the boundaries between the organization and its suppliers, customers, and regulators.
4. **Geographic:** the boundaries between nations, cultures, and markets.

Leverage The search for efficiencies through standardization (or at least global platforms that can be adapted to local wants and needs) is a common characteristic of global companies. One estimate suggests that standardization in manufacturing "can create savings of 20 to 30 percent, as a company operates fewer plants, buys from fewer suppliers, and reduces duplication. Globalization thus gives companies the leverage to reduce costs, achieve breakeven earlier, and increase profits over the widest possible markets."[5]

Ford is pushing hard toward a global infrastructure through its Ford 2000 plan. In its drive to leverage its global resources, Ford studied the operations of Volkswagen and Toyota as well as those of General Electric, Hewlett-Packard, and Xerox. It estimates annual savings of $3 billion through globalizing its product development, purchasing and supply, marketing, sales, and other activities. These savings would come from pooling resources and reducing destructive turf wars. Such savings would be used to finance projects in the high-potential markets of China, India, and Southeast Asia. The basic idea is to create and use the same systems and processes worldwide to produce products that can be built and sold in many different places with only small differences. This requires drawing on best practices wherever they can be found. As part of this process, Ford is merging its European and North American operations with plans to fold in Latin America and Asia-Pacific at a later time. Currently Ford's European and American cars have no parts in common![6]

---

[5]Ibid., p. 264.
[6]James B. Treece et al., "Ford: Alex Trotman's Daring Global Strategy," *Business Week,* April 3, 1995, p. 97.

The efficient management of worldwide assets is necessary but hardly sufficient for global success. The tangible and intangible resources of the organization must be employed to their fullest and in new combinations that continue to add value and create new sources of competitive advantage. Successful companies are those that leverage their capabilities across products and markets. Resources are not finite; we possess the capabilities to invent and reinvent our resource pool. Organizational learning matters here. Without a commitment to ongoing learning and its rapid deployment, organizations will fail to create and leverage resources to fuel growth.

Optimize   Everyone wants best results, but in what sense? Global organizations have multiple stakeholders (including customers, investors, communities, and associates). Each group wants to have its needs met, but these needs may not always be compatible with one another. Suppose an organization wants to service a high-potential market efficiently and effectively. The market in question says, "OK, but you must hire a certain number of local people and use a high percentage of local natural resources." This may not be the best way to maximize results in the short term, but it may increase long-term viability and performance given that the market is high potential.

Likewise, one part of the business may be producing superior results but in a relatively mature market. On the other side of the world is a market overflowing with potential but lacking resources for its development. For the sake of the total organization, resources may need to be taken from the mature success to the immature potential. Not an easy decision, but one that is necessary to prevent maximization in one area from destroying the potential of another. Only a mindset that thinks optimization and interdependence rather than maximization and independence can make these decisions effectively.

Global Organizations: Six Capabilities

If integration, flow, leverage, and optimization are key drivers of global businesses, what are the core capabilities these companies need to function effectively? There are at least six, and I call these **Global SMARTS** for short: strategy, momentum, agility, relationships, technology, and spirit.

Strategic Focus: Organizational Leadership through Concentrated Effort

Operating in a complex global marketplace without a strategy is like sailing in the boat described by Lewis Carroll in which "the bowsprit got mixed with the rudder sometimes."[7]
What does a global strategy do?

- It communicates a vision and provides the shared mental infrastructure for channeling energy and resources to wherever they can add most value, regardless of boundaries.
- It highlights the major operating drivers of a business (e.g., a product / service concept or a sales / marketing method) and the skill sets needed to support those drivers (e.g., quality, product / process development, and customer service).
- It presents the world as a total entity, not just a collection of individual subsidiaries or national markets.
- It addresses both market opportunities and competitive challenges.
- It answers such questions as: What products and services should lead our global efforts? Are there key markets we should target in the short term and the long term? Are there preferred ways to enter those markets? Given our current capabilities, how quickly should we expand? How should we distribute and organize our operations to gain maximum competitive advantage and synergy?

In developing strategy, global organizations cannot afford to lock the strategy-making process into a rarefied strategic planning function. Good strategy does not always begin in thinking and planning. It may begin in an action taken at a relatively low level in the organization. Such strategic flexibility only can be achieved in a leadership culture in which everyone understands "the connection between their daily actions and the business strategy, and who have the drive and skills to get their ideas implemented. . . . Whatever you are in the organization, whether you're a member of a project team,

---

[7]Lewis Carroll, *The Humorous Verse of Lewis Carroll*, New York: Dover Publications, 1960.

or a manager, or a corporate executive, you are already part of the strategy process. Your actions can propel or derail the success of the current strategies. Your actions can also be the basis for the evolution of entirely new strategies."[8]

Momentum: Organizational Leadership through Speed toward Goals

Slow and steady used to be the mantra for many organizations, but times have changed. As Bettye Hill of Avon said to me, "Where it used to take us two years to get to market, now we are developing some products from concept to market in a matter of months. If you don't get out there fast, someone else will." Organizational size has been sidestepped by speed and execution.

Zenith Electronics Corporation has been learning this global lesson. Zenith has been bleeding to death, with one profitable year in the last decade and huge market share losses to foreign competition. Radical change was the only answer. Albin Moschner, president and chief operating officer of Zenith, told the 1995 Business Week President's Forum that his company was losing an average of 10 percent of additional business opportunities each month because its cycle times were too slow. A fundamental review of design methodologies drastically reduced product development cycle time and resulted in productivity improvements of almost 100 percent. The freed resources were used to develop innovative products such as Zenith's high-definition television system and create value-added product enhancements. While not yet out of trouble, Zenith has moved a long way toward building momentum and reestablishing global competitiveness.

In an age in which products and services can be replicated quickly and easily, getting to market first is an advantage, no matter how short-lived. A whole new academic industry has been spawned to explain the success of the QWERTY keyboard over rivals such as DHIATENSOR (the 10 letters said to be needed to spell 70 percent of English words) or the VHS video format over Beta.[9]

---

[8]Stephen J. Wall and Shannon Rye Wall, *The New Strategists: Creating Leaders at All Levels,* New York: The Free Press, 1995, p. 10.

[9]Steve Lohr, "Business Often Goes to the Swift, Not the Best," *The New York Times,* August 6, 1995, p. E3.

Ford knows that while it is doing well, its competitors are more efficient at getting models to market faster. The redesign of the popular Taurus model took five years; the Japanese reworked competing models in four years. Chrysler's Neon subcompact was brought to market in 31 months. Part of generating speed at Ford has been a study of best practices in America and Europe and even outside of Ford. One result has been the breaking down of machining a new engine prototype into stages that can be done simultaneously. The time from engine design to testing has been reduced from 24 months to 100 days. Aiding the process are "no-fault" meetings in which the problem, not the messenger, gets attacked.[10]

Agility: Organizational Leadership through Versatility

The traditional organizational pyramid worked well in an environment where change was relatively slow and somewhat predictable. Today experts are talking about spider web organizations, starbursts, matrices, and other exotic structures. What all of these exotics have in common is that they are attempts to promote organizational flexibility and responsiveness and to unlock shareholder value and release human potential.

Companies never know where their next challenge will come from. Deregulation, privatization, and technological change are throwing open the doors to unexpected competitors. "Car companies are competing with banks in the credit card war," says *Fortune*, "and software and cable companies are vying for the right to transport tomorrow's consumer on the information superhighway."[11] Such dynamism requires organizations that can harmonize with ongoing change rather than continually battling it.

In an effort to become more responsive to customer and competitor changes, many organizations are looking toward process-driven, horizontal structures. This new operating model stresses core processes such as product development, client acquisition, or, in the case of Ford's Customer Service Division, fixing it right the first time on time, supporting dealers and handling customers, engineering

---

[10]Treece et al., "Ford," p. 95.

[11]Jaclyn Fierman, "When Genteel Rivals Become Mortal Enemies," *Fortune*, May 15, 1995, p. 90.

cars with ease of service in mind, and developing service fixes quicker.[12] Related work is combined, and work that doesn't add value is eliminated. Department heads are being replaced with process owners, and cross-functional teams are the site for much of the work that takes place in the organization. Results often center on customer satisfaction and retention measures.

One company that is used to agility is Bechtel. Pat Morgan, human resource manager, told me, "Our work is very project based. We have to build teams very quickly, get them up to efficiency, execute the project, and disband the team. We've been doing that for years and feel very comfortable with it, although I know a lot of organizations don't. A proposal becomes known to us, and we very quickly identify a project manager. We generally have team members identified in the proposal, and they could be based anywhere in the world. This comes down to leadership; you need to focus on project managers that can pull cross-functional and cross-cultural teams together and have them perform."

Relationships: Organizational Leadership through Communication and Partnering

If policies and procedures and power structures were the heart of industrial organizations, relationships are the heart of the global, information-rich enterprise. Donna McNamara, director of global education and training at Colgate-Palmolive, says, "We are a relationship-based company to the core. That's how information and knowledge gets transferred, that's how trust is built, that's how things get done quickly. Our company brings people together from across the diversity spectrum and gives them the sense that they are part of a common cause. The relationship piece of the global puzzle is critical. I really endorse that."

In a global economy, many new relationships are being forged:

+ *People and organizations:* The assumption of lifetime employment with continuous growth and development is no longer viable in a world of intense global competition and

---

[12]Rajiv M. Rao, "The Struggle to Create an Organization for the 21st Century," *Fortune*, April 3, 1995, p. 94.

rapid change. What company can guarantee it will need an individual's skills five years from now? Increasingly, men and women working in business organizations will be contractors or employees of contract employment firms.

◆ *Internal relationships and activities:* With increased competition, companies want to focus on where revenue is coming from. Activities that don't produce revenue are being outsourced to other vendors, such as maintenance, housekeeping, or data processing.

◆ *Team collaboration:* Global business is placing increasing demands on people to work together. This is very difficult in cultures that have emphasized individual achievement.

◆ *Interorganizational partnerships:* New growth is becoming dependent on alliance partnerships that bring capital, technologies, and expertise together to create new, powerful entities to drive innovation and the winning of market share.

One consequence of these trends is that new levels of trust need to be generated between people and organizations, organizations and outsourcers, and partners within alliances.

In a world where ideas can be transmitted at the speed of light, a product or services can be replicated before the ink dries on the patent. Trusting relationships, however, are extremely difficult to replicate. Relationships are forged only over time and through shared experiences. In a global economy, relationships often make the difference between winning and losing.

Technology: Organizational Leadership through the Generation, Distribution, and Application of Knowledge

Competitive advantage is increasingly being tied to knowledge, "intellectual capital," "know-how," and so on. Much of this knowledge is generated, distributed, integrated, and applied via one of the many technologies shaping our new organizations. Without technology, the flow characteristic of global organizations would be impossible. Technology also provides the means for coordinating global activities and aligning global businesses, reducing product cycles, maintaining management reach and communication, driving product customization to fit customer needs, and building the infrastructure for organizational learning and innovation transfer.

The speed of technological change is staggering, and with it comes increased power at reduced cost. Today's microprocessors are almost 100,000 times faster than those of the 1950s. When inflation is factored in, these microprocessors cost about 1,000 times less. If current trends continue, "one desktop computer in 2020 will be as powerful as all the computers in Silicon Valley today."[13] In addition, wireless networks are revolutionizing telephone delivery services and opening up new markets for such items as personal digital assistants (PDAs). The number of cellular users is growing by approximately 50 percent per year in North America, 60 percent in Western Europe, 70 percent in Australia, and more than 200 percent in the larger markets of South America.[14] High-speed fiber optic networks, intelligent software programs that know users' interests and act on their behalf, interactive TVs, smart credit cards, neural network fuzzy logic systems, and virtual reality systems are no longer the stuff of science fiction dreams. Our bodies and minds are being extended into time and space.

These new technologies are transforming the way we work. Innovations such as groupware are deemphasizing the physical spaces in which we work and reemphasizing the conceptual spaces. Increasingly, the computer screen itself is becoming the cyberspace office with links to colleagues all over the world, as well as suppliers, subcontractors, consultants, and even customers.

Ford has placed its international design operations under what it calls an "electronic roof." Through satellite links, undersea cables and land lines, engineers, manufacturers, and suppliers around the world can be integrated into the design process at an early stage. This helps reduce the 40 percent of costs that are incurred after the car is built.[15]

The level and speed of organizational collaboration that such a technology can deliver promises increased responsiveness, greater

---

[13]David A. Patterson, "Microprocessors in 2020," *Scientific American*, September 1995, p. 63.
[14]Ibid., p. 67.
[15]Julie Edelson Halpert, "One Car, Worldwide, with Strings Pulled from Michigan," *The New York Times*, August 29, 1993, p. 7.

flexibility, increased levels of empowerment throughout the organization, and an easing of communication across boundaries. But remember, to paraphrase a recent Northwest Airlines advertisement, "You can't fax a handshake, or the look in someone's eye." Business is still very much an emotional activity, and interpersonal "chemistry" is a powerful ingredient in what makes business happen, particularly globally, where so much depends on trust and solid relationships.

Spirit: Organizational Leadership through Company Character

Spirit is perhaps the most intangible capability in our list of capabilities, but it is one of the most important. A global spirit is embedded in the culture of an organization and provides the context of expectations and values in which associates work and derive meaning from their work. The corporate culture will either promote global leadership or act as a power brake.

What kind of spirit needs to shine through a global corporate culture? It is hard to define global competitive spirit precisely, but it can be seen and *felt* in many forms: an inspirational global corporate vision and mission; an obsession with current and future customer needs around the world; corporatewide experimentation and innovation and a deep commitment to sharing best practices across the organization; an embracing of the difficult challenges that emerge from change; a rejection of dependency and an acceptance of accountability at all levels; the continuous need to achieve; resilience in the face of crises and persistence in the face of obstacles; the valuing of differences, but an energetic drive toward discovering common working ground. The list could go on and on.

Spirit has more to do with feeling than with intellect or ego. American companies, on the whole, are shaped by analysis and technique; they are creatures of intellect. Winning, however, is often a matter of passion and relationships.

One company in which spirit is clearly evident is Avon Products. "The spirit is unbelievable," said Bettye Hill during our interview. "There's something about direct selling that is very motivational. It's built on heavy relationships, and there's lots of enthusiasm for who we are and for the women who make us [representatives]. If it wasn't for the representatives, none of us would be here. There is an absolute respect for them. In every Avon social function there is a toast to representatives, even if none are present. This part of the culture is so strong.

"A story is often told in the company of a young woman in South America who was bent over from continuously carrying wood. This was all her social class would allow her to do. She was recruited by Avon to sell. A year or so later she was standing upright, wearing a suit, and obviously very proud. She had taught herself to read and write all through her association with Avon. These stories tug at your heart. It's unbelievable. But this is the culture and the spirit. I'm a cynical New Yorker, but I've never seen anything like this. It gets to you. You see the opportunities opening up for these women. It's magical!"

AN AGENDA FOR BEING WORLD CLASS

While being a global company and building the capabilities listed earlier does put you in the game, it may not be enough to win in the global marketplace. Winning comes from achieving and beating world-class levels of performance.

One thing we can be sure of is that a mix of definitions of *world class* exists. In a study of 21 British companies, Constantinos Markides and John Stopford, professors at the London Business School, made some very interesting observations about how companies relate to the idea of being world class:[16]

- Some companies emphasized *asset efficiencies*, that is, survival, relative costs of supply, and programs of cost improvement.
- Others broadened the scope and emphasized *competitive effectiveness:* being more responsive than local competitors, being among the top-performing companies, or having the ability to compete on level terms with the best in the company's chosen markets.

---

[16]Constantinos Markides and John M. Stopford, "From Ugly Ducklings to Elegant Swans: Transforming Parochial Firms into World Leaders," *Business Strategy Review* 6, no. 2, Summer 1995.

DIALOGUE BOX

How do you rate your company on the core capabilities needed to be effective globally? Share your responses with others and discuss the differences in the group.

1 = Low; 5 = High

Strategic focus (Organizational leadership through concentrated effort)

1   2   3   4   5

Why did you give this rating?

Momentum (Organizational leadership through speed toward goals)

1   2   3   4   5

Why did you give this rating?

Agility (Organizational leadership through versatility)

1   2   3   4   5

Why did you give this rating?

Relationships (Organizational leadership through communication and partnering)

1   2   3   4   5

Why did you give this rating?

Technology (Organizational leadership through the generation, distribution, and application of knowledge)

1   2   3   4   5

Why did you give this rating?

Spirit (Organizational leadership through company character)

1   2   3   4   5

Why did you give this rating?

♦ A smaller number stressed the ambition to be the "exemplar competitor" and be recognized as world class by both competitors and customers.

♦ In a number of companies, several definitions were present at the same time and at different levels. It was not uncommon for the CEO and the business unit heads to be operating with different definitions. A definition with which the majority of participants could agree stressed the ability of a company to compete with anybody in its chosen markets. For the study authors, being world class was also "an aspiration to achieve world-best standards of achievement in all activities and functions," and in this sense *world class* is a state of mind rather than an existing operational reality.

What does it take to be world class? Markides and Stopford found that leading global companies tend to do more than others on 10 management dimensions. The following list is adapted from their work.

1. Goal stretching. An ambitious goal, based on the recognition of a gap between present position and where the company would like to be in 5 to 10 years, stimulates imaginations, motivates sustained action, and promotes the building of new capabilities. Charles Jones of EDS's management consulting unit says, "If you don't demand something out of the ordinary, you won't get anything but ordinary results."[17] Stretch targets have driven innovation in such areas as inventory, product development, and manufacturing cycles. Incremental targets drive companies toward mediocrity. Aiming for maximum impact, some consultants have referred to stretch targets as BHAG (Big, Hairy, Audacious Goals).[18]

PepsiCo is fighting Coca-Cola around the world by aggressively entering those markets where Coca-Cola has felt safe from stiff competition. The battle cries are: Embrace risk. Act quickly. Innovate constantly. Deliver what's perceived as best value. In taking on this challenge, Christopher Sinclair is setting goals that can appear outrageous. He tripled Pepsi-Cola International's revenues between 1989

[17]Shawn Tully, "Why to Go for the Stretch Targets," *Fortune*, November 14, 1994, p. 145.

[18]James C. Collins and Jerry I. Porras, *Built to Last: Successful Habits of Visionary Companies*, New York: HarperCollins, 1994, p. 91.

and 1994 and is now targeting "five by 95" ($5 billion in sales, which is more than double 1993's $2.2 billion). He believes is that you focus the mind by aiming high and taking on a competitor who wants to wipe you out. In summary, "You have to get people thinking about *dramatic* growth," says Sinclair. "Growth is not going to come by attracting business away from the small players. If you act like No. 2, you'll always be No. 2." Britain's chief of PepsiCo, Stacey Clark, says, "Whenever you get within reach of the [performance] bar, Chris is already raising it."[19]

2. Inclusive leadership. Leaders need to build confidence and pride and a belief that change not only is possible but individuals can influence the outcome. The CEO must galvanize a top leadership team, and that process must be driven deeper into the organization to include as many people as possible. World-class companies work at framing the competitive challenges in terms that associates can relate to. One company in the study sent union representatives and fitters to Japan to see for themselves what competition they faced. The abstractions management talked about came to life, and there was an increase in the amount of creative ideas coming from the shop floor. Most important, people in the organization took *ownership* of the competitive challenges the company faced. Ownership promotes engagement, which in turn stimulates leadership at all levels.

To promote dialogue, a common vocabulary needs to be fostered. Individuals need to be talking the same language when they discuss "global" or "world-class." Leaders at the center of the organization can promote the necessary shared understanding.

At the same time, one of the most important tasks of leaders on the frontlines of the organization is to keep the center in touch with reality. One danger of breeding global minds at the center is that they start to see the world in standardized terms and pursue only economies of scale. Confronting and challenging the center is the primary value of leaders in the field. A mature leadership in the center will actively hold those in the field accountable for pushing reality through the doors of the executive suite.

3. Proactive measures. A focus on profitability, market share, and other financial indicators can be misleading. They are measures

---

[19]Patricia Sellers, "Pepsi Opens a Second Front," *Fortune,* August 8, 1994, pp. 71–76.

of *past* investment. A balance of measurements is needed; that is, a company also needs to focus on strategic indicators that depict how the company might do in the future. These indicators include customer satisfaction, associate morale, the company's financial health relative to its competitors, the company's strategy relative to industry trends, feedback from distributors, customers, and so on. If a company pays attention only to financial factors, it can operate only in a reactive mode. Strategic indicators allow managers to react before a crisis hits.

4. Best practices. Quickly adopting the latest management fad is likely to result in wasted money and increased cynicism. Strategy and benchmarking are examples of two initiatives that often get applied without an organizationwide understanding of what they mean, what benefits can be expected, and how they can be best used in the specific organization and cultural setting. Strategy can become an interesting intellectual exercise for a specialist in planning, but it may just end up in a three-ring binder on the shelves of senior managers. These managers may keep referring to *the* strategy, but no one else feels any ownership for it or really knows what it is or what their role is in implementing it.

5. Efficiency *and* effectiveness. Successful companies pay attention to the top *and* bottom lines, sales volume, and net income. Too many companies pay attention to one or the other. The bottom-liners are always seeking to improve the ratio of outputs to inputs, so they devote attention to financial controls and systems, the elimination of waste, cost-saving programs, increased productivity rates, and meeting budget and profitability targets. The top-liners, on the other hand, are always looking to make improvements in the company's capabilities. The drive is for growth and an improved capacity for production. Strategies for doing this include making investments in skills and capabilities, taking calculated risks and experimenting with new ways of doing things, and promoting learning development and transfer.

Successful companies in the British study seemed to follow a path of achieving efficiencies and then moving on to developing effectiveness. Unsuccessful strategies can be of at least two types: aiming for effectiveness without achieving the necessary levels of efficiency and seeking only to achieve efficiencies and not moving on to effectiveness. One major challenge for the organization is to achieve a balance between what Sumantra Ghoshal, a leading authority on global business issues, once called the Sweet (Effectiveness) and the Sour (Efficiencies).[20] The rewards of creating efficiencies are the resources for developing effectiveness.

6. Continuous innovation. In a world of fast-flowing information, no competitive advantage can last forever. Access to information means that competitors can replicate innovations quickly. Staying ahead means creating a restless organization in which new ideas are generated constantly. This involves risk. In all likelihood, successes may remain more the exception than the rule. Stan Skalka, president of Victor Stanley, Inc., in Dunkirk, Maryland, said it all when he commented, "You have to kiss a lot of frogs before you meet the princess."[21]

The authors of the British study talk of "strategic innovation" as opposed to technical innovation. The latter refers primarily to incremental improvements in techniques and technologies. The former refers to changing the fundamentals of the industry, that is, the rules of the competitive game. This type of innovation push aims to reinvent an industry, not just an organization. It aims, as Gary Hamel and C. K. Prahalad point out in *Competing for the Future*, to change the rules of engagement (as we have seen in discount brokerage services), redraw the boundaries between industries (as is taking place in the computer and communications fields), or create entirely new industries (as Apple did with personal computers).[22]

7. Building capabilities. Knowing which capabilities to develop, when, and how is specific to an organization within given industry and competitive conditions. Understanding which capabilities to build will depend to a great extent on where the competitive advantage of the company lies. Michel Robert, in *Strategy Pure and Simple: How Winning CEOs Outthink Their Competition*, lays out certain capabilities that should be addressed depending on the strategic driver of the company (see Figure 1–2).[23]

---

[20]Sumantra Ghoshal, "Personnel Managers Should Learn to Cook 'Sweet and Sour,'" *Personnel Management*, May 1994.

[21]Ferdinand Protzman, "U.S. Companies Looking to Go Global Get Help from Home," *The New York Times*, October 16, 1994, p. 4.

[22]Gary Hamel and C. K. Prahalad, *Competing for the Future*, Boston: Harvard Business School Press, 1994.

[23]Michel Robert, *Strategy Pure and Simple: How Winning CEOs Outthink Their Competition*, New York: McGraw-Hill, 1993.

FIGURE 1–2
Strategic Capabilities

Strategic Drivers	Strategic Capabilities
Product/service concept driven	Quality/product and process development (Japanese automakers)
	Service (IBM)
User/customer class driven	Market/user research (Procter & Gamble)
	User loyalty (Johnson & Johnson)
Market type/category driven	Market/user research
	User loyalty
Production capacity/ capability driven	Manufacturing/plant efficiency (Guilford Mills)
	Substitute marketing (paper, plastic, and concrete companies)
Technology/know-how driven	Research (Sony)
	Applications marketing (3M)
Sales/marketing method driven	Recruitment (Avon)
	Selling effectiveness (Avon)
Distribution method driven	Most effective distribution method (FedEx)
Natural resource driven	Exploration (Exxon)
Size/growth driven	Financial management (Colgate-Palmolive)
	Information systems (ITT)
Return/profit driven	Financial management
	Information systems

Source: Adapted from Michel Robert, *Strategy Pure and Simple: How Winning CEOs Outthink Their Competition*, New York: McGraw-Hill, 1993.

Strategic drivers are those areas that management emphasizes in doing business. Strategic capabilities are those areas of excellence a company deliberately needs to cultivate over time to keep its strategy on the competitive edge. These capabilities need to be performed at levels higher than competitors perform. They are the engines that propel the business forward.

A process of "imagineering" can be performed to identify potential capabilities needed in the future. An ambitious but realistic objective can be established for 10 years into the future. Working backward from that long-term objective, medium-term goals could be set at different intervals, such as, two, five, and seven years. With the long-term objective and medium-term goals in mind, needed capabilities can be identified and developed. New capabilities can be added to older ones in the manner of a strategic capabilities staircase. This proactive approach to change may prevent the dramatic ruptures businesses inflict on themselves and the alienation and resistance that result.

8. Paradox management. It is now a cliché to say that those working in a global business environment must learn to handle paradox. Typical dilemmas include building capabilities while remaining flexible to new opportunities; achieving differentiation and low cost at the same time; achieving consistency and flexibility in a dynamic environment; meeting short-term financial goals while maintaining long-term vision; balancing needs for decentralization and centralization in the organization; maintaining needed hierarchy and functional strength while encouraging flow across levels and boundaries; building a global corporate culture while recognizing the value-added of local differences; and building partnerships with past, current, or future competitors.

Global leaders should not waste valuable energies trying to eliminate these dilemmas. Such an endeavor would not be feasible or desirable. While these dilemmas should be minimized to stop them from becoming dysfunctional, it should be recognized that they provide valuable creative tension in our new organizations. This tension helps safeguard against too easy solutions to complex problems.

Interestingly, the authors of the study found that some managers "were so task oriented they could not recognize a dilemma at all." This suggests too narrow a focus and an overreliance on linear versus systems thinking.

9. Intelligence gathering. Learning from the best in the world regardless of industry or location is critical. Benchmarking against a national base of companies is inadequate; the competitive standards are set globally.

Learning can come from unexpected sources. Arthur Anderson has a Global Best Practices Initiative that investigates companies worldwide to identify value-added corporate process methods.[24] Searching widely for best practices can yield surprising results.

---

[24]Robert Hiebeler, "To Compete Better, Look Far Afield," *The New York Times*, September 18, 1994.

Southwest Airlines looked to improve the turnaround of its aircraft at airports. Instead of looking at other airlines, the company studied the practices of pit crews at the Indianapolis 500. New ideas emerged about equipment fittings, materials management, and teamwork that resulted in a 50 percent reduction in turnaround time.

Granite Rock Company wanted to improve how it loaded gravel into its trucks. By studying bank automatic teller machines, Granite Rock came up with the idea of providing drivers with cards they could insert into special machines. This eliminated the need for drivers to leave their trucks to fill out lengthy and time-consuming paperwork. In the same vein, a gas utility company studied FedEx to generate new ideas about delivering fuel. British Airways studied caring for individuals at hospices for terminally ill patients.

10. Acting out. Encouraging calculated risk taking, trial and error, and experimentation is essential to global success. Business is a continuous search for sources of competitive advantage—for what works in the marketplace—not a pursuit for intellectual elegance and truth. Information is useful to decision making, but can never replace judgment and a willingness to act. There is never enough information available to lead to the perfect action. While analysis and thought can provide business leaders with a conceptual foundation and direction, they can also act as a barrier to understanding and action. Concepts are a roadmap, not the territory itself. Too often senior management is insulated from the realities confronted on the front lines of action. Strategic plans, projections, sales figures, and financial reports tell a story but cannot convey the feel, smell, taste, and texture of working close to customers.

LEADERSHIP COMMUNITIES: MAXIMIZING COLLECTIVE INTELLIGENCE

One of the key conclusions of an ICEDR/Gemini Consulting project was that *"Leadership has traditionally been reserved for the few; it now must be unleashed and made available to as many as possible."*[25] Top leadership in our global organizations is not going to have all the answers; the world is simply too complex and changeable. Increasingly, we must look to draw from the collective intelligence in the organization.

---

[25]D. A. Ready, *Champions*, p. 26.

DIALOGUE BOX

1. What does the term *world class* mean in your company? Is there a shared definition within the organization? What are the key differences among levels, units, and individuals, and what impact could these different definitions have on overall performance?
2. What initiatives are in place in your company to achieve or maintain world-class performance?

   ◆ Setting stretch goals.
   ◆ Developing leaders throughout the organization.
   ◆ Putting proactive measures in place.
   ◆ Finding best practices within the industry and beyond.
   ◆ Driving for efficiency and effectiveness.
   ◆ Encouraging continuous innovation.
   ◆ Building strategic capabilities.
   ◆ Managing paradoxes.
   ◆ Gathering intelligence.
   ◆ Taking action.

3. What are your competitors doing to be world class?

In the past, we faced a relatively stable world and created highly centralized, bureaucratic organizations to maintain that control. In so doing, we created the conditions for our own passivity and dependence. In a highly complex world with rapid change and organizational units spread worldwide, we need to enhance our flexibility and responsiveness by dramatically expanding our leadership base—and not just by small increments. It's time for leadership to be democratized and the accountability for results that underpins leadership to be an expected element of our organizational cultures. We want cultures that promote the independence and autonomy of strong individuals and units while also having them recognize their part in the whole, that is, their interdependence.

What are some of the major barriers to building our leadership resources and maximizing our collective intelligence?

   ◆ **Traditional notions of leadership**. Traditionally, the leader was the individual who set the rules. He or she would tell everyone where to go, how to get there, and allocate the resources. In the new conditions of global uncertainty, no one has a total grasp on the ends or the means. Increasingly, leaders are being looked to for guidance and support on adapting to challenges rather than giving specific direction. You can see this new sense of leadership emerging at Chrysler.

What is the secret of Chrysler's successful turnaround? CEO Robert Eaton says, "If I had to use one word it's empowerment. That's the biggest reason."[26] When Chrysler wants to produce a new model or rework an existing one, it creates a team of some 700 designers, engineers, marketing, manufacturing, and finance personnel. A vice president performs the role of "godfather" to the team, but multiple leaders below the vice president direct the work and the group organizes itself according to how it can best get the work done.

Prior to the start of the project, Eaton and about a dozen senior managers meet with the leaders of the team. They outline a vision for the new vehicle and work out stretch targets for the group in terms of overall design and performance, fuel consumption, and cost. This early stage is really about developing a "contract" between senior management and the team. The team works out how to best achieve the targets, and doesn't get back to management unless a major problem develops. Since Eaton has been at Chrysler, every vehicle has come in below its investment target and its cost-per-car target. The real progress made at Chrysler is involving its people. According to Eaton, the greatest difference between Japanese and U.S. companies in the 1970s was that the Japanese firms were engaging their people and the U.S. firms were not.

A master at the "you-figure-it-out" style of global business leadership is Ralph Larson at Johnson & Johnson. He is quite aware that people in his highly decentralized organization criticize him and want him to "Do something! Do anything!" His comeback is, "managers come up with better solutions and set tougher standards for themselves than I would have imposed."[27] Does this mean Larson abdicates a leadership role? Absolutely not! Johnson & Johnson's results speak for themselves. Larson, like other senior global leaders, is under pressure to simplify and consolidate decision-making processes to make them more global. Larson understands, however, that he

[26]Marshall Loeb, "Empowerment That Pays Off," *Fortune*, March 25, 1995, p. 145.

[27]Brian O'Reilly, "J&J Is on a Role," *Fortune*, December 26, 1994.

can quickly destroy morale and stultify leadership by issuing edicts from headquarters. "We do best," he says, "when we take the time to describe the problem and let them come up with a solution."[28] Maintaining a fine balance between developing nicely engineered global solutions and building global leadership in the organization is at the heart of today's competitive agenda.

Concepts of collective or distributed leadership offer us a constructive way forward. Fred Kofman and Peter Senge make the point that what makes "the myth of the great leader so appealing is that it absolves us of any responsibility for developing leadership capabilities more broadly."[29] From their system's perspective, we tend to opt for the symptomatic rather the fundamental solution (see Figure 1–3).

FIGURE 1–3
Shifting the Burden

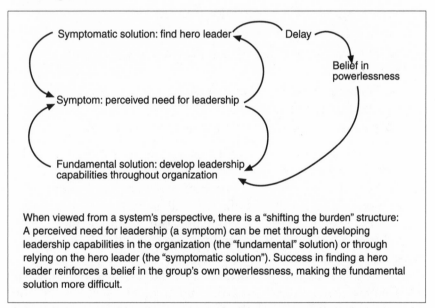

When viewed from a system's perspective, there is a "shifting the burden" structure: A perceived need for leadership (a symptom) can be met through developing leadership capabilities in the organization (the "fundamental" solution) or through relying on the hero leader (the "symptomatic solution"). Success in finding a hero leader reinforces a belief in the group's own powerlessness, making the fundamental solution more difficult.

Source: Adapted from Fred Kofman and Peter M. Senge, "Communities of Commitment," in Learning Organizations: Developing Cultures for Tomorrow's Workplace, ed. Sarita Chawla and John Renesch, Portland, OR: Productivity Press, 1995.

---

[28]Ibid.

[29]Sarita Chawla and John Renesch, eds., *Learning Organizations: Developing Cultures for Tomorrow's Workplace*, Portland, OR: Productivity Press, 1995, p. 35.

Our challenge in new organizations is to find a balance among three ways of relating to one another: autonomy, cooperation, and control. In the most productive organizations, the tension between distributed leaders and formal leaders will be a creative source of energy. In *The Age of the Network*, Jessica Lipnack and Jeffrey Stamps make the important point that "Networks are leaderful, not leaderless. Each person or group in a network has something unique to contribute at some point in the process. With more than one leader, the network as a whole has greater resilience."[30] At any one time, leadership in a group may shift depending on an individual's technical or functional expertise, global experience, or connections. There may also be a coordinating leader in the group, someone who knows the organizational system well and can mobilize effort and resources to get things done. Lipnack and Stamps suggest you ask the following questions to gauge whether you have fewer bosses and more leaders:

+ Do you hear only one voice at meetings?
+ Are there subgroups with task leaders?
+ Does more than one person make commitments and take responsibility?
+ Do people feel heard and believe they have a voice in decision making?
+ Do they participate, or at least feel they can?[31]

By driving leadership to all levels, the organization will evolve into what Kofman and Senge call a "leadership community." The barriers to creating such communities are many, and change will depend on will as much as skill. The will is critical because certain mind shifts need to take place to realize our vision of fluid leadership. These mind shifts relate to how we conceive of and manage organizational energies.

+ **Leadership and management: false opposites**. Over the past decade or so, we have set up artificial barriers between leadership and management. Leaders have become a separate species with their

---

[30]Jessica Lipnack and Jeffrey Stamps, *The Age of the Network: Organizing Principles for the 21st Century*, Essex Junction, VT: Omneo, 1994, p. 18.

[31]Ibid., p. 94.

own unique characteristics and capabilities. If you don't think we have drawn a line between leadership and management, think about the following quotation from C. K. Prahalad: *"It is the appetite for this process of reexamining and reinventing that will separate the builders (leaders) from caretakers and the undertakers (managers and cautious administrators)."*[32] Such an analysis is a double-edged sword. On the one hand, it encourages us to pay attention to the need for leadership qualities in a world of continuous change and global competition. On the other hand, it sets leadership above the "mundane" but critical work of managing.

Such a viewpoint is reinforced in the work of Warren Bennis.[33] For example:

The manager administers; the leader innovates.

The manager is a copy; the leader is an original.

The manager maintains; the leader develops. . . .

The manager does things right; the leader does the right thing.

Rather than release human potential, such dichotomies can serve to lock people into static categories. They can act as another self-limiting straitjacket for ourselves and others.

The separation of leader and manager roles was useful for a time. It allowed us to see the value-added that leadership qualities bring to organizations seeking to invent their futures and mobilize action toward their goals. But now those privileged few identified as leaders are put on pedestals. *The unintended consequence of this is to create leadership passivity in others.* Leadership becomes a specialized, deified commodity. The negative aspects of this are alluded to in a *Fortune* profile of Yotaro Kobayashi, chairman of Fuji Xerox. The major idea expressed by Kobayashi is that we should "lift the veils that give leaders their aura of majesty and mystery; once young people can recognize their heroes as human, they can begin to find heroism in themselves."[34]

---

[32]Ashkenas et al., *The Boundaryless Organization*, p. xiv.

[33]Warren Bennis, *On Becoming a Leader*, Reading, MA: Addison-Wesley, 1989, p. 45.

[34]Stratford Sherman, "How Tomorrow's Best Leaders Are Learning Their Stuff," *Fortune*, November 27, 1995, p. 100.

American culture is well known for its orientation to analysis, for separating parts from wholes. Leadership has been picked apart and analyzed, but the time is ripe for reintegrating it into the wider sphere of management. The German language doesn't make such a separation between leadership and management. *Fuehrungskunst* (management) is the "art of leadership."[35] I have met no one during this book project whom I would categorize as being just either a leader or a manager. The great value these individuals bring to their organizations is that they are both leaders and managers as appropriate to the challenge at hand. As leaders they are forever stretching the bounds of the possible, and as managers they are firmly grounded in the realities of how to set imagination in motion toward concrete goals. If we set expectations for managers to lead, they will lead; if we expect leaders to manage, they will manage. If we expect both sets of behaviors, anything is possible! Expectations are the key, and expectations are embedded in culture.

    ♦ **Superiority**. In a global organization, one barrier to developing a leadership community is the assumption of superiority in the so-called developed countries. Doug Reid, senior vice president of human resources at Colgate-Palmolive, has this to say:

> The terms "developed country" and "developing country" are misnomers. The assumption is that in the developed country you're sophisticated, and that you can really help the developing countries come along. My sense is that "developed" means mature and that "developing" means young, growing, and learning. One of the reasons I enjoy going to developing countries is that I learn so much. I was in Malaysia a couple of weeks ago and they came up with a human resources approach that I think is terrific and I want to take it around the globe. After World War II, the United States did have something of a monopoly on management technology. Some managers in the United States still feel they have the upper edge on management technology, but that advantage is long gone. I just came back from Thailand, and the way they have established the distribution center out there is something we can learn from and apply elsewhere in the world. One of the big complaints I got from Asia on my recent trip—after I'd asked what can we do for you back at global headquarters—was, "Listen. Listen to what we're saying. Listen instead of selling."

[35]Helmut Maucher, *Leadership in Action: Tough-Minded Strategies from the Global Giant*, New York:, McGraw-Hill, 1994, p. vii.

Paying attention to such feedback allows companies such as Colgate-Palmolive to maximize their collective intelligence and build a leadership community.

A GLOBAL LEADERSHIP PROCESS

While leadership style and priority differences occur across cultures, the underlying leadership process is essentially the same. The image that has guided me in defining this process is the complex Hindu deity Shiva. Shiva combines multiple qualities that appear contradictory but weave themselves into a rich tapestry: creativity and destructiveness, benevolence and vengeance, asceticism and sensualism. In some forms he is portrayed as having six faces, signifying his many-sidedness. He also has a third eye that aids inward vision. Shiva embodies energy and change; creation and destruction, for example, are not opposites but part of the same cycle of regeneration. You may be familiar with the representation of Shiva as the Cosmic Dancer, Nataraja. In this form, Shiva performs the Dance of Life within a ring of fire. He is not consumed by the fire, but appears to draw on the energy of the fire for his own vitality.

While not wanting to stretch the image too far or trivialize Hindu thought, I see the global manager at the center of a ring of fire. This ring of fire is called Global Competition. The global leader can either be consumed by the fire or embrace its energy to generate higher levels of performance. From this analogy, we can formulate a generic leadership process (see Figure 1–4). This process can be broken down into three major steps; we could also refer to them as habits of global leadership:

1. Framing global competitive challenges as opportunities.
2. Generating personal and organizational energy.
3. Transforming energy into world-class performance.

FIGURE 1–4
The Global Leadership Process

The global leader . . . converts the challenges of global competition into personal and organizational energy for creating worldwide stakeholder value in order to build and sustain world-class performance.

1. Framing global competitive challenges as opportunities.
This step begins with summoning the courage to apply the creative
destruction capability. Eckhard Pfeiffer, president of Compaq Computer Corporation, is very conscious of the need for this approach in
the global computer industry. In 1991, Compaq faced its first real
crisis. Problem: Global competitors were producing excellent clones
at lower prices, and Compaq's customers were rolling in that direction. Compaq sales dropped, and the stock fell by two-thirds. Pfeiffer
recognized that if Compaq was not only to endure but prosper, the
frame had to be broken. He had to unlearn what had led Compaq to
its initial success.

2. Generating personal and organizational energy. Having
embraced the challenge, Pfeiffer led the way to taking on the global
competition. The worldwide work force was cut from 12,000 to 10,000;
dealerships were expanded from 3,500 to 38,000; and suppliers were
pressed to give more favorable deals. In addition, Pfeiffer expanded
Compaq's presence in the home, education, and small-business markets, created 24-hour mail-order and customer service phone access,
and drove home the need for focus and efficiency throughout the
organization. Perhaps the most important element in generating energy around the global challenge was his setting the stretch goal to
make Compaq the biggest producer of PCs by 1997.

3. Transforming energy into world-class performance. Since
Pfeiffer took over as chief executive in 1992, Compaq sales have more
than doubled to $10.9 billion, and profits have increased four times to
$867 million. Compaq made its stretch goal in 1994! It shipped 4.8 mil-
lion PCs in that year, beating out the 4 million attained by both Apple
and IBM. In terms of worldwide market share, Compaq's rose from
4.8 percent to 10.0 percent, IBM's fell from 10.0 to 8.3 percent, and
Apple's dropped from 8.5 to 8.3 percent. And what's next? At the
January 1995 meeting, Pfeiffer set another global challenge: to triple
Compaq's sales to $30 billion by the year 2000. After announcing this
goal and challenging everyone to "scale new heights," a cable lifted
him 150 feet off the stage and through the ceiling of the auditorium!

This is a fine example of the global leadership process at work.
Eckhard Pfeiffer saw opportunity in crisis and mobilized energies
toward the creation of outstanding performance.

Another example is David Whitwam at Whirlpool (sometimes
referred to as Worldpool).

1. Framing global competitive challenges as opportunities. Whitwam took over Whirlpool in 1987. At that time, Whirlpool was the number two domestic appliance maker in the United States and had made a few small inroads into international markets. Since the 1950s Whirlpool had been exporting to Asia on a small scale, and in 1958 it bought an interest in a Brazilian appliance maker.

Whirlpool, by any standard measure, was a successful company. Like most successful companies, it wasn't adept at thinking in terms of life cycles. Charles Handy, in his powerful book *The Age of Paradox*, illustrates life cycles by means of the sigmoid curve. This curve has a horizontal S shape and describes how life, products, organizations, and so on, proceed through stages of slow experimentation, takeoff, and then decline. As he says, "The secret to constant growth is to start a new sigmoid curve before the first one peters out."[36] Luckily for Whirlpool, this principle came naturally to Whitwam.

By the late 1980s, Whitwam was focusing on two issues that shaped his consequent thinking. First, the United States was rapidly becoming a mature market; the chances for vigorous growth were next to zero. Second, concentration of appliance makers into a small number of global firms was increasing. David Whitwam could have accepted slow growth until the time when one of the global Goliaths swallowed him up. Instead, he decided that if globalization was an inevitable trend, he would make Whirlpool one of its leading exponents. Sweeping the threat of a slow, painful death aside, he reframed the competitive threat into a vision of global opportunity.

2. Generating personal and organizational energy. In a bold move, Whitwam paid out $1.1 billion for NV Philips, a large Dutch electronics firm. It was a high price for a company that was hardly making a profit. Many analysts thought he was making a huge mistake. His vision was to transform "two parochial, margin-driven companies into a unified, customer-focused organization capable of using its combined talents to achieve breakthrough performance in markets around the world."[37] But Whitwam was not satisfied with what

---

[36]Charles Handy, *The Age of Paradox*, Boston: Harvard Business School Press, 1994, p. 51.
[37]Regina Fazio Maruca, "The Right Way to Go Global: An Interview with Whirlpool CEO David Whitwam," *Harvard Business Review*, March–April 1994, p. 135.

he calls "flag planting"; his vision was to create one company world-wide—not an easy task given the fragmentation of the NV Philips operation. For example, when Whirlpool took over, the washing machines made in Italy and Germany had no common components, not even one screw!

Whitwam is working on building an integrated, synergistic company; a company in which the whole is greater than the sum of its parts. His goal is to take the best of what he has and leverage it world-wide. This means creating standard platforms and processes for products that will be sold with local variations (Whitwam is well aware that a "one size fits all" mentality won't work even within the same national borders, although the search for global efficiencies goes on). It means creating an "exchange" organization in which the transfer of systems, processes, and knowledge is fluid and turf battles are reduced to a minimum. This, in turn, depends on creating a field of common ground, a territory of shared understandings among members of the total organization, old and new. "One-company challenges" were introduced shortly after the European acquisition. These challenges have included the creation of global product strategy review and product creation processes and a talent pool system for human resources.

Patience has been key. Rather than jumping into a focus on Philips's performance, Whitwam dedicated time to trust and vision building, allowing employees themselves to discover the web of mutual interests and interdependencies that underpin the performance of a global organization.

A sensitivity to culture has also played its part in this one-company worldwide process. A conscious decision was made not to "invade" NV Philips with expatriate Americans. During the first year, only two Americans worked in Europe. In the second year, there were six. Now there are approximately 30. The integration was slow and deliberate. While short-term profits might have been better by charging in with quick fixes, the long-term hostility toward an American "occupation" could have been very damaging. The teamwork among units seems to be working. In 1994, Whirlpool won a competition sponsored by electric utility companies. The challenge was to develop a more energy-efficient refrigerator. Whirlpool's entry was designed by engineers in Europe, North America, and Brazil.

Becoming a leading global company also meant paying attention to the big picture and building lasting stakeholder relationships through creating value. When Whitwam started the global transformation process, he would tell employees that the reason for the company's existence was to create value for shareholders. In terms of generating energy within the organization, that approach was a nonstarter. Whitwam broadened the scope of value creation and reinforced the concepts of interdependence and empowerment. In creating value for shareholders, Whirlpool was also generating value for its other stakeholders, including employees, their communities, and suppliers. Employees were motivated to "think like owners" and to take more accountability and responsibility for how the work gets done. This was reinforced with a pay-for-performance compensation system that rewards higher productivity and quality results and the linking of other benefits, such as 401Ks, to the achievement of return-on-equity and return-on-net-asset goals.

Generating and channeling energy at Whirlpool was not simply about creating a vision and a mission. It was also about persistence and follow-through, maintaining focus in a climate of uncertainty, paying attention to multiple details, and encouraging ownership of and accountability for results. Too much of the leadership literature focuses on the glamour of being a visionary and too little on the hard work of making it happen.

3. Transforming energy into world-class performance. The results are in. Whirlpool has become a world leader in the appliance business. It sells home appliances under 10 brand names in more than 120 countries and manufactures in 12 countries. In terms of sales it ranks number one worldwide, in North America, and in Latin America and number three in Europe. It is now positioning itself to be a significant player in the huge Asian market; Asian sales are expected to grow three to four times faster than those in the United States over the next several years.

The examples of Eckhard Pfeiffer and David Whitwam might suggest that only those people at the very top of large organizations—or "mahogany row," as it is sometimes called—can demonstrate global leadership. Such thinking would be a big mistake. Global leadership is less a position than a desire to embrace the challenges posed by global competition, an ability to mobilize personal and organizational energies to meet those challenges, and the transformation of those energies into world-class performance.

Global leadership may be demonstrated by an executive formulating and communicating an inspirational global strategy or vision for the whole company. It can be equally well demonstrated by a team leader attempting to build common working ground on a multicultural product development team that is struggling to move ahead on its project. Leadership could also come from a service representative who takes the initiative to tap into expertise around the world to solve a customer's problem. Then again, it could come from an engineer in a Japanese subsidiary who recognizes the potential global impact of a manufacturing process innovation in his or her plant and persuades the supervisor to organize a videoconference to speed its possible adoption in facilities in China, the United States, Germany, and Brazil.

A wonderful example of the power of distributed global leadership is given by Stephen and Shannon Wall in their book *The New Strategists: Creating Leaders at All Levels*.[38] Foreign competition was severely hurting Milacron, a Cincinnati-based plastics injection-molding machines manufacturer. Two people—Harold Faig, a product manager, and Bruce Kozak, a salesperson—decided to try and do something about the continual loss of sales to Nissei and Toshiba. Imports had taken over 50 percent of the U.S. market in less than 10 years. Over a Sunday morning cup of coffee, they brainstormed the specifications a machine would need to compete effectively with the Japanese. Faig then went to his boss and said, "Look, if you're not in a position to defend this and keep the wolves away, it will never happen." Much to Faig's and Kozak's surprise, the "do it" signal was given. A cross-functional team was formed, and a new Vista machine was developed in nine months (less than half the time it usually took to develop a new product). Milacron is the surviving major producer of this type of injection-molding machine in the United States.

---

[38]Wall and Wall, *The New Strategists*, pp. 6–7.

DIALOGUE BOX

---

1. To what extent is your organization developing its global leadership resources to maximize its collective intelligence?

   1 = Not at all; 5 = To a great extent

   1   2   3   4   5

   Why did you give this rating?

2. Have you seen examples of the global leadership process at work in your company, that is, individuals or groups who (1) embrace global challenges as opportunities, (2) generate personal and organizational energies to meet those challenges, and (3) transform organizational energies into world-class performance? What challenges triggered the process? Who were the key players, and what personal qualities did they possess? What were the results?

SUMMARY CHECKPOINT

Thrust into an arena of fierce global competition, many of our organizations face new levels of vulnerability. To be responsive, fast, and adaptable in this environment requires the development of active leadership resources throughout an organization.

What is a global company, and what type of leaders do we need to work in them? A global company is one that pursues integrated organizational strategies to maximize the flow and leverage of resources worldwide to produce optimal results for the *total* organization. The underlying capabilities needed to succeed globally are strategic focus (organizational leadership through concentrated effort), momentum (organizational leadership through speed toward goals), agility (organizational leadership through versatility), relationships (organizational leadership through communication and partnering), technology (organizational leadership through the generation, distribution, and application of knowledge), and spirit (organizational leadership through company character).

While the above capabilities help companies become global companies, management constantly needs to pursue certain practices if the company is to generate world-class levels of performance. These practices are setting stretch goals to challenge the organization to new levels of performance, driving leadership to all levels, establishing proactive measures of performance that gauge strategic health, implementing best practices, pursuing efficiency and effectiveness, promoting continuous innovation as the norm, an ongoing commitment to building capabilities, identifying and balancing paradoxes, gathering intelligence from a wide range of sources, and taking action.

Our traditional view of leadership, one built on an out-of-date military command and control model, has created high levels of passivity in our organizations. To generate higher levels of competitiveness, we must develop leadership cultures that seek to utilize the collective intelligence of the organization. In such a culture, global leaders—at whatever level or location—will (1) embrace the challenges of global competition, (2) generate personal and organizational energies to confront those challenges, and (3) transform the organizational energy into world-class performance.

SOME ACTION IDEAS

Individual

- ◆ Deepen your familiarity with your company's global initiatives and overall intent: strategic markets, products and services to lead the global effort, organizational structure, and so on.
- ◆ Understand your company's global capabilities in relation to its customers and competitors. Can you add value to your company's actual or potential capabilities?

Organization

- ◆ Place the building of global leadership resources throughout the company as a priority item on the competitive agenda.
- ◆ Work to create a common language in the organization for discussing "globalization," "world-class" performance, and "leadership."

Individual

- Demonstrate readiness and willingness to take ownership of the challenges posed by global competition.
- Analyze your local and global spheres of influence. What can you do within these spheres to energize the drive toward world-class levels of performance?
- What blockages can you remove from the flow of information and resources?
- Look at what you do in the company from a global and local perspective. Do you see opportunities for greater leverage or optimization of results?
- Help focus energy on achieving world-class results, not generating more activity.
- Recognize that leadership can be demonstrated at any level of the organization. Take risks and demonstrate accountability. Encourage others to do the same. Think like an owner.

Organization

- Benchmark those companies in the world that do what they do better than anyone else (inside and outside your industry), and then think well beyond their achievements.
- Communicate challenges from global competitors in an honest and direct fashion. Let the multiple leaders in the company rise to the occasion.
- Survey the primary management practices in the organization, and evaluate whether or not they support the drive to world-class performance.
- Identify what the company may have done in the past to encourage leadership passivity, and stop doing it.
- Aggressively work against any feelings of superiority in the home country. Listen to ideas from all over the world, and integrate the best.
- Set *one-company challenges* in the organization to build consistency and leverage.

CHAPTER **2**

Global Leadership Capabilities

[Leadership] is a role in which anyone engages whenever he or she attempts to redirect resources or attention in order to accomplish a larger goal. Leadership acts can occur whenever problems are solved, decisions are made, or information is acted on. When someone attempts to change things or to influence others to take new or different directions that will better serve multiple stakeholders for the future, he or she performs a leadership act.

Patricia McLagan and Christo Nel, The Age of Participation[1]

Preview

♦ Building global leadership benchstrength requires organizational and individual investments in building capabilities. A key question is: What capabilities to develop?

♦ In presenting a model of the capabilities needed to be a successful global leader, three competency clusters are identified: business acumen, relationship management, and personal effectiveness. We call these clusters the Global Leadership Triad. An over- or underemphasis on one or two clusters will produce suboptimal results. The central driving force in this model is an individual's engagement with personal transformation.

---

[1]Patricia McLagan and Christo Nel, *The Age of Participation: New Governance for the Workplace and the World,* San Francisco: Berrett-Koehler, 1995, p. 98.

- The Global Leadership Triad provides a starting point for companies wishing to produce their own set of global leadership competencies. It is important that each company build internal ownership of any competency list.
- The profile that emerges from the Global Leadership Triad is a desired, ideal type. Individuals need to demonstrate continuous learning and ongoing behavioral effectiveness in each of the competency clusters.
- One of the major challenges in our organizations is the elimination of limiting beliefs, particularly in regard to women and global assignments.

THE GLOBAL LEADERSHIP TRIAD

In *Leading Minds: An Anatomy of Leadership,* Howard Gardner states that leadership has too often been represented as being either unproblematic ("you too can be a leader") or unreachable ("the born leader").[2] Rather than think about leadership in such simplistic terms, he suggests that we recognize that leadership is a subject that can be mastered and a role that can be achieved if one is willing to make the needed investments. What kinds of investments are needed if we are to develop successful global business leaders? Companies will need to commit human and financial resources to designing strategies, structures, and systems that promote and reward leadership actions throughout the organization. They will also need to commit to necessary corporate culture changes where formal and informal norms and values are not clear and consistent about expected leadership contributions from members. Certainly individuals will need to invest their time, energy, and commitment in building their global leadership capabilities. But what capabilities need to be developed?

Being an effective global leader requires a blending of three competency clusters: business acumen, relationship management, and personal effectiveness. We will call these competency clusters the Global Leadership Triad (© Terence Brake, 1996).

---

[2]Howard Gardner, *Leading Minds: An Anatomy of Leadership,* New York: Basic Books, 1995, p. 304.

Why business acumen? Without a comprehensive understanding of the overall business and an excellent grounding in the professional knowledge and skills required to do his or her specific job, a global leader will never gain the credibility needed to be effective. Based on the actual and potential needs of the company's multiple stakeholders, he or she also needs to pursue opportunities with an entrepreneur's spirit while understanding how to get things done in a complex organization.

Why relationship management? The world of the global organization is dependent on people from different cultural backgrounds working together toward common goals under conditions of rapid change. In organizational environments in which the flow of resources is critical and structures are somewhat fluid, the quality of relationships is fundamental to successful mobilization of effort and the achievement of world-class results. Successful global leaders are agents for the necessary changes. They work to build often temporary communities aimed at fostering worldwide collaboration.

Why personal effectiveness? No matter what strategies, structures, and systems we put in place, global leadership depends on individuals taking accountability for their own growth and development and having the desire and maturity to experience the unfamiliar world around them with an openness of mind. It also depends on these men and women having the agility and resilience to deal with the unexpected and to keep moving forward toward goals with a sense of optimism.

From an individual perspective, the leader must create a suitable blend of all three competency clusters.

In *Seeing Organizational Patterns: A New Theory and Language of Organizational Design,* Robert Keidel presents a triadic way of looking at human organizations.[3] In Keidel's view, there are three basic ways in which human beings can interact with one another: control, cooperation, and autonomy. An effective organization balances all three types of interaction. Our model of the individual global leader is also triadic, and the three competency clusters relate closely to Keidel's variables: business acumen (control), relationship management

---

[3]Robert W. Keidel, *Seeing Organizational Patterns: A New Theory and Language of Organizational Design,* San Francisco: Berrett-Koehler, 1995.

(cooperation), and personal effectiveness (autonomy) (see Figure 2–1).

At the center of our model is a philosophy of the Transformational Self, a philosophy of possibility and personal engagement with the world—that is, a drive toward meaning and purpose through activity strengthened by reflection, personal mind management, and openness to change. This is fundamental to leadership, whether global or local. Engagement is driven by vision and values. Without vision and values, a leader has no momentum and consistency, no integration. In a complex and often dramatically unfamiliar global environment, vision provides the driving and directional force and values the stabilizing force. Both are critical to global leader effectiveness over time. (We will talk more about this aspect of the model in Chapter 5, "Toward a Culture of Possibility.")

FIGURE 2–1
The Global Leadership Triad

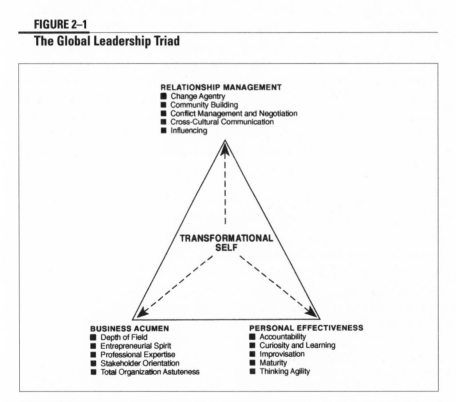

© Terence Brake, 1996.
Source: Inspired by Robert Keidel's triadic view of organizations in *Seeing Organizational Patterns: A New Theory and Language of Organizational Design*, San Francisco: Berrett-Koehler, 1995.

The following breakdown of our global leadership competencies is based on comprehensive literature research, interviews, and a review of the global competencies developed by several major companies. This list aims to offer a starting point for globalizing companies as they seek to profile the qualities needed by men and women in their organizations. It can only be a starting point. Every organization needs to develop and take ownership of its own profile. Several of those interviewed made a comment similar to the following composite statement:

> We hired a consultant to develop a set of competencies for us. When we showed them to the field, there was a strong negative reaction. Managers kept saying, "These don't fit with our realities out here." We pulled together a global task force to develop our own competency set. The funny thing was that when they had finished, our competencies looked very similar to those developed by the consultant. But now we *owned* them!

Business Acumen

The ability to pursue and apply appropriate professional knowledge and skills to achieve optimal results for the company's global stakeholders.

1. Depth of field. Demonstrates a willingness and an ability to switch perspectives between local and global / functional and cross-functional needs and opportunities.

> *a.* Perceives the enterprise as being *one* organization and aims to do the right thing for the total organization, not just his or her function, unit, process, division, or subsidiary.
>
> *b.* Continuously looks to transfer value-added ideas from a local to a global level and between functions.
>
> *c.* Creates opportunities on a regular basis to broaden his or her perspective on the local and global challenges faced by the organization.
>
> *d.* Pays attention to potential synergies created by a diverse organization operating in multiple environments and actively pursues partnerships across and between organizations to achieve world-class results.

    e. Supports the translation and integration of the company's vision, mission, and core values to build connections between the global and the local.

2. Entrepreneurial spirit. Demonstrates the initiative and courage to take calculated risks based on the identification and analysis of high-potential local and global business opportunities.

    a. Takes the initiative to capitalize on the challenges posed by global competition and seeks ways to meet them with new and enhanced quality products and services, techniques, methodologies, and so forth.

    b. Maintains a "can-do," proactive orientation despite high levels of environmental complexity, uncertainty, and resistant organizational barriers.

    c. Drives for results in priority areas rather than just pursuing activities that may or may not add value.

    d. Maintains a posture of creative dissatisfaction that consistently challenges the organizational status quo to uncover new opportunities.

    e. Demonstrates a sense of urgency in fulfilling tasks and achieving results.

    f. Grounds discussions of "internal" business issues in a language centered on global and local customer satisfaction, needs, and wants.

    g. Inspires others to become product and service champions.

3. Professional expertise. Demonstrates a commitment to the ongoing development of his or her business knowledge and skills to world-class levels.

    a. Establishes credibility quickly through displaying the highest standards of technical, functional, and management competence and product/service knowledge.

    b. Seeks knowledge and expertise beyond the specific boundaries of his or her position and understands the global interdependencies among units, functions, processes, positions, and so on.

    c. Drives to stay up to date on the major global trends that are shaping the industries and markets in which the company competes.

  d. Seeks out and utilizes global best practices from inside and outside the organization.

  e. Understands and utilizes financial concepts and principles to analyze business challenges and opportunities and promote the development of a common financial vocabulary throughout the global organization.

4. Stakeholder orientation. Demonstrates a willingness and an ability to balance the sometimes conflicting needs of stakeholders to achieve optimal results for the organization.

  a. Establishes open channels of communication between the organization and stakeholders (particularly customers) and uses them to gather accurate and timely input on existing and anticipated needs and wants.

  b. Balances stakeholder needs (including those of organizational units) based on an analysis of potential short- and long-term business impact (positive, neutral, and negative).

  c. Seeks to minimize barriers to organizational responsiveness within his or her sphere of influence (e.g., making recommendations for streamlining a process).

  d. When appropriate (when the individual feels the organization's interests will be better served in the short or long term), acts as an advocate for stakeholders when the company is showing resistance to positive change.

  e. Acts as a role model in continuously seeking value-added improvements in the creation and delivery of world-class products and services that will excite and delight customers and other stakeholders.

  f. Builds stakeholder needs (including those of communities) into organizational decision-making and planning processes.

5. Total organization astuteness. Demonstrates insight into "how the business works" above and beyond his or her immediate area and seeks to use this knowledge to get things done within and among organizational units.

  a. Draws on a range of information-gathering skills (direct questioning, observation, use of third parties, etc.) to build

a realistic profile of the global organization (above and
beyond those presented in annual reports and organization charts).

b. Creates or utilizes multiple internal networks for sourcing
business intelligence, expertise, global best practices, and
resources and for promoting coordination of effort and so
on.

c. Recognizes the key constituencies and decision makers in
the organization (within and outside of the formal chain of
command) and uses political savvy (an understanding of
power relationships rather than destructive manipulation
based simply on one-sided self-promotion) to create
alliances and foster collaboration to meet global goals.

d. Recognizes the deeply held assumptions and mental
models (conventional wisdom) embedded in the
organization's culture and helps them to surface for review
in the light of global business change.

e. Understands key organizational processes, systems,
standard operating procedures, working methods, and so
on, and promotes their continuous examination in relation
to achieving and sustaining world-class competitiveness.

f. Demonstrates a good sense of timing in putting forward
new ideas and proposals.

g. Analyzes key global trends and predicts their impact on
the organization's strategy, structure, and systems.

Relationship Management

*The ability to build and influence collaborative relationships in a complex
and diverse global network to direct energy toward the achievement of business strategies.*

   6. Change agentry. Demonstrates a receptivity to new and different ways of doing things and mobilizes others to identify and
implement desired changes.

a. Recognizes that change is the only constant in a global
business environment and that proactive change ("if it's
not broken, break it") is critical to long-term global competitive advantage.

b. Defines and communicates a compelling vision of the future that provides the sense of meaning, purpose, and optimism that sustains the change process.

c. Works to minimize barriers to change and utilizes key leverage points in the organization to facilitate required changes (e.g., resource allocation system, reward system, recruitment and selection, education and training).

d. Feels the pulse of the organization—where the energy is focused—and works with those energies to achieve and build momentum for change.

e. Communicates what it takes to succeed in the changed environment and coaches, mentors, and develops others in new expectations and accountabilities.

f. Empowers others to take ownership of the strategic change by identifying and implementing tactical solutions that fit with the change.

7. Community building. Demonstrates a willingness and an ability to partner with others in forging reciprocal, interdependent relationships aimed at the achievement of shared business goals.

a. Builds the commitment and engagement of others through communicating respect, developing trust, sharing information, and establishing a common purpose.

b. Encourages team diversity while working toward building common working ground that fosters collaboration and inclusion (e.g., shared norms of behavior, common goals and objectives, complementary working methods).

c. Creates opportunities for everyone to contribute to the achievement of shared goals (through planning, decision making, etc.) regardless of cultural style of working.

d. Ensures that members have the resources they need to accomplish their goals, (e.g., finance, people, training) while encouraging initiative and a sense of personal accountability for getting results.

e. Continuously builds relationships across the organization that can later be used as the foundation for developing and launching key global initiatives.

f. Works to develop the bench strength and potential of the team through providing feedback, recruiting global and local talent, and so forth.

8. Conflict management and negotiation. Demonstrates both assertiveness and sensitivity in using conflict to generate constructive outcomes.

a. Recognizes conflict as an integral part of human relationships and seeks to use it to generate creative energy for directing global organizational challenges and opportunities.

b. Recognizes and adapts to cultural differences in the display and handling of conflict, making decisions, and reaching binding agreements.

c. Anticipates potential conflicts and strategizes to minimize their destructive impact on relationships (e.g., through focusing on the problem, not the person; being flexible and patient; spending time on building relationships, not just making deals; building a climate of trust and mutual respect).

d. Works toward synergistic agreements based on shared interests rather than conducting win/lose battles of opposing positions (while also having a strong sense of the nonnegotiables).

e. Asserts viewpoints against resistance without becoming defensive or losing control.

f. Maintains a perspective aimed at establishing long-term benefits.

9. Cross-cultural communication. Demonstrates an ability to identify cultural differences and adapts his or her behavior to facilitate the achievement of shared understandings.

a. Recognizes his or her own dominant cultural orientations and has a well-developed sense of and respect for the visible and relatively invisible cultural differences among groups.

b. Appreciates the added value that different perspectives can bring to the table and is open to, and always listening for, different and more effective means for achieving shared objectives.

c. Continuously works to move beyond ethnocentrism, the use of national stereotypes and generalizations, and toward authentic relationships with individuals.

d. Demonstrates patience, civility, tolerance, empathy, and adaptability in seeking for, and responding to, substance over style in cross-cultural relationships.

e. Is aware of and sensitive to the cues communicated through nonverbal cross-cultural communication (e.g., hand gestures, facial expressions, silences).

f. Demonstrates a willingness and an ability to pursue learning other languages.

10. Influencing. Demonstrates an ability to move others to action without a reliance on positional authority or proximity.

a. Seeks power to champion critical initiatives for the organization rather than pursuing personal gains made at the expense of others.

b. Anticipates the effect of taking a certain action or conveying a specific message and strategizes to gain maximum appeal and persuasiveness (e.g., identifies key decision makers, appeals to organizational vision and values, uses compelling data and concrete examples of success, uses high-impact experts or other third parties to exert direct or indirect influence, uses appropriate timing, creates dramatic effects, and builds political coalitions).

c. Identifies and utilizes organizational sources of energy (sense of purpose, symbols, stretch goals, etc.) to minimize institutional barriers and build and sustain optimism and enthusiasm.

d. Maintains and communicates to others a sense of ethical integrity that builds trust, commitment, confidence, and authentic communication.

e. Acts as a role model for demonstrating courageous, decisive leadership when his or her expertise and/or personal strengths are required to reduce uncertainty and ambiguity and push initiatives forward.

    f. Uses all available means to build and sustain quality relationships over distances of time and space.

Personal Effectiveness

The ability to attain increasing levels of maturity to perform at peak levels under the strenuous conditions of working in a global enterprise.

    11. Accountability. Demonstrates a commitment to "owning" problems and takes responsibility within his or her sphere of influence for the achievement of business objectives.

    a. Feels a strong sense of stewardship about the organization and looks to ensure that its assets and resources are used to maximize benefits for existing and future stakeholders.

    b. Engages with the work of the organization and holds self and others accountable for achieving agreed-to goals and objectives that support business strategies.

    c. Sets high expectations for self and others and makes sure these expectations are well-defined and communicated with precision.

    d. Spends time reflecting on personal strengths and weaknesses and commits to a lifelong process of growth and development to increase effectiveness.

    e. Looks to make the best out of a difficult situation through persistence, hard work, and the driving need for a sense of accomplishment.

    f. Continually looks not to place blame but to get results.

    12. Curiosity and learning. Demonstrates a willingness over time to seek out challenging new experiences and an openness to learn from them.

    a. Approaches work in a global organization with a sense of adventure, openness, and a strong, intrinsic desire to experience the world (and the self) in new ways.

    b. Avoids limiting assumptions about the capabilities of self or others; recognizes the power of expectations in transforming performance from average to outstanding.

c. Reflects on new experiences and looks to draw lessons from what succeeded and what failed; translates those reflections into hypotheses for testing in future situations.

d. Is able to tolerate the discomfort caused by continuous new learning and lack of an achieved sense of mastery.

e. Looks to share learning with others to increase the pool of global expertise in the organization.

13. Improvisation. Demonstrates adaptability to changing circumstances and an ability to generate creative responses that add value under conditions of high uncertainty.

a. Demonstrates an ability to sense changing realities and the need for a new strategy.

b. Derives personal energy from uncertainty; recognizes the situation as an opportunity for play and experimentation.

c. Recognizes the need to move beyond habitual responses in a global business environment defined by rapid change, information overload, and increasing options for customers.

d. Creates an atmosphere that draws others into the creative process.

e. Respects standard operating procedures as a framework for action, but applies them based on an *objective* view of what will work locally and with the purpose of achieving the organization's larger goals and objectives.

14. Maturity. Demonstrates a strong and stable sense of self with a capacity for resilience when faced with crises and setbacks.

a. Demonstrates self-confidence (not arrogance) in the face of significant challenges.

b. Maintains a sense of balance in a rapidly changing environment, based on a deep set of personal values.

c. Demonstrates an ability to recover quickly from mistakes or outright failure, without becoming defensive or defeated, and to persist in moving toward the desired objective.

d. Maintains a sense of humor and perspective in challenging times.

e. Uses experience to anticipate and prepare for challenges and opportunities that are not obvious to others.

15. Thinking agility. Demonstrates a willingness and an ability to attack problems from multiple angles while maintaining a bias toward action.

a. Applies different thinking styles (strategic, analytical, systemic, inductive, deductive, etc.) based on each one's appropriateness to solving a problem or working with an idea.

b. Mixes and matches individual and social problem-solving processes based on given circumstances (e.g., need for quick response, need to build consensus).

c. Gathers input from global and local information sources to build and expand a knowledge base aimed at identifying opportunities and managing problems.

d. Avoids either/or thinking when faced with contradiction and works to develop rich solutions that contain elements of both sides of the dilemma; alternatively, seeks to develop a radically different approach.

e. Maintains an openness to counterintuitive data; avoids a rush to judgment.

f. Moves toward action without attempting to achieve a single "correct" answer or search for perfect information.

This list of competencies may seem overwhelming, but it is no more than many companies are currently seeking in their global leaders. The question should not be "Can this person demonstrate abilities in all of these competencies to the desired level?" but "Does this person show the ability and willingness to engage in a long-term pursuit of learning in these competency areas?"

The work of Professors McCall, Spreitzer, and Mahoney at the University of Southern California may offer some guidelines for identifying such people early on.[4] High-potential people, in their view; tend to exhibit the following attributes:

---

[4]Tom Richman, "Identifying Future Leaders," *Harvard Business Review,* November–December 1995, pp. 15–16.

+ They demonstrate commitment and take action.
+ These characteristics get them noticed, resulting in development opportunities.
+ They are less likely to stay in the same job past the point of learning from it.
+ They are more likely to take on new and demanding tasks, including overseas assignments.
+ If the organization doesn't offer them opportunities to develop, they are likely to create their own, despite risk to their careers.
+ Their integrity and interpersonal skills help establish trust with others, which enables them to get valuable feedback.
+ They are more likely than others to change as a result of feedback and mistakes.

Identifying such high-potential people and matching them with the kinds of experiences they will need to develop their business acumen, relationship management, and personal effectiveness competencies is the key to building global leadership bench strength. Does this mean taking a longer-term, strategic view of global leadership development? Yes, it does. The longer a company delays in setting up a selection and development process, the more it will confront a shortage of global talent in the years ahead. Global leaders cannot be pulled out of domestic, international, or even multinational hats.

GLOBAL LEADERSHIP COMPETENCIES IN ACTION

Lists of competencies are useful, but they don't help the reader get a *feel* for what is entailed. During the writing of this book, one interview in particular helped me put shape and substance to the qualities I was hearing global leaders needed to be successful. That interview was with Philip B. Evans, senior vice president, strategic alliances and joint ventures, at Avon Products, Inc. Quoting at length from my interview with him will help put flesh on the bones of some of the competencies listed above.

Of Phil Evans's 29 years with Avon, 26 have been spent on the international side of the business. After spending seven years with

DIALOGUE BOX

1. How do you rate yourself in each of the 15 competencies? (1 = Low, 5 = High). You could also have others you trust rate you. Return the favor.

Business Acumen	Relationship Management	Personal Effectiveness
◆ Depth of field ___	◆ Change agentry ___	◆ Accountability ___
◆ Entrepreneurial spirit___	◆ Community building___	◆ Curiosity and learning___
◆ Professional expertise___	◆ Conflict management and negotiation___	◆ Improvisation___
◆ Stakeholder orientation___		◆ Maturity___
◆ Total organizational astuteness___	◆ Cross-cultural communication ___	◆ Thinking agility___
	◆ Influencing ___	

2. Do you rate yourself much higher in one or two competency clusters? Did your partners' ratings confirm your results?

3. Why do you think the current imbalance exists? (What life experiences and choices on your part gave you your current competency profile?)

4. What do you think are the consequences of the imbalance that may keep you from being a successful global leader?

5. What can you do—inside and outside the organization—to correct the imbalance?

Avon in Canada, he helped the company open up the market in Japan. After Japan he was sent to New York, where he has had responsibility for heading up Avon businesses in Latin America, the Pacific, and Europe. The quotations from my interview with Phil Evans have been categorized under the three major competency cluster headings described in the leadership model. The reader will soon realize, however, that one quotation may reveal several competencies at work and that the categorization is somewhat arbitrary. Each quotation is followed by some of my own notes (in italics).

Business Acumen

1. "First, and foremost, the individual has to be good at what he or she does. The person must be a successful, above-average performer in the home environment so that they can bring skills and capabilities to the new environment and gain respect for what they know and are able to do."

Relevant competency: professional expertise. *Too often, individuals have been chosen to work in the international arena only because they possessed the right technical skills for the project. While we are gradually shifting to a more comprehensive view of the capabilities needed, we should not swing the pendulum too far and lose sight of the power and credibility that cutting-edge professional knowledge and skills bring to an initiative.*

Furthermore, those individuals with experience in overseas markets and operations become part of the intellectual capital of the company. Companies need to understand the role such knowledge assets can and should play in shaping and implementing their organizational strategies and how their competitors compare in global knowledge. They also need to answer such questions as: Who has what knowledge? Where are they now? Where can that knowledge add most value? What kind of investments do we need to make to close important gaps in our global knowledge portfolio? How can we make this knowledge more accessible to others?

Does access to knowledge make a difference? In 1994, Monsanto's chemical business lost a large order to a competing firm. In reviewing what had happened, headquarters in St. Louis learned that a sales representative, located somewhere else on the globe and in a different business unit, had heard rumors about the sale, but the difficulties caused by time zones and organizational boundaries had buried the information until it was too late.

Monsanto has now begun piloting a program on a Lotus Notes database that links salespeople, major account managers, and competitor-intelligence analysts. This Knowledge Management Architecture (KMA) provides a tool for helping to exploit customer and competitor intelligence, reveal best practices, and make highly informed decisions.[5]

One of the key capabilities of future leaders will be an ability to absorb and digest large amounts of technically sophisticated information while being able to communicate what is essential to the "unschooled mind."[6] The avoidance of either trivialization or distortion is becoming increasingly difficult.

2. "On the product side, the challenge was to convince Avon senior management and the board of directors to invest money in product research and development for a new line in the Japanese market. This was at a time when our business there was very small and when we had never developed a product for any market other than the U.S. (apart from conducting formula adaptations based on the legal/regulatory requirements of specific countries). Since that time, the Japanese product line has evolved, and in many ways is very different from the rest of Avon's product world."

Relevant competencies: entrepreneurial spirit; stakeholder orientation; total organizational astuteness. *From a relationship management perspective, change agentry and influencing are also highly relevant here, as is accountability from the personal effectiveness cluster. The Japanese market was very different from others encountered by Avon. Phil Evans was able to identify the need for change and the opportunity for Avon and its stakeholders. Beyond this, however, he used his organizational knowhow to help transform opportunity into results. Sometimes it's not easy being heard, but leaders persist. Jodie Kavanagh, an employee at Honda's East Liberty, Ohio, paint shop, came up with an idea to simplify the design of plastic bumper covers for the Civic model. Honda executives visiting the plant listened to the idea but rejected it. Instead of giving up, she came up with several alternatives. Eventually a compromise idea was reached, and Honda's savings in the United States alone are $1.2 million.[7]*

3. "A company can get a feeling that it is extremely well represented in terms of its global management by having people with different passports in key senior management positions. But these

---

[5]Thomas A. Stewart, "Getting Real about Brainpower," *Fortune,* November 27, 1995, p. 201.

[6]Gardner, *Leading,* p. 305.

[7]Edith Hill Updike, David Woodruff, and Larry Armstrong, "Honda's Civic Lesson," *Business Week,* September 18, 1995, p. 76.

people with different passports need to be put into the same kind of cross-cultural experiences that we expect of the home office people if they are to make a contribution to the global business. When you look to them to wear the other hat, that corporate hat, it's much harder for them to do so if the only role they have ever experienced is to be a member of the management team of one piece of the whole. Pulling up stakes and moving to France to run the French company or to Thailand to run the Thai company forces a change in perspective on the *whole* thing."

Relevant competency: depth of field. *Being a global company is about more than having people of different nationalities in management positions. It is also about providing those individuals with opportunities to gain a global perspective on the business. It is about wearing different hats (e.g., local and global) and developing depth of field to produce optimal results for the total organization.*

Optimizing is necessary in a complex system in which the achievement of certain objectives can negatively affect the achievement of others. Creating optimization is "deciding which compromise between conflicting goals will give the greatest benefit on balance. 'Satisficing' is a weaker form, in which the decision is merely to choose a compromise that can be accepted, and that meets certain minimum requirements."[8] Al Zeien, CEO of Gillette, gives the following example. A manager in Sweden needs to decide if he is going to increase his sales force in the northern part of the country. Most of the Swedish population lives in the south, but adding more salespeople in the north could increase sales. Zeien wants the manager to think about the money the entire Gillette world will make by adding those salespeople. This kind of decision can be facilitated by a good accounting system, as well as a performance rating system that rewards the manager for taking the company's global profitability picture into consideration.[9]

Relationship Management

1. "From a business point of view, my role when I went out there [Japan] in 1973 was really one of training and developing—and, to some extent, selecting—people to staff the marketing function. When

[8]Ruth Carter et al., *Systems, Management and Change: A Graphic Guide*, London: Paul Chapman, 1984, p. 112.

[9]Charles M. Farkas and Philippe De Backer, "There Are Only Five Ways to Lead," *Fortune*, January 15, 1996, pp. 109–12.

I went there, we hadn't realized the extent to which we would have to adapt and change the system in order to be successful. Somehow or other, whether it was part of my makeup or someone suggested it to me, I realized early on that listening was a very important skill to have in an overseas assignment. It became clear after a certain amount of time had passed that by creating an open channel of communication with my staff, we could begin to understand the needs of the marketplace rather than proceeding on the assumption we knew how to do it because we had done it in the United States, in Brazil, in Mexico, and this is how it gets done everywhere. Too often, companies look to local people to be implementers of a predetermined plan rather than participants in the development of the right iteration of that plan for that marketplace. I'm not sure what brought that into focus, but I think the fact that we were having more challenges making the kind of growth we were used to making in the early stages of a market entry made us realize we didn't have it quite right and we'd better adapt."

Relevant competencies: cross-cultural communication; and, from a personal effectiveness perspective, thinking agility. *Phil Evans talked during the interview of hearing counterintuitive advice from his Japanese staff. It was his ability to open the channels of communication and to listen to the advice (even though it meant changing a very successful Avon system) that led to successful entry into Japan. Listening (not just hearing) demonstrates respect and builds trust. Without listening, the advantages of diversity (different and more effective means for achieving shared objectives) are lost. His ability to be open to the counterintuitive data he was receiving and to integrate it into his problem-solving process demonstrated great mental agility.*

The problem of adaptation is by no means unique to Avon. Every globalizing company, at some point, hits a barrier when the tried and true system doesn't work, and managers need to pay very close attention. IKEA, for example, had adaptation problems in the United States. Based on previous successes, it assumed it could sell the same product to Americans that it had to the Swedes and the Swiss.[10] IKEA approached the United States from an exporter's mentality rather than that of an in-country enterprise. Swedish beds—measured in unfamiliar European centimeters rather than American inches—were too narrow for most Americans. IKEA had also not

---

[10]"Furnishing the World," *The Economist*, November, 19, 1994, p. 79.

thought to sell matching bedroom suites, which many Americans like. In addition, the IKEA kitchen cupboards were too narrow to accommodate pizza-size dinner plates. The American taste for lots of ice in drinks made the IKEA drinking glasses too small for practical use. To overcome this problem, many Americans were buying flower vases for drinking purposes. Healthy financial resources in Europe helped the company survive the early losses in the States. Now a large percentage of IKEA goods sold in the United States have been adapted to the local market, and sales have tripled.

Even McDonald's, that flagship of American standardization, has learned how to be adaptive. In markets that it finds difficult to "read," it takes on joint venture partners (the Far East) or licenses its name without taking on the risk of committing equity capital (the Mideast). Variations in the menu also cater to local wants and needs. Veggie burgers, instead of beef, will be the staple fare in India.[11]

2. "The individual must be able to convey to the people in the new environment that their interest in being there is to create success for that enterprise rather than success for him- or herself. All cultures are, I think, pretty quick to spot someone who comes into a situation and their primary goal is just to get noticed for what they're doing, or have their card punched before moving on. I would also not want to overstate becoming integrated into the team. You can go into a foreign culture and get buried in the team and not be able to exert your influence. It's finding the right balance between establishing respect and communicating that your role is to help that organization be more successful by introducing new and different ideas. 'Going native' can be a problem. You can easily lose the external perspective you were supposedly bringing to the party."

Relevant competencies: change agentry; community building; conflict management and negotiation; influencing; and, from a personal effectiveness perspective, accountability. *Effective global leaders understand that their primary challenge is not to be liked by everyone they encounter internationally but to create the conditions for organizational success under a different set of conditions. They have a sense of stewardship about the company. It means dealing with the paradox of being part of international groups while also challenging, if necessary, some assumptions held by groups (without destroying relationships).*

Some global leaders will find themselves acting as a bridge between

---

[11]Greg Burns, "All the World's a McStage," *Business Week*, May 8, 1995, p. 8.

cultures. Hendrik (Henk) van Baaren, president of flavors at International Flavors and Fragrances (IFF) and a Dutchman, remembers being sent by IFF in New York to head the European operation: "I think the Americans trusted me enough to offer me the job; they considered me to be in their camp. But the Europeans felt that I understood them, that they could talk to me about European points of view, problems and gripes. I was always explaining the one side to the other. The short-term view of the American approach caused difficulties. The Europeans often wanted a long-term cautious approach. They wanted to contemplate a little longer, be less aggressive, try things out a little bit. The Europeans wanted to put time and money up front. The Americans were always saying, 'What does the next quarter look like?'"

Pat Morgan of Bechtel also told me of instances in which his company has formed teams to act as cultural bridges: "Some years ago, we were asked to get involved in the Chunnel project [a rail tunnel between England and France]. Our role was a kind of management role to help the umbrella organization. We had a long discussion on what the team should be. It's well known that the British and the French don't always see eye to eye. How do you structure a team that can function well in that context? We settled on a team with a large Canadian representation. We found this was a very nice way to bridge some of the cultural issues. Many times, in looking at a strategy to win the work, we'll consider the cultural mix up front, and we'll communicate to the client that we've thought about these issues."

3. "Cultural adaptability is, I believe, very important. I used to think language skills were as important as cultural adaptability, but I now believe adaptability is far more important. Increasingly, those of us who don't possess great skills in foreign languages can be successful. It can be very dangerous to pick people because they have language skills and then find out they have very little cultural adaptability *and* little interest in adapting. You need a strong willingness to understand what it is that causes the people of another culture to behave the way they do so that you can be effective in listening and offering leadership. Perhaps it isn't so much adapting as it is becoming sufficiently 'tuned in' to the way people think and behave. In Japan, for example, you need to be very cognizant of the importance of 'face saving' and not immediately expose—particularly if you're the boss of a group—what it is that *you* want to do. You need to encourage the input before you display your point of view because there simply isn't the give-and-take we are used to."

Relevant competencies: cross-cultural communication; influencing. *There can be no doubt that cultural adaptability is a top priority for global leadership success. The issue of language skills is problematic. A 1995 survey on the abilities international managers need revealed different attitudes between English speakers and others. American and British participants considered language ability as "useful, but not essential."[12] Those managers whose first language was not English stressed the importance of speaking more than one language. One European said he would not consider hiring someone if "by the age of 40, the person still has not made an effort to learn another language." Interestingly, the British and the Americans also played down the importance of cultural differences.*

Henk van Baaren of IFF Flavors is very clear on the importance of learning about cultures and language. In our interview he said, "If you want to do business globally, you really must take your time to understand what makes another culture tick. Get firsthand experience. Go and work in another culture for a few years—not because you have to, but because you want to. Do it because it's exciting and interesting and you want to explore. Focus as if you're always going to be there. You should try and learn at least one language from the area. Addressing people in their language is very impressive; people feel you have taken the trouble to get to know their country and their culture."

4. "Strategic alliances and joint ventures are the way in which companies will expand their business in the future. People who have a relationship orientation are more likely to be successful in a situation where they don't have control."

Relevant competency: influencing. *Of interest here is the new concept of emotional intelligence (EQ). A study at Bell Laboratories found that those engineers who were most productive and valued on teams of up to 150 people did not measure at the highest levels on IQ or achievement tests or have the best academic qualifications.[13] Instead, determining factors in their success were congeniality, rapport building, empathic understanding, persuasiveness, and consensus building. These qualities helped them integrate well into information and communication networks so that often their requests were dealt with before others. On a more psychological level,*

---

[12]Leigh Ann Collins Allard, "The New International Manager," *Management Review*, August 1995, p. 6.

[13]Daniel Goleman, "The Decline of the Nice-Guy Quotient," *The New York Times*, September 10, 1995, p. 6E.

they were able to be in touch with and define their own feelings; control their immediate impulses (including anger, anxiety, and greed); calm themselves; and, under difficult conditions, stay resolved and hopeful. No doubt as work in this area moves forward, we will learn more about its practical applicability to success in cross-cultural situations.

5. "We must also be able to use our leadership skills in ways that are appropriate to the circumstances. In an Asian environment, for example, influence is probably more important than standing up with the flag and saying 'follow me.' In a Western context, you might have to use a very different set of your capabilities to galvanize the team. Ideally, you want it to be coming from some sort of consensus from your team as to where they all want to go, but there are always times when, as the leader, you have to say, 'This is the direction we're going in,' and bring people who are not fully with you into line. When you think about the full range of potential situations globally, the nature of those leadership skills varies from market to market . . . In the main, it is far better to work with a culture than against it, but there are times when you need to go against the grain. Let me draw an analogy. Do you use market research to tell you what to do all of the time? When you have ideas, market research is a very effective tool in determining how successful that idea is likely to be. Sometimes you are thinking about something consumers are not able to think about themselves. There may well be times in a new situation where, instinctively or for the right set of reasons, you believe strongly enough that it needs to be done a certain way, although that doesn't necessarily match up with what the people you've hired from the local environment think is the right way to go. That's a leadership trait at some point. You've heard the input and thought about the pros and cons, and you've taken your own set of experiences, and you say, 'We're going to do it this way.' More often than not, it's a question of going with the flow and adapting."

Relevant competencies: conflict management and negotiation; influencing. *From the business acumen cluster, professional expertise will play a large role, as will accountability from the personal effectiveness cluster. Phil's quote raises a key question: When does adaptability slip over into abdication of leadership responsibility? Obviously, judgment is called for in every situation, and that judgment needs to based on the weight given to several factors in the situation. Those factors will include*

+ *The importance of the task to be accomplished.*
+ *The nature and importance of the relationships.*
+ *The relative business acumen of all the involved parties.*
+ *The time pressures.*

One thing needs to be clear to all global leaders: Cross-cultural relationships are highly important to the success of the business, but the goal is not to create "Happy Families" based on harmony, peace, and love.[14] Leadership is about having or taking responsibility to redirect attention or resources to make the right things happen for the organization and its stakeholders. Adaptability does not equal adoption or accommodation. Adaptability is about switching communication style and so on, to facilitate working together. A skilled leader can still get things done his or her way if appropriate and keep the relationships intact. Use of indirect communication is often a good way to make a point without creating huge amounts of resistance. Klaus Roithner, an engineer with Siemens of Germany, has worked on a joint venture with IBM. After analyzing IBM's pilot manufacturing system, he made some proposals for improving it. IBM staff simply accused him of wanting to do things the Siemens way. Changing his style, he says, "I indirectly suggest an idea to IBM engineers, and let them think they have come up with it themselves."[15]

Personal Effectiveness

1. "First of all [in terms of what it takes to be successful in working internationally], a genuine interest in what's going on in the rest of the world and, probably more than anything—fostered by the three years I spent in Japan—a sense of adventure and curiosity."

Relevant competencies: curiosity and learning. *Every global leader I've spoken to has had this sense of adventure and curiosity. This "call to adventure" is captured well in* <u>The Adventure of Working Abroad: Hero Tales from the Global Frontier</u> *by Joyce Sautters Osland.[16] She uses a framework based on the journey of the mythical hero to describe the*

---

[14]Tony Eccles, *Succeeding with Change: Implementing Action-Driven Strategies*, London: McGraw-Hill, 1994, p. 168.

[15]E. S. Browning, "Computer Chip Project Brings Rivals Together, but Cultures Clash," *The Wall Street Journal*, May 3, 1994, p. 1.

[16]Joyce Sautters Osland, *The Adventure of Working Abroad: Hero Tales from the Global Frontier*, San Francisco: Jossey-Bass, 1995, p. 710.

experience of working overseas. The first stage is the Call to Adventure, which involves stepping into the unknown. Crossing over boundaries (physical and cultural) is difficult. It is the equivalent of Jonah being swallowed by the whale. Sometimes help is given by a protective figure, such as a mentor.

The second stage is Initiation. The "hero" undergoes tests and ordeals that must be overcome. A transformation takes place as difficulties are managed and insights are gained. It involves a process of letting go of old perceptions and behaviors and taking on new ones. The "hero" has a new source of power that ultimately derives from increased self-awareness and the knowledge that she or he has have the inner capacity to overcome difficult situations.

The third stage is Return, which again is often far from an easy adjustment. When successful, the "hero" is able to move across the boundaries with ease. He or she also has a heightened consciousness of self and the surrounding world.

Without a desire for experiencing the unknown and a willingness to undertake a difficult journey of understanding self and others, I cannot imagine anyone succeeding globally.

2. "The biggest personal challenge was recognizing that you could cope in a place where everything is as different as it is in Japan, where your skills with the language are minimal at best."

Relevant competency: maturity. *One of the greatest challenges of working globally is that successful individuals in one environment are asked to perform at similar levels in an unfamiliar setting. This can be extremely disorienting. What has worked for them in the past no longer creates the results they are used to. This can be as basic, as one manager said to me recently, as trying to buy bleach in a store or as complex as trying to formulate a joint strategy when all the parties approach the strategy-making process with very different thinking patterns. When working across cultures, we are often thrown back into more childlike (dependent) modes of learning. This can be very uncomfortable for highly successful people who are used to getting results quickly. Self-confidence in one's underlying capabilities and resilience in seeing things through are a must.*

3. "From a personal point of view, the opportunity to work in a global company in a variety of different roles, markets, countries, and cultures really needs to be seen by the individual as both rewarding from a business point of view—in terms of opportunities for career progression—but also as a fantastic life experience to be enjoyed! There are enormous opportunities for personal growth and development whether they ultimately prove useful to the company or not. At various stages of one's career, you say, 'Well, that was kind of a waste of time. It doesn't seem to have gotten me anywhere,' but in reality you've developed some confidence or an understanding which 2, 5, or 10 years down the road, comes back to be a valuable asset."

Relevant competency: accountability. *While many managers gauge their success by rising to new heights in their organizations or obtaining increased compensation packages, many global leaders I've met seem to work with a different set of criteria. Promotion and pay are important, of course, but many talk in terms of personal growth and development. They feel deeply enriched by the experience of working across cultures and of becoming more self-aware. I once heard someone on the radio talking about the space program say, "The real benefit was the challenge it posed." Many global leaders express the same sentiment about working internationally.*

4. "Avon, at that stage, had successfully expanded into Latin America and Europe essentially doing what most companies do as they expand internationally: taking the concept that has been successful in the home market and rolling it out. Japan was the first market we encountered where the Avon 'system' just didn't work.

There were two significant differences from our other markets at that time. One was product driven; the local cosmetic market was dominated by Japanese companies, and the Japanese consumer perceived their products to be designed specifically for their needs, the sensitivity of their skin, etc. They were very loyal to those Japanese companies. The second difference was cultural. The direct selling that Avon was used to doing wasn't a comfortable cultural fit. Avon's style of direct selling was somewhat casual and relaxed, with friends and neighbors dealing with one another. The Japanese style of direct selling was a more highly structured, formal, and professional system. Early on we had to think about how to adapt the Avon formula to this market. Interestingly, in order to distinguish ourselves from the entrenched Japanese companies, we chose to become even more informal and relaxed in our style of selling."

Relevant competency: improvisation. *It requires a high level of flexibility to let go of a tried and trusted idea and take a risk that may or* *may not produce better results. What Phil Evans did in Japan worked, even though it was a departure from the Avon system. A flair for improvising has been common among the successful global leaders I've talked with. I remember one individual in particular. His company sold medical devices, specifically bags for capturing fluids from wounds. Because of his knowledge of the products, he was sent to head a booth at a trade fair in Mexico. At first, he didn't have much luck. The Mexicans, he noticed, tended to socialize and discuss business with people they already knew. No one was stopping at his booth. After the first day, he was struck with an idea. Visiting the business center at the fair, he created an invitation to free drinks at the pool the following evening. He strategically placed these invitations at eating and drinking places at the fair and hoped for the best. The following evening he waited for people to turn up at the pool, and they did—in droves. Rather than serving drinks directly from bottles, he had poured each bottle into a different style of surgical bag and hung them over a makeshift bar. The bags soon became the topic of discussion at the pool, and, of course, relationships were quickly made and business followed.*

Heineken has a reputation for being a company that finds and develops excellent global managers. Han de Goederen, production manager in the Netherlands, told Business Week *of his 4 ½ years in Africa when very often the telephones didn't work: "That was good training for making your own decisions without the support of the group in Holland."*[17]

Bechtel has also proven to be adept at improvising when necessary. Pat Morgan, a human resources manager with Bechtel, told me of the time when his company was contracted to provide support and logistics in Kuwait after the Gulf War: There was no labor in Kuwait, and so in the space of about four months we mobilized about 15,000 people from around the world into the country. We tapped into our operations in Thailand, Philippines, Indonesia, and so on. In doing that, you need to innovate. Kuwait at the time was heavily mined, and we couldn't put our people onto the land. So we moved a ship into Kuwait harbor and had our people live on the ship. We also had to bring in mine disposal experts to clear the areas we were going to work in. At that time, just after the war, there was also no Kuwait immigration department, so we were faced with the issue of how to get people into the country. I went in as air freight, and we took a lot of people in that way. But because I had gone in as air freight, I couldn't get out when

[17]Julia Flynn and Richard Melcher, "Heineken's Battle to Stay Top Bottle," *Business Week*, August 1, 1994, p. 61.

it was time for me to leave. When you're operating internationally, very little gets done by the textbook."

OVERDOING STRENGTHS, NEGLECTING WEAKNESSES

The challenge for the global leader—and, consequently, for his or her organization—is in how to blend the competencies into an effective mix for specific situations. High potential managers tend to build competency strength in one area but neglect the others. It is not unusual, for example, for a high-potential manager to be very strong in business acumen but relatively weak in relationship management and personal effectiveness. As already mentioned, many expatriates have been selected in the past because of their technical expertise in or knowledge of the business. The high failure rates among of expatriates are a testimony to the inadequacy of a one-dimensional approach to global leadership.

Leaders who overemphasize business acumen will tend toward overcontrol in working with others. Such leaders pay very close attention to consistent and very well-defined structures. A focus will be placed on the task at hand, and the relationships through which the task will be completed will be neglected. Good results may be

DIALOGUE BOX

1. What difficulties has the company as a whole experienced in operating globally? (Be candid.)

2. Do these difficulties suggest that the company needs to be paying more attention to building strength in specific global competency areas?

3. What do you think the company as a whole should be doing to address the competency deficits?

4. What can you do within your sphere of influence to close the competency gaps?

achieved in the short term, but long-term results will tend to decline and the work climate will be strained and lacking in innovative spirit and collaboration. Those at the center of global organizations need to be cautious about an overemphasis on control. Rather than working *with* others in the global organization, overcontrollers work *at* others and can disempower and alienate those in the subsidiaries. When you weave a tendency toward "I know what I'm talking about. This is the way to do it" with fears of cultural imperialism and imposed policies and procedures dictated by the home office, you have a potentially explosive mix at worst or a recipe for unproductiveness at best.

On the other hand, an underemphasis on business acumen and control will lead to a lack of respect and credibility and a lack of consistency across the organization. If the leader cannot gain respect overseas through knowledge and expertise, the assignment is doomed from the beginning. Those who underemphasize business acumen will also neglect the financial perspective necessary for competitive operations and a concern for effectiveness and efficiency.

An overemphasis on relationship management on the part of the global leader will result in a lack of structure and clarity in terms of accountabilities and authority lines, indecisiveness, frustration, and a loss of individual recognition and a sense of personal achievement. The cooperative situation may "feel good" but be lacking in needed results. Well-intentioned managers in cross-cultural business interactions may spend inordinate amounts of time and energy on networking, building cooperation, incorporating diversity, and gaining consensus when what may be needed is a clear direction and a structural framework in which to operate. Not every decision can or should be reached in a collaborative manner. If the global organization is to work in an integrated fashion, some decisions will need to be mandated and others delegated.

An underemphasis on relationship management will result in undercommunication, confusion, lack of feedback and trust, an overabundance of self-interested power games, opportunism, and minimal collaboration. In a time of intense competition, complexity, and change, relationships are a competitive advantage. Competitors can replicate products and services fairly quickly. On the other hand, relationships among members of the organization and between organizational members and customers are difficult, if not impossible, to reproduce.

An overemphasis on personal effectiveness creates mavericks who do things in their own self-interested way. Action takes place in an environment that can be defined in Darwinian terms as "the survival of the fittest." As Robert Keidel says, "there is a notion of personal liberty and freedom, without a concomitant sense of responsibility and community."[18] When personal effectiveness becomes an end in itself, the individual part manipulates the environment for its own ends, whether or not the actions taken will benefit others or the organization as a whole.

An underemphasis on personal effectiveness, however, destroys incentive, aspiration, creativity, and, perhaps most important, personal accountability. What we are witnessing in corporate America today are the dying and painful last breaths of business dinosaurs built for an industrial rather than an information age. These industrial organizations emphasized control and paternalism in a relatively stable environment. We have become used to the comfort and shelter they offered us, but competitive times have changed and our organizations are changing with them.

Morris Shechtman describes this new environment as "high risk" and emphasizes that individuals no longer have the job security, career advancement, and organizational stability they have come to expect.[19] The rules for success in these new times revolve around taking accountability for our personal growth and development and holding others accountable for their own. While such a view may seem to overdo the personal effectiveness element of the triad, the intended outcome of Shechtman's approach is not only accountable individuals but non-codependent, reciprocal, and interdependent relationships based on mutual interest.

THE GLOBAL LEADERSHIP GENDER CHALLENGE

Only about 3 percent of global managers are women compared with domestic manager positions, where they hold 37 percent of the jobs. Something seems wrong here! Can women be effective global managers? Yes, of course they can. But, as Nancy Adler makes clear, a

---

[18]Keidel, *Seeing*, p. 18.

[19]Morris R. Shechtman, *Working Without a Net: How to Survive and Thrive in Today's High Risk Business World*, Englewood Cliffs, NJ: Prentice Hall, 1994.

number of myths need to be challenged before the numbers rise significantly.[20]

Myth 1: Women are reluctant to take on global roles. The reason most often given for failed expatriate assignments in the past has been "failure of spouse and/or children to adjust." As Adler points out, "companies have confused a role (unemployed spouse) with a gender (female) and concluded that women do not adjust well to life abroad." In a survey of more than 1,000 graduating MBAs, Adler found an equal number of men and women wanting to pursue an international assignment in their careers. The limiting beliefs come from those with the power to determine assignments (some of whom may be women). Typical beliefs may take forms such as: "I don't think you'll have the stamina to survive in the tropics"; "We shouldn't send a woman (particularly a single woman) to that part of the world."

Myth 2: Women in dual-career marriages are poor candidates. In Adler's study, more than three-fourths of the human resource executives interviewed said that dual-career marriages were a reason companies avoid sending women abroad. A man with a working wife would be considered, but not vice versa! Dual careers can be a problem, but not necessarily. Many careers are increasingly portable, and other spouses find positions overseas.

Myth 3: Women managers face more foreign prejudice than men do. Prejudice against local women is often used as a basis for predicting the failure of an expatriate woman. Adler surveyed more than 100 women managers on international assignments. Almost all (97 percent) said their assignments were successful. Almost half (42 percent) described their gender as an advantage; 16 percent found both advantages and disadvantages; and 22 percent saw their gender as irrelevant. Only 20 percent saw their gender as a disadvantage. What became clear is that foreigners are seen as foreigners above all else; a foreign woman is not expected to act as a local woman would. The limiting cultural expectations imposed on local women therefore do not apply to the female expatriate. Novelty may be a factor in acceptance, but so is a respect for professionalism. Many women expatriates report what they call a "halo effect." Men in the host nation

---

[20]Nancy J. Adler, "Women Managers in a Global Economy," *Training & Development*, April 1994, pp. 31–36.

recognize that women international managers are rare, and so those that do exist must be outstanding in order to represent their company. Situations can occur in which managers and customers in the host country assume the woman expatriate is not a manager. I have personally known of such cases in Japan, the Middle East, and Latin America where the women were actually sent to be team leaders. In such instances, male colleagues need to take the initiative in making sure that host-country nationals understand the status and authority of the woman before loss of face or damage to her ability to perform effectively occurs.

Women can do a number of things to help pave the way to their success:

- Establish yourself as a foreigner.
- Take a first-class flight, and stay at a first-class hotel.
- Be introduced by the company's highest-ranked representative in the region or a well-respected third party.
- Emphasize the prestige of your company.
- Have your CEO send letters of introduction.
- Translate your business card (including definitions of your title).
- Produce an organizational chart showing your position in the hierarchy.
- Quickly establish your decision-making power and authority (in Japan, this will mean sitting at the center of the table).
- Speak forcefully with few qualifiers.
- Be very well prepared (better than your male colleagues).
- Display professionalism and femininity in clothing and manner (while showing respect to the other culture).
- Find a mentor for local mores, and pay attention to the details (like bringing an odd number of flowers to a host in Germany).
- Don't take male-dominated cultures personally.[21]

---

[21]Carol Steinberg, "Working Women Have Their Work Cut Out for Them Overseas," *World Trade*, February 1996, pp. 22–24.

Companies engaged in building global leadership bench strength must look to their men *and* women. Limiting beliefs and assumptions must be challenged whether they relate to race, color, creed, or gender. Women need to be considered for international work as often as men, and for assignments that are not just temporary or experimental. Assumptions about foreign discrimination need to be given less prominence in our thinking. We need to be realistic; some women (like some men) will fail in their assignments. But we must not generalize beyond that point; we need to focus on identifying and making use of talent. We also need to create benefits packages that offer greater support and flexibility to dual-career families and single men and women. Adler also has a number of good suggestions for creating more constructive policies: greater lead time in announcing international assignments (allowing greater preparation time for those in dual-career relationships); access to executive-search services for partners with careers; benefits aimed at helping people stay in touch if they choose some form of commuting arrangement (e.g., telephone or airfare allowances); and appropriate titles and status.

Perhaps the first challenge many companies will face is getting the issue of women in international assignments onto the corporate agenda. As Pat Morgan of Bechtel said to me in our interview, "If global assignments are part of the career path in the organization, we have to make sure that women (particularly those with children) and minorities have access to the assignments and tools they need to succeed. You have to be proactive." How many U.S. or foreign companies can say they are looking at this issue proactively?

One final word needs to be said here about gender. Creating strength in all areas of the Global Leadership Triad—business acumen, relationship management, and personal effectiveness—applies to men and women equally. Some of the literature seems to emphasize the strengths of women in terms of relationship management only. Kathryn Leary, CEO of the Leary Group, an international marketing firm based in New York, says that women have certain advantages over men when operating in a global business environment.[22] These advantages include greater skills in nurturing

---

[22]Rhonda Reynolds, "The Personal Touch," *Black Enterprise,* July 1995, p. 42.

relationships, empathy, adaptability to the needs of others, and listening. This may be true, but these strengths need to be made firm by balancing them with the other elements of the triad.

SUMMARY CHECKPOINT

The development of global leadership requires organizational and personal investment in those capabilities that make a difference. Being an effective global leader requires a blending of three competency clusters: business acumen, relationship management, and personal effectiveness. Business acumen is the ability to pursue and apply appropriate professional knowledge and skills to achieve optimal results for the company's stakeholders. This cluster consists of five competencies: depth of field, entrepreneurial spirit, professional expertise, stakeholder orientation, and total organizational astuteness. Relationship management is the ability to build and influence cooperative relationships in a complex and diverse global network to direct energy toward the achievement of business strategies. It consists of change agentry, community building, conflict management and negotiation, cross-cultural communication, and influencing. Personal effectiveness is the ability to attain increasing levels of maturity to perform at peak levels under the strenuous conditions of working in a global enterprise. This cluster contains accountability, curiosity and learning, improvisation, maturity, and thinking agility.

DIALOGUE BOX

1. Do you believe there are prevailing myths about the roles and capabilities of women and minorities as global leaders in your company? What are those myths, and how do they show themselves?

2. What can you do within your sphere of influence to challenge such myths?

3. To what extent do current benefits packages and company policies facilitate or inhibit women and minorities taking global leadership positions?

The primary question to ask of an individual is not "Can this person bring abilities in all of these competencies to the desired level?" but "Does this person show the ability and willingness to engage in a long-term pursuit of learning in these competency areas?" Every company should be setting up an appropriate selection and development process or face a severe shortage of global leaders in the years ahead.

A key challenge for individuals is to develop strength in all three competency clusters. Too often, high-potential managers build competency strength in one cluster (e.g., business acumen) but neglect the others.

A major challenge for organizations is to develop the global leadership talent of its men and women. Too many myths operate in our companies rationalizing why women are inappropriate for global assignments. These limiting beliefs must be challenged wherever and whenever they arise. It is not only the right thing to do; it also makes business sense in a world short of global talent.

SOME ACTION IDEAS

Individual	Organization
◆ Assess your desire for working and leading in a global business environment. To begin with, do you have the motivation? Does the idea of working globally *really* engage you?	◆ Assess the need to develop a set of global leadership competencies in the organization. How would they add value to strategy development and implementation? You might want to share the Global Leadership Triad with influential colleagues and begin informal discussions. Relate these discussions to plans the company has for building and/or sustaining its global leadership position.
◆ Discuss the global plans of your company with your manager. What are the pathways into playing a significant global leadership role (e.g., high-potential programs). What needs to be done to get into such programs?	

Individual	**Organization**
• Use the Global Leadership Triad as a tool for identifying your personal development needs. Gain feedback from others on how they perceive your global capabilities.	• Identify champions in the organization who could drive the competency identification process. Enlist their support in widening the debate. Whenever possible, enlist the support of influential line managers. Note: Ideally, the human resource function would facilitate, but not drive, the process.
• Identify the top three things you must absolutely do now to strengthen your global leadership capabilities.	
• Identify work and nonwork opportunities to build competencies.	• Establish a global task force of line managers and human resource personnel. Use the Global Leadership Triad as a starting point for analysis. Relate the triad back to your specific business plans and strategies.
• Consider the competencies listed in the Global Leadership Triad in relation to your own company. Are there competencies missing that you believe are key to success in your *specific* business environment? Discuss these with your manager.	
	• Use the task force to formulate a plan on how best to proceed (e.g., surveys, focus groups). Choose methods that will create maximum ownership of the final competency list.

CHAPTER 3

Leadership in a Collaborative Global Enterprise

There may be born leaders, but there surely are far too few to depend on them.

Peter Drucker[1]

Preview

- Productive collaboration among worldwide units is a distinguishing mark of the successful global enterprise. Global leadership at all levels must foster deep rather than surface collaboration.

- Four key facilitators are identified for achieving successful global collaboration: global competency development, global context-building, global values clarification, and global skill development. Global leaders must drive these facilitators through the organization.

- Global leadership levels within an organization can be divided into four broad bands (the global leadership spectrum). Collaboration within and among bands is

[1]Peter Drucker, "Foreword: Not Enough Generals Were Killed," in *The Leader of the Future: New Visions, Strategies, and Practices for the Next Era*, ed. Francis Hesselbein, Marshall Goldsmith, and Richard Beckhard, San Francisco: Jossey-Bass, 1996, p. xi.

enhanced when associates understand their global roles and accountabilities. Global leadership competencies provide a framework of expected behaviors and traits and facilitate a shared understanding of priorities.

+ To function collaboratively, associates need a shared contextual understanding of the organization, the business, and the global environment in which the business competes. Leadership cannot emerge and thrive in an information-starved working climate.

+ Collaborative values must exist at the macro (world) and micro (team) levels, and they must be embedded in performance measures and reward systems. Shared values, such as respect and responsibility, help build common working ground. Such values cannot be imposed, but must be constructed in an open dialogue.

+ While role clarification, context-building, and value clarification make global collaboration possible, communication, leadership, and organization skills make it happen. Global leaders are continuously building and refining these skills in themselves and others.

THE COLLABORATIVE GLOBAL ENTERPRISE

Along with superior financial performance, high levels of customer satisfaction, excellent employee morale, and the power of the company to attract top-notch recruits, productive collaboration among the worldwide units of the enterprise is a sure sign of health in the global company. Leadership at all levels must foster collaboration among the scattered locations or the organization will stagger along at suboptimal performance and eventually die.

When successful, global collaboration generates outstanding results. One example is the IBM ThinkPad 700C.[2] Reflecting the idea of a traditional Japanese lunchbox, *Shokadou Bentou*, which has a simple exterior and a complex interior, the 700C was an intensive effort across three continents: the United States, Japan, and Europe.

---

[2]Kiyonori Sakakibara, "Global New Product Development: The Case of the IBM Notebook Computers," *Business Strategy Review*, Vol. 6, no. 2, Summer 1995, p. 25.

The talent network was based in the IBM Yamato Design Center in Japan (industrial designers and engineers); Milan, Italy (industrial design consultant); the IBM Almaden Research Center in San Jose, California (researchers); and the IBM Corporate Design Program in Stamford, Connecticut (strategy and coordination staff). Communication during the development process was almost daily. Technology played a major part in facilitating the collaboration; a Sony image system, fax machines, telephones, and electronic mail provided the continuous linkages and helped build an integrated, empowered team.

To talk of collaboration, however, is not enough. We need to distinguish between *deep* and *surface* collaboration. In surface collaboration, engagement with the process and the outcome is enough only to get the job done satisfactorily. Individuals and units work within a shared plan, but their focus is on their own specific interests and outcomes rather than the group interests and outcomes. There is no sense of a deeper purpose or mission. We might call this cooperation rather than collaboration. Deep collaboration occurs when there is the full engagement of participants and an intense focus on a shared singular purpose that transcends the interests of individuals or units. There is a seamless integration of the parts, and the outcome appears to have been produced by a "single good mind."[3] Both types of collaboration are positive, but real breakthroughs and synergies take place at the deep level, as in the IBM ThinkPad example. Leaders who blend individual and local interests with collective interests and demonstrate the value of interdependence create the winning global teams.

What can a global organization do to promote collaboration among and within its multiple locations? There are at least four major factors (see Figure 3–1).

+ **Global competency development:** Competencies are the driving needs of the business articulated in statements about the desired characteristics of organizational members. They provide a framework of expected behaviors and traits and facilitate a shared understanding of priorities.

---

[3] John B. Smith, *Collective Intelligence in Computer-Based Collaboration*, Hillsdale, NJ: Erlbaum Associates, 1994, pp. 2–3.

- ◆ **Global context-building:** Context provides the shared understandings of the world, the organization, and the business that facilitate the collaborative process. Too few people in our organizations have a good, functional understanding of the business in which they work, and of the global environment in which the business is trying to succeed.

- ◆ **Global value clarification:** It is difficult to imagine a global organization functioning effectively without being saturated with a well-articulated set of collaborative values. Such values make possible the deep collaboration the organization needs to operate at peak performance. Writing corporate value statements is not enough. Professional, collegial values at the macro (world) and micro (team) levels must drive everyday decision making at all levels and locations.

- ◆ **Global skill development:** Communication, leadership, and organizational skills take us beyond the realm of values and make collaboration happen. Transnational teamwork is where the global agenda and local agenda meet in a creative tension that can be generative of value or entropic.

FIGURE 3–1

Global Collaboration: Key Factors

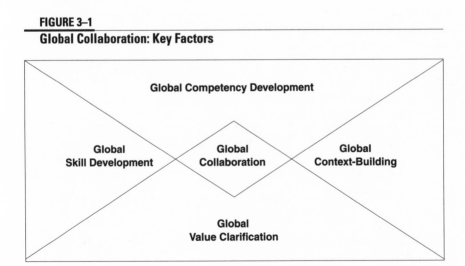

With clear roles, accountabilities, and competency requirements; an understanding of the world, business, and organizational contexts in which they work; well-defined sets of collaborative values under which to operate; and the skills to make transnational teamwork a reality, leaders across the spectrum can maximize the collaborative power of global organizations.

GLOBAL COMPETENCY DEVELOPMENT

The previous chapter presented a generic model of global leadership competencies, the Global Leadership Triad. This provides a foundation for further competency development and customization. By providing a map of required competencies, an organization helps communicate and reinforce its strategic intentions and needs. Collaboration is enhanced when people understand the big picture and their part in it and can support one another in fulfilling roles and accountabilities, compensating for competency gaps, and getting results. Roles and competencies need to be understood and aligned so that the organization is achieving maximum focus and synergy.

What can an organization do to develop its competency profiles? There are at least five steps (see Figure 3–2). The number of steps followed depends on the depth of analysis required. Step 1, "analyze the actual and potential global business environment," will provide leadership profiles that can be useful—at a very general level—for recruitment and selection. Driving the analysis down to step 3, "identify roles and responsibilities within bands," will generate a list of global leadership competencies for the organization as a whole. One step further and the competencies will be matched to the different bands on the company's global leadership spectrum. Finally, at step 5, global leadership competencies will be generated for specific jobs in different functional areas. The choice of how deep to go will depend on the objective (what will we use the competency lists for?) and the availability of human and financial resources.

Collecting data for this process usually involves focus groups of job occupants, their managers, direct reports, and even customers, suppliers, and other stakeholders. Critical event interviews, surveys, and direct observation techniques may also be used.

FIGURE 3–2

Competency Development

Step	Description
1. Analyze the actual and potential global business environment	Identify the dynamics of the current and future global business environment of the company. Produce broad profiles of the types of men and women needed to drive competitiveness into the next century.
2. Identify global leadership bands in the company	Identify the logical demarcation points on the company's global leadership spectrum. Describe the major differentiation factors between each leadership band.
3. Identify roles and responsibilities within bands	Analyze the major roles and responsibilities within each leadership band on the spectrum, and produce a list of global leadership competencies relevant to the total organization.
4. Define competencies in relation to each leadership band	From the organizational list (e.g., the Global Leadership Triad), link competencies to each leadership band. Rework competency descriptions, when necessary, to relate to the specific roles and responsibilities of each band.
5. Identify competencies for specific jobs/functions	Select jobs with actual or potential global impact and analyze roles and responsibilities, primary tasks and performance criteria, and behavioral indicators.

Step 1: Analyze the Actual and Potential Global Business Environment

Understand the actual and potential dynamics of the organization's global business environment, including its industries, markets, technologies, and so on. Look 5 and 10 years beyond the present time. Analyze the company's strategic response to these dynamic changes and what this response means for the types of people the company needs. Develop profiles of the types of individuals needed to build and sustain the company's global leadership. Senior managers are often a good source for this type of information.

Step 2: Identify Global Leadership Bands in the Company

Within any global corporation, there will be what I call a *global leadership spectrum*. Within this spectrum, I distinguish four broad bands: individual associate, first-line, middle, and senior. Individuals may be based in different locations around the world but be members of the same band and share very similar roles and competency requirements. Certain differentiating factors are important in distinguishing among the bands, although no hard and fast boundaries exist. (See Figure 3–3.)

    1. More complex mental tasks. There is no doubt that the types of problems dealt with at senior levels are more complex and demand a sophisticated range of thinking skills. The number of variables tends to be much greater and the relationships among them more complicated and dynamic. In moving away from technical and functional problems to global, systemwide problems, the senior manager also encounters increased levels of uncertainty in the reliability or usefulness of data, a shift away from the concrete to the abstract, an environment given to dramatic change, a greater variety of options and trade-offs, and an increased need to rely on judgment forged out of experience rather than analysis per se.

FIGURE 3–3

Five Differentiating Factors

Individual Associate	First-Line Manager	Middle Manager	Senior Manager

a. More complex mental tasks ————————————————————→

b. Wider and more powerful circles of influence————————————→

c. Increased risk and complexity of international contact ————————→

d. Increased time span ——————————————————————→

e. Decreased level of technical input ————————————————→

Elliot Jaques and Kathryn Cason have pinpointed a number of mental processing patterns.[4] The first is what they call *declarative processing;* that is, a position is explained by articulating a number of separate reasons. No connection is made between the reasons. The second type is called *cumulative processing;* a position is explained by pulling together a number of different ideas. None of the reasons by itself makes the case, but taken together they add up to one. The third pattern is called *serial processing;* a position is explained by putting together a chain of thought made up of a sequence of reasons, and each one builds to the next one. The final pattern is called *parallel processing;* several positions are created by means of serial processing, and the chains of reasoning or scenarios are held in parallel and connections are made among them. Elements of one scenario may be put into another; the final position may be a combination of elements from several chains.

While all types of mental processing can be useful across the spectrum, many of the problems faced at the senior and middle levels of global management require sophisticated parallel mental processing. Developing a global strategy, for example, requires the creation and linkage of multiple possible scenarios.

Rosabeth Moss Kanter clearly sees the need to stress thinking in our new models of global leadership, particularly at the senior level:

> The intellectual functions of leaders have often been neglected in discussions of leadership. Charisma, force of personality, or interpersonal skills have often been stressed more than the brainpower required for leaders to think through problems and find new solutions. . . . In the global economy of the information age, ideas and events are reshaping—or threatening to reshape—every social and economic institution. . . . Trying to lead while the system itself is being reshaped puts a premium on brains: to imagine possibilities outside of conventional categories, to envision actions that cross traditional boundaries, to anticipate repercussions and take advantage of interdependencies, to make new connections or invent new combinations.[5]

---

[4]Elliott Jaques and Kathryn Cason, *Human Capability,* Falls Church, VA: Cason Hall, 1994, pp. 30–31.

[5]Rosabeth Moss Kanter, "World-Class Leaders: The Power of Partnering," in *The Leader of the Future: New Visions, Strategies, and Practices for the Next Era,* ed. Francis Hesselbein, Marshall Goldsmith, and Richard Beckhard, San Francisco: Jossey-Bass, 1996, p. 97.

As we go deeper into the global age, we may look to our business leaders to resemble the philosopher kings so beloved by Plato in *The Republic*.

2. Wider and more powerful circles of influence. As people move up the organizational pyramid, their formal power increases and they enter into more formal leadership positions. They can influence a greater number of people and at more powerful levels. But that is only part of the leadership story. At whatever level people are in, they can maximize their leadership impact by focusing their energies on issues they can do something about and people they can influence directly. Stephen Covey discusses this concept in *The Seven Habits of Highly Effective People*.[6] We all have "Circles of Concern" in our lives. These circles tend to be very large, and they contain many things over which we have no real control. Within the Circle of Concern is a smaller one containing those things we can do something about: our "Circle of Influence."

By focusing personal and organizational energy on this smaller circle, we tend to enlarge it and to become more empowered. Concentrating energy on the Circle of Concern will leave us feeling inadequate and helpless, victims of circumstance.

3. Increased risk and complexity of international contact. List the kinds of international contact individuals have in your organization. You may end up with a list that looks like this:

International Managers. The multilingual elite who fly from place to place making deals.

Expatriates. Those who relocate to another country for several years.

Inpatriates. Subsidiary personnel who relocate to headquarters for an extended period of time.

Technicians. Specialists who may spend weeks or months in a foreign location installing equipment or setting up operations.

Occasional Parachutists. Troubleshooters who move in and out of foreign locations very quickly.

---

[6]Stephen Covey, *The Seven Habits of Highly Effective People*, New York: Simon & Schuster, 1989, pp. 81–89.

Domestic Internationalists. Home-country personnel who have regular contact with subsidiaries or global customers, suppliers, distributors, foreign governments, and so on.[7]

Senior and middle global leaders operate in a wider variety of cross-cultural situations with a greater degree of complexity. The terrain to be walked by senior global leaders is the whole world. The degree of risk is particularly high if the company is negotiating strategic relationships and making acquisitions across borders. Bringing together companies with national and organizational cultural differences creates a high degree of uncertainty and vulnerability. Strategic alliances in particular are always open to the possibility of a total withdrawal of cooperation. Legal contracts alone will not manage this kind of complexity and vulnerability.[8] Closing the deal is just a small step on the road to building effective transnational relationships.

Such complexity and risk differ from that experienced by someone trying to open a new market, work on a global team, or visit an overseas site to install new equipment. These activities tend to have more clearly defined opportunities and constraints and a smaller number of people and situations to contend with.

4. Increased time span. Elliott Jaques has again been instrumental in demonstrating how the level of work in a role—the felt weight of responsibility and its complexity—is related to what he calls the *time span of discretion.*[9] This measure looks at the longest targeted completion times of tasks assigned to a role, such as 1 day, 3 months, 1 year, 5 years, 10 years, 20 years, or 50 years. As individuals move up the organization, the time span of discretion increases and likewise the felt responsibility and complexity. The CEO of a global corporation may be grappling with issues 20 to 50 years out from today, while the individual associate is working in a time span of one day to three months.

5. Decreased level of technical input. One of the few variables that tend to decrease as people move up the organization is the level

---

[7]Derek Torrington, *International Human Resource Management: Think Globally, Act Locally,* New York: Prentice Hall, 1994, p. 6.

[8]Wendy Hall, *Managing Cultures: Making Strategic Relationships Work,* Chichester, U.K.: John Wiley, 1995, p. xviii.

[9]Jaques and Cason, *Human Capability,* p. 13.

of technical input expected. Cutting-edge technical skills are expected of those lower down in the organization at the individual associate and first-line manager levels. Middle and senior managers operate more strategically, with a greater emphasis on conceptual thinking skills and mental processing.

Step 3: Identify Roles and Responsibilities within Bands

The roles individuals play in different parts of the global leadership spectrum will differ by company, but some generalizations can be made.

Senior Band

This elite group on the global leadership spectrum tends to be on the road most of the time, coordinating and integrating the pieces of the global system. It will include the CEO and other senior officers of the company and business heads. Rosabeth Moss Kanter uses the term "Cosmopolitans" to refer to this group. In her view, they

> lead companies that are linked to global chains. Comfortable in many places and able to understand and bridge the differences among them, cosmopolitans possess portable skills and a broad outlook . . . Cosmopolitans are rich in three intangible assets, three C's that translate into preeminence and power in a global economy: concepts—the best and latest knowledge and ideas; competence—the ability to operate at the highest standards of any place anywhere; and connections—the best relationships, which provide access to the resources of other people and organizations around the world.[10]

Christopher Bartlett and Sumantra Ghoshal define the major roles to be played by corporate global managers as follows:[11]

- They lead (in the broadest sense, e.g., communicate global vision, values, and general strategic direction). They define reality for the organization and set the inspirational tone. They are in many ways the voice of the company.

---

[10]Rosabeth Moss Kanter, *World Class: Thriving Locally in the Global Economy,* New York: Simon & Schuster, 1995, p. 23.

[11]Christopher A. Bartlett and Sumantra Ghoshal, "What Is a Global Manager?" *Harvard Business Review,* September–October 1992.

- They identify and develop talented business, country, and functional managers who can translate company strategies into effective worldwide operations. This is often done through job rotations around the world early in the manager's career and challenging international assignments of shorter duration. The key challenge for the corporate manager is to identify, track, and draw talent from the worldwide talent pool.
- They balance negotiations among the often conflicting needs of business, country, and functional managers.

These managers are ambassadors, champions of shareholder value, defenders of brand equity, and mobilizers of organizational capability. They are the stewards of the organization's past, present, and future.

The primary roles of the senior business or product-division managers, according to Bartlett and Ghoshal, are determined by their need to drive toward global scale efficiencies and competitiveness by integrating operations worldwide. Their roles are to

- Act as strategist for their specific organizations. The strategy needs to encapsulate the often opposing needs of local markets and scale efficiencies. This is often done through task force teams brought together to identify convergence of market segments across national borders. From such an analysis, regional or even global brands may be fashioned.
- Be the architect of the organization's worldwide asset and resource configuration through decisions aimed at creating the most efficient and effective infrastructure. Efficiency and effectiveness often need to be finely balanced, and trade-offs will be common. The location of plants, design centers, research and development facilities, and sales and marketing offices, for example, is a political, economic, and capability issue of great complexity. A concentration of power does need to be achieved to champion globalization, but not at the expense of disempowering local men and women and generating passivity. Economic rationalization is critical to reduce redundancy and costs, but not at the expense of destroying capabilities that have been built up over years of investment, education, and training.

◆ Coordinate transactions across national borders to maximize the value-added flow of resources, products and services, technologies, and so forth. Methods for coordinating will include management from the center; the management of exceptions through formal policies and procedures; the establishment of set ranges for negotiations; use of cross-functional teams and task forces for shared development, implementation, and problem resolution; and use of informal communication channels.

Middle Band

Middle managers—country managers, for example—have the difficult role of trying to maximize the results of their specific organizations while ensuring the flow of best practices and resources across the organization to optimize results for the total organization. Robert Allen, CEO of AT&T, makes this point when he says to his management team, "Come to our management meetings and represent your businesses. But there are times when I ask you to put on my hat on behalf of the shareholders and help me make decisions that cross business-unit boundaries."[12]

The primary roles of country managers, according to Bartlett and Ghoshal, are to

◆ Be a sensor to the opportunities and needs of the local marketplace, including meeting specific customer needs, meeting the challenges of other competitors, and responding to the requirements of local governments. These roles require an ability to gather and interpret intelligence, determine possible outcomes, and communicate significant intelligence to senior management. The import of information often spills over borders. As Bartlett and Ghoshal say, "Consumer trends in one country often spread to another; technologies developed in a leading-edge environment can have global significance; a competitor's local market testing may signal a wider

---

[12]Jessica Lipnack and Jeffrey Stamps, *The Age of the Network: Organizing Principles for the 21st Century,* Essex Junction, VT: Omneo, 1994, p. 11.

strategy; and national legislative initiatives in areas like deregulation and environmental protection tend to spill across borders."[13]

◆ Build local resources and capabilities, particularly human capabilities, into corporate assets. Smart country managers recognize the importance not only of responding to local markets but of building their enterprises, whenever possible, into global centers of excellence.

◆ Contribute to and be an active participant in implementing global strategies.

First-Line Band

Managers of departments within business units will fall into this category. They are the men and women who provide the key functional expertise in the organization. Their potential contribution to the global network is huge, but too often neglected. As Bartlett and Ghoshal point out, "at a time when information, knowledge, and expertise have become more specialized, an organization can gain huge benefits by linking its technical, manufacturing, marketing, human resources, and financial experts worldwide."[14] The primary objective of these individuals is to facilitate the process of organizational learning and innovation through technology transfer and linking resources and capabilities worldwide. To do this, they must

◆ Scan the world for value-added, specialized information. While an innovation or a trend may seem insignificant within a single market, it may be of strategic importance when looked at globally.

◆ Cross-pollinate knowledge and best practices. Acting as "linchpins," functional managers—often working in cross-functional teams—can be the creators of synergy by seeking and utilizing connections among specialty groups. One of the key capabilities global organizations need is the ability to find, evaluate, integrate, and deploy new knowledge into the organization as quickly as possible. Functional managers are the key players in making this happen,

---

[13]Christopher A. Bartlett and Sumantra Ghoshal, "What Is a Global Manager?", p. 128.
[14]Ibid., p. 129.

through both formal and informal communication networks.

♦ Be a strong advocate for those innovations and best practices that can be leveraged globally.

Individual Associates Band

Individuals in this category may have some supervisory responsibilities, but their primary responsibilities are technical, service oriented, and/or administrative. Although these people are at the lower end of the spectrum, they are often the ones who have most contact with customers. They may not be first-line managers, but they are front-line staff and can make or break relationships with clients.

Individual associates may also be heavily involved in global issues. Customer service representatives may be dealing with global customers; technical people may be sent to any part of the world to install or service equipment; and cabin crews on airlines are the "face" of the company to customers from around the globe.

One critical need of any global company is to create alignment among these roles so that they work in parallel, and not against, one another.

From a relatively brief analysis of the roles and responsibilities in the organization, a generic list of global leadership competencies for the company can be developed. The Global Leadership Triad is aimed at this level of analysis.

Step 4: Define Competencies in Relation to Each Leadership Band

From this broad analysis, an organization can produce a global leadership competency map (see Figure 3–4). In the left-hand column are the core global leadership competencies outlined in the Global Leadership Triad. The next four columns represent the four bands in the global leadership spectrum. By using a simple code (e.g., N = Nice to have; I = Important to have; and C = Critical to have), we can make some distinctions among the bands. These distinctions would need to be explained in some detail and, whenever necessary, the competency description changed to more fully capture the requirements at a particular level. For example, what does "stakeholder orientation" mean at the level of your individual associates as opposed to the level of your senior managers?

FIGURE 3–4

Global Leadership Competency Map

Triad	A. Individual Associate	B. First-Line	C. Middle	D. Senior
Business Acumen				
1. Depth of field	I	I	C	C
2. Entrepreneurial spirit	N	N	C	C
3. Professional expertise	N	C	C	C
4. Stakeholder orientation	I	I	C	C
5. Total organizational astuteness	N	C	C	C
Relationship Management				
6. Change agentry	N	N	C	C
7. Community building	N	C	C	C
8. Conflict management and negotiation	N	I	C	C
9. Cross-cultural communication	C	C	C	C
10. Influencing	C	C	C	C
Personal Effectiveness				
11. Accountability	I	I	C	C
12. Curiosity and learning	N	I	C	C
13. Improvisation	I	C	C	I
14. Maturity	N	I	C	C
15. Thinking agility	N	I	C	C

I have placed codes in all of the boxes in the competency map not because these are the "right" answers (organizations need to determine their own set of answers) but because they can provide a starting point for discussion. We could debate the appropriateness of the codings for some time, and that is just what should happen. Let me give you my reasoning for at least two sets of boxes.

Let's start with boxes 2A, B, C, and D (entrepreneurial spirit). I coded these N, N, C, and C, respectively. Ideally, we would have individual associates who are entrepreneurial and always looking to identify and pursue opportunities. But their primary focus should be on implementing operational systems and processes to achieve world-class standards of excellence. If individual associates can highlight opportunities for growth, the channels for communicating them should be open. They should also be rewarded for bringing them to light. The focus for first-line managers should be on attaining and sharing functional excellence, whether it is finance, marketing, manufacturing, sales, and so on. Again, they should be encouraged to seek out opportunities, but entrepreneurship is not their primary focus. Entrepreneurship starts to become critical as we enter into middle and senior levels of management. Middle managers in particular must be sensors to the opportunities available in the local marketplace. They must also be open to recognizing global potential when it exists. Senior managers perhaps do not need to be *the* entrepreneurs as such. What is critical for them is an ability to create an environment in which entrepreneurship can flourish.

What about boxes 13A, B, C, and D (improvisation)? I coded these I, C, C, and I, respectively. Being able to improvise at the individual associate level is important, because these people often interface directly with the customer, and customers often have unique needs. British Airways currently has a program in place called Breakthrough. This program, aimed at ground staff and cabin crews, encourages individuals to "respond to customers' needs as individuals and not rely on textbook rules and regulations." As we move into first-line and middle manager levels, improvisation becomes critical. No matter what systems are put in place, when working across borders, middle managers need to be able to adapt very quickly to local circumstances. At the more senior levels, managers are often dealing with longer time horizons, and the need for quick improvisation is often less critical.

Step 5: Identify Competencies for Specific Jobs/Functions

An organization can choose to drive the global leadership competency analysis deeper by identifying competency needs for specific functional jobs within each band, for example, customer service representative/marketing services (individual associate band).

At this level, it is important to identify the job's global roles and responsibilities, the primary tasks and performance criteria, and the specific behaviors that demonstrate the required competencies, i.e., who does what, how do they do it, when is it done, and who else is involved? It is also important to establish performance levels for each competency for appraisal and development purposes.

Performance levels indicate increasingly higher levels of competency achievement. What might these levels look like? In Figure 3–5, the left-hand column lists the performance levels (expert/leader, etc). The criteria column describes the behaviors that are typical of a specific performance level. The third column is for the manager to check off the observed performance level. The fourth column provides space for the manager to list the individual's development priorities, along with any required or suggested developmental opportunities, such as training programs, observing an expert performer, or a formal coaching session.

FIGURE 3–5
Performance Levels

Title: Customer Service Representative/Marketing Services
Competency Area: Cross-Cultural Communication

Performance Level	Criteria	Check for Ranking	Developmental Action Plan
Expert/leader	Consistently takes the initiative to teach/ influence others in how to recognize cultural differences and make appropriate adaptations in communication style to maximize responsiveness.		
Proficiency	Is consistent in recognizing cultural differences and adapting communication style to the customer and being responsive. Is inconsistent in taking the initiative to teach/ influence others.		
Developing	Is beginning to recognize differences in cultural communication styles. Is inconsistent when adapting his or her style to customers from other cultures.		
Not demonstrated	Consistently demonstrates no awareness of cultural differences or adaptability when interfacing with customers from other cultures; displays ethnocentric attitudes and behaviors.		

DIALOGUE BOX

1. What would be the most logical set of bands in your company's global leadership spectrum?

2. What are the major roles and responsibilities of the men and women in each of your leadership bands?

3. How do the competencies listed in the Global Leadership Triad relate to your leadership bands?

4. Can you create a global leadership competency map for your company?

GLOBAL CONTEXT-BUILDING

It never fails to amaze me as I work inside different business organizations how little most employees know about the context in which they perform their tasks. Many employees know *how* to do something, but far fewer know *why*. Context is about what people need to know to perform at their best and collaborate with one another.

As we enter into a more interdependent global age with an increasing reliance on dynamic collaboration across business units and functions, and with greater accountability and responsibility driven down the organization, employees need to understand the *meaning* of what they and others do if they are to contribute most effectively. They need to be able to see the connections among the parts and understand how they can affect the results of the whole by being a leader within an ever-increasing circle of influence. To some extent, this will require organizations to make a mindset shift from training to education.

There at least two components to the required education: an understanding of the global environment context and the organization's business context.

Global Environment Context

No matter where leaders fall on the spectrum, if they are to be successful they need to have a clearer understanding of the global context in which they live and work. One urgent task of global leaders is to help themselves and others overcome parochial educational backgrounds. The deficits in geographic understanding of most Americans is well known. In 1989, Casper Weinberger, secretary of defense, commented, "When we are told by a former Superintendent of Public Schools in the District of Columbia that one in four students questioned could not locate the Soviet Union on a map, and when she also tells us that their surveys showed that one in seven Americans cannot find the United States on a map, it is time to do more than worry or just throw up our hands."[15] A parochial education is the fate of most of us on this planet, but we can educate ourselves to become more cosmopolitan.

One way to map this new context is to look at the trends. A WORLD 2000 project sponsored by the World Future Society looked at the major trends shaping our emerging global system.[16]

Trend 1: A Stable Population of 10 to 14 Billion   From its current level of 5.5 billion people, the world's population is expected to stabilize at somewhere between 10 to 15 billion by the mid-21st century. This growth will be largely in developing countries. The disparities between the developing countries of the South and the developed countries of the North do not appear to be shrinking. Average income in the South is about 6 percent of that in the North. Population growth will exacerbate the problem. Asia will contain the vast majority of the world's population, with approximately 59 percent. China, India, and Indonesia alone will hold about 40 percent.

Trend 2: Industrial Output Will Increase by a Factor of 5 to 10   Material consumption will increase dramatically as many parts of the world drive toward creating standards of living equivalent to those seen in the United States, Europe, and Japan. At the same time, throughput is expected to grow less as efficiency increases.

With this increase in output will come the inevitable pollution. About 25 billion tons of industrial pollutants flowed into waterways

---

[15]Christopher L. Salter, *Missing the Magic Carpet: The Real Significance of Geographic Ignorance,* Princeton, NJ: Educational Testing Service, November 1990.

[16]William E. Halal, "Global Strategic Management in a New World Order," *Business Horizons,* November–December 1993, pp. 5–10.

in China in 1991. This created more toxic water pollution in China than in the entire Western world.[17]

Trend 3: The Wiring of the Globe   The spread of information technology (IT) brings the world together into a global communications network. The technological bases of our societies are shifting from physical to information technologies, and knowledge is becoming the source of power. Undoubtedly, some areas of the world will be information rich and others information poor. Those that are information poor will become increasingly alienated from the world community. (See Appendix 2, "The Global Leader and the Internet," for some addresses that can help you keep up with many issues in international business.)

Trend 4: The High-Tech Revolution   New breakthrough fields are emerging in the mapping of DNA, genetic therapy, robotics, materials research, sustainable environmental technology, automated transportation, and the technology of consciousness (including virtual reality).

Trend 5: Global Integration   The creation of a global economy and a shared communications system is moving us toward a shared international culture (driven mostly by the spread of American popular culture), open trade, global banking, perhaps a common world currency (or regional currencies), and some form of world governance (or at least the need for greater international collaboration).

Trend 6: Diversity and Complexity   While the previous trend leads us toward integration, this trend leads to increased fragmentation. The fall of communism has led to the reemergence of ethnicity and culture as the basis of shared identity. While on one level the world moves toward commonality, on the other it moves toward increased differentiation.

A future clash of ideals is likely between Muslim states and the liberal, secularized West, and both—as Brian Beedham of *The Economist Publications* argues—may be headed toward "an argument with

---

[17]Jane H. Lii, "Boom at-a-Glance," *The New York Times,* Sunday Magazine, February 18, 1996, p. 27.

the materialist authoritarianism (and racialism) that seem to lie behind 'Asian values', the concept so popular among modern politicians in the old Confucian culture zone."[18] The centers of world power—Europe, America, China, Russia, and Japan—may increasingly find themselves at odds as they maneuver themselves to maximize political and economic self-interest (this will particularly be the case with China and Russia). Who knows what turbulence we will see in East Asia as China sinks once again into warlordism or seeks to force its will on Korea, Vietnam, or Taiwan?

Wars in the 20th century have largely been fought on an east-west axis; those of the 21st century may well be fought on north-south coordinates, particularly in southern Asia and much of Africa.

Trend 7: A Universal Standard of Freedom   Although it shifts in political and religious winds, a concern for human freedom and human rights has gained momentum around the globe. Democracy and various forms of capitalism have become established throughout a significant portion of the world, at least in name.

This is perhaps one of the weakest trends in the World Future Society survey. When the Berlin Wall collapsed, there was a great deal of optimism about the triumph of democracy. That optimism has dissolved. Many African countries, as well as China, look to the so-called "soft authoritarianism" of Singapore rather than the United States for their model society. America, in the meantime, is no longer sure that for strategic reasons many parts of the world should be democratic (a radical change in approach). Autocratic regimes in Latin America, for example, have often proven to be more effective in putting down the drug trade. In the Middle East, American officials are not loudly promoting democratization for the region. The relatively stable and pro-American autocracies of Egypt and Saudi Arabia are deemed more compatible with American interests than governments formed on the foundation of militant Islam.[19]

---

[18]Brian Beedham, "The World's Next Wars," in *The World in 1994*, London: The Economist Publications, 1993, p. 13.

[19]Judith Miller, "At Hour of Triumph, Democracy Recedes as the Global Ideal," *The New York Times*, Sunday Magazine, February 18, 1996.

Elections in many parts of the world have often produced what Berkeley political scientist Ken Jowitt calls "mimic democracies."[20] While there are elections, such states often lack the civic virtues such as free speech, separation of church and state, property rights, and pluralism on which democracies are built.

Linked to the use of arbitrary power is governmental and business corruption. The Political and Economic Risk Consultancy group in Hong Kong report's that paying off officials to gain business can add 5 percent to operating costs in China. Transparency International, a research and advocacy body based in Berlin, has published what it calls a Corruption Index. The Index ranks the world's most and least corrupt countries. Those found most corrupt were Indonesia, China, Pakistan, Venezuela, Brazil, Philippines, India, Thailand, and Italy. Least corrupt were New Zealand, Denmark, Singapore, and Finland.[21]

Trend 8: Continued Crime, Terrorism, and War   As the world goes through traumatic change, there will be disgruntled individuals and groups whose alienation leads to violent conflict, although widespread global wars seem unlikely.

The globalization of business will contribute to the instability in the world. The founder of the World Economic Forum, Klaus Schwab, and its managing director, Claude Smadja, have been very candid in their analysis of the potential consequences of globalization.[22] They argue that while irreversible, the process of economic globalization is creating feelings of helplessness and anxiety in Western democracies. They argue that four key elements need to be kept in mind:

♦ The great speed with which capital crosses borders, the rapid development of technological changes, and changing marketing and management requirements increase the pressure on companies to make structural adjustments. These adjustments strain the social fabric of societies. We have not found ways to help people cope with such transformational changes or to persuade them that such changes

---

[20]Ibid., pp. 4-1, 4-5.

[21]Barbara Crossette, "New Watchdog Group Ranks Nations in Corruption Index," *The New York Times*, August 13, 1995, p. 6.

[22]Klaus Schwab and Claude Smadja, "Start Taking the Backlash Against Globalization Seriously," *International Herald Tribune*, February 1, 1996.

will lead to increased prosperity. The 1995 revolt in France was just the tip of an iceberg of discontent.

♦ Globalization is reshaping the distribution of world economic power, which will change the distribution of political power. The authors argue that as we approach 2000, we will enter into an era of strategic economic parity among the United States, East Asia, and Europe: "East Asia is a net beneficiary. Results for Europe look much less certain. The United States has recovered ground lost in the 1980s but at the cost of an actual decline of real wages."

♦ Long-held assumptions about how the world works are being challenged by globalization. For example, it has been assumed that technological change and productivity increases would translate into more jobs and higher wages. Instead, change has eliminated more jobs than it has created. An environment is emerging that "leads to winner-take-all situations; those who come out on top win big, and the losers lose even bigger." Those able to ride out globalization tend to be those who are knowledge and communication oriented.

♦ Public opinion in Western democracies is growing increasingly skeptical about the hypothetical benefits of the global economy. There is doubt that globalization leads to win-win scenarios. The globalization process is "delinking the fate of the corporation from the fate of its employees." Traditionally, higher profits were linked to higher wages and increased job security. Surviving in a globally competitive world may just mean further layoffs. The ties of loyalty between corporation and employee, if not severed, have been frayed. One only has to read about the delayering, restructurings, and downsizings—many related to pressures powered by global competition—to understand that the change is uncomfortable to many.

Trend 9: Transcendent Values   People in advanced, postsurvivalist cultures will continue to strive for quality of life defined in nonmaterial terms (e.g., spirituality, self-fulfillment, art, community). This is not to say that consumerism and materialism have run their course—far from it.

Any business leader looking at these trends will see opportunities, challenges, and a multitude of questions. (See Appendix 3, "Staying in Touch: The Printed Word," for a list of useful periodicals that will help you stay in touch.)

Organization's Business Context

An important key to empowerment and building global leaders is information sharing. If we want to create global leaders at all levels of the organization, we must be willing to let the information loose. How can people be expected to buy into an organization they don't understand?

Alan Randolph studied 10 companies looking to make a transition from a bureaucratic to an empowered work force. He found that the "first critical (and often misunderstood) key is information sharing."[23] He tells stories of companies that had put their people through leadership training, team building, problem solving, and conflict resolution training with little success. The resistance was often stronger than the training.

The turning point occurred when senior managers started sharing sensitive financial information about the company, its structure, market share, growth opportunities, and competitor strategies. When people understand the challenges, they can and very often will rise to the occasion and take ownership of the problems. In addition, the level of trust in these companies has risen exponentially, and trust is a key to collaboration. People with information also set more challenging goals for themselves and take more risks in using their talents.

GLOBAL VALUE CLARIFICATION

We live in an interdependent world that drives us to greater levels of collaboration and partnering, but that world is also a world of difference. If we are to collaborate successfully, we need to clarify and communicate our values at two levels: the macro and the micro. This involves open, professional dialogue and understanding the context in which cultures, including our own, make decisions about what is acceptable behavior. We may decide (hopefully we do) that there are certain nonnegotiables. In this case, we need to communicate them and explain our reasoning. We also need to listen.

---

[23]Alan W. Randolph, "Navigating the Journey to Empowerment," *Organizational Dynamics,* March 22, 1995, Vol. 23, no. 4, p. 19.

DIALOGUE BOX

1. What world trends are going to have the biggest impact on your business in the next 5, 10, 15, and 20 years? What kinds of impact do you think they will have: positive or negative?

2. How would you rate the extent and quality of information sharing in your company, particularly as it relates to global strategies and intentions?

   Poor   Excellent

   1   2   3   4   5

   Why did you give this rating?

3. What additional kinds of information would you like your company to share with you?

4. Do you think the sharing of this information would make a significant difference to how you and others do your current jobs, the level of interest in your jobs, your commitment to the company, and your career plans?

Macro

As players on the world stage, global companies face moral and ethical choices on a daily basis. Should I be moving this process from the First World to the Third World to avoid tough new environmental standards that will raise my costs and make us uncompetitive in many markets? Should I be partnering with this manufacturer, who uses child labor and practices few health and safety policies? Or who discriminates against certain minorities? The position taken by Levi Strauss is "to be ethically responsible for business issues it can control—such as responsible child labor conditions—as opposed to social conditions in a country that it has no control over."[24] In 1992,

---

[24]Charlene Marmer Solomon, "Putting Your Ethics to a Global Test," *Personnel Journal*, January 1996, p. 74.

Levi Strauss produced company guidelines for selecting business partners; they cover issues ranging from the environment to health and safety. When the guidelines were formulated, the company conducted audits of its worldwide contractors. Ideally, the audits create a win/win situation. In 1992, Levi Strauss began to bear down on contractors that violated the International Labor Organization's standards barring the employment of young people under 14. Two firms in Bangladesh were found in violation. The contractors argued that the children, ages 11 to 13, were the sole economic support for their single-parent families. In a compromise arrangement, Levi Strauss asked the contractor to continue to pay the wages of the children and hire them back when they reached 14. In turn, Levi Strauss would pay for the children to attend school.

A collaborative stance to clarifying international business principles has been taken by a group known as the Caux Round Table. The group was formed in 1986 by a former president of Philips Electronics, Frederik Philips. Participants in generating the world standards for ethical behavior included Canon, Chase Manhattan Bank, ITT, Matsushita, Siemens, and 3M. In essence, the group believes that business can promote human welfare by improving the lives of customers and employees by providing products and employment. (See Appendix 4 for a complete set of the Caux Round Table principles.)

DIALOGUE BOX

1. How would you rate your company in terms of the *clarity* of its international business principles and its *commitment* to them?

   Poor   Excellent

   1   2   3   4   5

   Why did you give this rating?

2. Do you think the Caux Round Table international business principles in Appendix 4 are a reasonable framework in which to conduct global business? Do you disagree with any of the statements? Is anything missing?

Micro

While there is, consciously or unconsciously, a global organizational culture in which people operate, groups of people working together in multicultural teams must develop their own minicultures if they are to be effective. This requires a concerted effort to build common principles and practices while maintaining diverse perspectives. Although each team needs to negotiate its own principles, here is a starting point:

Caring. Everyone demonstrates a genuine concern for the well-being of others in the group. Genuine caring is not manipulative or patronizing. It does not seek to create dependence or control. We respect individual feelings and seek to pay attention to one another's needs.

Confidentiality. Everyone respects boundaries. Team decisions may leave the room (whenever appropriate), but team discussions stay in the room. We work hard to build trusting relationships.

Fairness. Everyone deserves to be treated in an equitable manner, without bias or prejudice. We relate to one another as fellow human beings, not as stereotypes.

Honesty. Everyone is encouraged to express his or her needs. We look to understand and clarify one another's needs when they may not be expressed directly.

Openness. Everyone avoids closing off ideas and opinions too soon. We focus on what adds value, not surface style. We recognize the importance of different perspectives in helping us achieve breakthrough thinking and results.

Participation. Everyone is expected to participate. Active participation is desirable in meetings, but if some members want to think about what is said and come to the next meeting with their ideas thought through, that's OK. Although the styles of participation may differ, everyone is expected to give their best. We look continually for new and better ways for everyone to contribute.

Respect. Everyone shows genuine consideration for the feelings of others in the group. Gossiping, backbiting, and talking behind someone's back are taboo. We do not threaten or bluff one another. We use humor to laugh at ourselves, not others.

Responsibility. Everyone takes responsibility for completing assigned tasks on time, attending sessions, being punctual, and catching up (when necessary). We best support one another when we take responsibility for ourselves.

Results. Everyone is focused on the purpose of the team and how to produce world-class outcomes quickly and efficiently. We value results, not activities.

Sharing. Everyone is expected to share information, knowledge, and expertise that are appropriate to getting the mission accomplished. We learn more when we share more.

Unity. Everyone is a critical member of the team. We refuse to divide into factions or play "us versus them" games in the group. We work to make the whole stronger than the parts.

Understanding. Everyone seeks to understand and be understood. Understanding does not mean agreement. It does mean listening while retaining the integrity to stand up for what we believe is right. It is a commitment to exploring differences and working toward common ground. When we seek understanding, we benefit the learning of the whole group.

GLOBAL SKILL DEVELOPMENT

A multicultural team has come together from the United States and Europe to select a manager for the Brussels office. The American was told by her boss to take charge of the meeting. The Europeans don't take kindly to the idea. According to the French woman on the team, "She has neither the competence nor the standing." Tough words! It is, perhaps, the only thing the Europeans can agree on. The Englishman on the team, the host, is looking to create some form of harmony and to be fair to everyone. The French woman wants someone to take charge. The German wants to put a system in place so that things will run smoothly. The Spaniard wants to postpone decisions until the American boss can be present. The scene is from a cross-cultural training video produced by Transnational Management Associates (TMA) of London and Paris. In trying to sort out this multicultural disaster area, the producers of the video present us with what they call the Culture Triangle (see Figure 4–2).

FIGURE 4–2
The Culture Triangle

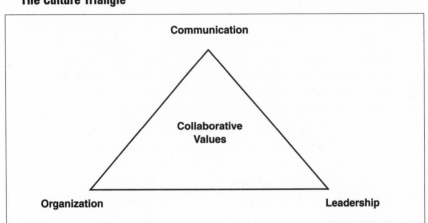

Source: Adapted from *Building the Transnational Team (video)*, Transnational Management Associates, 211 Piccadilly, London W1V 9LD and 92 rue de Levis 75017, Paris.

The components of the Culture Triangle—communication, leadership, and organization—relate closely to the Global Leadership Triad: communication (relationship management), leadership (personal effectiveness), and organization (business acumen). The Culture Triangle gives us a simple framework for talking about the skills and practices needed for global collaboration. Within the triangle, I have added collaborative values; these are at the heart of the team culture that needs to be built.

Following is a list of skills and practices that help to build minicultures and foster collaboration.

Communication: Facilitating the Exchange of Shared Meaning

♦ **Ask open-ended questions.** Asking open-ended rather than closed-ended questions allows for a freer range of expression. It gives everyone a better chance to discover misunderstandings, as well as providing the team with space for discovery about one another.

♦ **Be open to the counterintuitive.** Maintain mental alertness even when the going gets tough. What may seem counterintuitive may be exactly what you need to hear. You need to *be there* in mind, spirit, and body.

♦ **Be specific.** Make your statements as plain and down to earth as possible. Avoid abstractions and buzzwords; for example, if you use abstract terms such as *quality, empowerment,* or *success,* explain what you mean. Once on a roll, team successes tend to accumulate, but only if the team understands what is meant by *"success".* Also, provide the context for *why* something is important, not just *how* it needs to be addressed.

♦ **Challenge stereotypes.** When stereotypes are in operation, no one is communicating authentically. Any intended communication is missing its mark. Every member of the group needs to challenge the use of stereotypes in self and in others. It is perfectly reasonable to say, "You may have heard that most Americas (or English, etc.) want to make quick decisions and worry about the implementation later. Let me tell you about the way *I* like to make decisions. Then perhaps you can tell me your preferred way of decision making. We may be closer on this than you think." It is always important to remember that you are communicating with individuals, not cultures. Refuse to allow ethnic/racial or cultural jokes; everyone may laugh initially, but underlying resentment may work to destroy team relationships. One technique that helps to slow down the evaluation process is to think DIE: *D* stands for *describing* the behavior, *I* equals *interpreting* the behavior from the standpoint of the other person, and *E* is for *evaluating.* Usually we leap into the evaluation mode and get stuck in judging rather than perceiving.

♦ **Clarify assumptions and interpretations.** Continually check for possible differences in meanings. Paraphrase what others say, and summarize key points. Frequent summaries should be a key feature of all multicultural meetings. Use written, visual, and oral communication in combination to make meanings clear and precise. Make sure you avoid the use of jargon, colloquialisms, and slang.

♦ **Gather input.** Look for new ways to gather input from the team. Use audience response systems, e-mail, groupware, videoconferencing, and so on. Ask for input before giving input; otherwise you may hear only what others think you want to hear.

♦ **Listen with full attention.** Listen in the *here and now;* that is, avoid thinking too far ahead and losing the meaning of what is actually said. Others may have accents that are difficult for you to understand; give all your attention to the *substance* of what is being said, not the style.

◆ **Observe with full attention.** Look for body language that may tell you that someone is having trouble understanding or is disagreeing and doesn't want to raise the issue in front of the whole group.

◆ **Set a comfortable pace.** Find a pace that is comfortable for the whole group. For many, English will be the second language. Allow extra time for the processing and internal translation of information. Break the message into small chunks, and check for understanding after each one. Make sure everyone has enough time to speak without interruption. Don't try to fill silences; allow time for thought.

Leadership: Generating and Channeling Energy into Creating World-Class Performance

◆ **Be consistent.** Leadership statements and behaviors need to be consistent. A leader who says one thing and does another loses credibility and influence. When teams are not rich in resources (as they often aren't), they need to be rich in spirit. Playing favorites or suddenly changing the rules affects everyone and destroys morale. Any unwritten rules need to be explained.

◆ **Be proactive.** The leader needs to recognize potential problems, bring them to the surface, and deal with them before they spill over and affect team performance. This can be difficult when some cultures are very indirect in their expression of conflict. Patience and learning how to read the signs are critical. The sources of conflict need to be clarified and used as an opportunity to learn something about one another or to deepen relationships.

◆ **Break habits.** When the group starts to form habits, the leader should challenge them, or at least explore their value with the group. Certain habits can be very constructive and promote energy flow, but they usually have a life cycle. Habits grow stale, and they may eventually inhibit creativity. Certain behaviors should be challenged before they become habits (e.g., team members from the same culture always sitting together).

◆ **Build commitment to a vision.** Vision provides the energy and overall direction for the group. It is the motivational force that gives shape and purpose to team activities. Out of the vision should emerge the superordinate goals to which everyone feels ownership and commitment.

♦ **Coach.** The global team leader can be the coach in many areas. Apart from technical issues, he or she may have more experience in the company and the business. The leader can coach others in what it takes to succeed in the company and set expectations for what the company is looking for from the team. The leader can help team members wear the local hat and the global hat. She or he can also help the team surface and explore differences and help members shift their cultural orientations from an unconscious to a conscious level. The leader can also create opportunities for team members to coach one another. If necessary, the leader should tap into sources to provide just-in-time training.

♦ **Control the ego.** The ego wants things to be done its way. It wants control and the ability to express itself at every opportunity. It wants success to head in its direction. Unfortunately, a hyperactive ego can destroy the energy of the team. Team members from all cultures need to feel that they can participate (without having to battle to get their voices heard), that their contributions are recognized and respected, and that they can influence the process and the outcomes. Leadership in the team may need to shift depending on an individual's knowledge or expertise in an area. Controlling the ego doesn't mean the leader needs to be nonassertive. The level of assertiveness may need to be adjusted for the group. The leader's charge must be to ensure that things get done that are right for the business. Sometimes that means going against the flow.

♦ **Decide.** While the leader looks to build consensus, he or she cannot abdicate overall accountability. The leader needs to make clear or negotiate the decision-making responsibilities in the group. Who makes what decisions and when? Keep the needs of the business in the foreground.

♦ **Enable information flow.** Information, resources, and authority need to flow through the team. Withholding information creates mistrust and resentment. Those who take leadership roles should not be automatically selected from the host country or the country that is most technologically or economically advanced. Sometimes leaders are chosen from what are called "blender" countries such as Holland, Sweden, or Switzerland. Probably no one on the team would be carrying a lot of historical baggage relating to members from these countries, baggage that could interfere with team functioning and flow.

◆ **Give flexible feedback.** Giving and receiving feedback is culturally sensitive; the leader should work at finding out what different team members expect. In some cultures, a person may find out how she or he is performing from a third party who happens to say something like "I hear that your team leader thinks you should be paying more attention to your deadlines." That kind of indirection is not going to work with most Americans or others accustomed to direct communication.

◆ **Form relationships.** The leader needs to be conscious of the fact that members of different cultures form relationships in diverse ways. Americans are generally up front, sharing lots of personal information quickly. They move quickly into an egalitarian, informal mode, and they expect others to do the same. Many Europeans and Asians are slower to build; they cannot be rushed. Asians may want to spend time up front developing relationships; Americans and Germans may want to get down to business quickly. The leader will need to seek a balance depending on the composition of the team, the urgency of the task, and so on. At the first meeting, the leader might want to pass out a biography of each person.

◆ **Set team process expectations.** Early meetings are often not a good sign of what is to come. Let the members know they will experience highs and lows. If the members are relatively inexperienced, explain that teams often go through a building process (e.g., orientation, trust building, goal/role clarification, commitment, implementation, high performance, and renewal).[25]

◆ **Set challenging goals.** The leader needs to stretch the team's capabilities by setting challenges and high expectations. The leader must be influential in breaking down barriers within and outside the team, asking for innovative solutions, and maintaining the focus on getting results.

◆ **Solve problems.** Attention needs to be paid to fixing problems and not assigning blame. Placing blame wastes energy and doesn't solve the problem. Mistakes need to be seen as learning opportunities for everyone.

---

[25]Mary O'Hara-Devereaux and Robert Johansen, *Global Work: Bridging Distance, Culture and Time*, San Francisco: Jossey-Bass, 1994, p. 159.

Organization: Developing the Infrastructure That Enables Joint Work

◆ **Check team process.** How is the team working together? Very often teams get caught up in performing tasks and don't stop to think about the processes by which they are meant to be achieving them. Is the team staying with its original process for working together? If not, why not? What has changed? Is the change for the better, or are some members now feeling out of the loop? When things don't run as smoothly as expected, it is very tempting for the majority in a group to impose its own way (even unconsciously). We all have a tendency to recreate the familiar in times of stress. That means many members may feel alienated, betrayed, and resentful.

◆ **Create alignment.** It is important that the team understand how its work links to other teams and projects. First, the team needs to understand its specific role and accountabilities in relation to other initiatives; second, it needs to understand its context; third, a healthy competition can be generated among teams.

◆ **Establish purpose.** If the team purpose is unclear to everyone, how can the team get organized? How will it focus its energies? How will it effectively break down the work into meaningful units? How can it hope to work "like five fingers on a hand?"[26]

◆ **Leverage resources.** If there were only one way to accomplish something, we would all be doing it. We need to encourage the team to look for complementary ways of working rather than the "one way." But we also need to make these differences visible and known to one another. If we don't articulate differences, people make assumptions—usually wrong and damaging assumptions. At its best, diversity challenges "groupthink" and generates value. At its worst, it destroys cohesion and productivity. Work with people's abilities and interests. Ask the team to always look for continuous improvements.

◆ **Map processes.** Particularly on a large project, it will help the work process if the expected flow of work among team members is made visible. Who receives what, from whom, when, and where does it go from here? People need to understand who has accountability, who needs to be kept in the information loop, and who is

---

[26]Rajiv M. Rao, "Zen and the Art of Teamwork," *Fortune,* December 25, 1995, p. 218.

actually responsible for carrying out the work. All of this should be fed into an overall action plan for the group. Individual team members will be able to see the interdependencies and how their part fits into the achievement of the whole. This also promotes accountability.

◆ **Map tasks and accountabilities.** Vision, goals, and purpose are good, but sooner or later they must be translated into explicit roles, tasks, time frames, and outcomes. How formal this mapping needs to be will depend on the team and the complexity and length of the project.

◆ **Record decisions, issues, etc.** Someone on the team needs to be given accountability for producing summaries of meetings: decisions made, open issues, tasks to be accomplished before the next meeting, and so on. This should be given to all team members as soon after the meeting as possible. If any misunderstandings arose because of language difficulties, they should be resolved as quickly as possible after the meeting. The written word is often easier to absorb than fast-paced talk. The group also needs to build a collective memory bank for easy reference.

◆ **Timing.** Collaborating in multicultural teams usually takes longer than in a monocultural team. You can cut the time by making sure everyone receives materials well in advance of the meeting. Plan meetings well ahead. Have realistic expectations about what can be covered in a specified amount of time.

◆ **Track progress against milestones.** Progress needs to be measured against milestones set in the action plan. Performance data need to be gathered and shared. Successful accomplishments need to be communicated to the whole group. The leader will need to be sensitive to differences in reward expectations. What matters most to the individual? Money? Title? Relationship? All three? The team must also be sensitive to what is going on outside of its jurisdiction: What changes are going on in the company, the industry, and the business environment that could affect the team's work?

DIALOGUE BOX

If you are in a global business team, how do you rate its performance in terms of demonstrating collaborative values and skills? Have your colleagues in the team complete the same questionnaire and compare results. Use the findings to identify areas for improvement. Have the whole team discuss the key issues and identify constructive solutions.

Use the following scale:

Poor   1   2   3   4   5   Excellent

Team Score

COLLABORATIVE VALUES

Caring	1	2	3	4	5	_____
Confidentiality	1	2	3	4	5	_____
Fairness	1	2	3	4	5	_____
Honesty	1	2	3	4	5	_____
Openness	1	2	3	4	5	_____
Participation	1	2	3	4	5	_____
Respect	1	2	3	4	5	_____
Responsibility	1	2	3	4	5	_____
Results	1	2	3	4	5	_____
Sharing	1	2	3	4	5	_____
Unity	1	2	3	4	5	_____
Understanding	1	2	3	4	5	_____

COLLABORATIVE SKILLS

Communication: Facilitating the exchange of shared meaning

Asking open-ended questions	1	2	3	4	5 _____
Being open to the counterintuitive	1	2	3	4	5 _____
Being specific	1	2	3	4	5 _____
Challenging stereotypes	1	2	3	4	5 _____
Clarifying assumptions and interpretations	1	2	3	4	5 _____
Gathering input	1	2	3	4	5 _____
Listening with full attention	1	2	3	4	5 _____
Observing with full attention	1	2	3	4	5 _____
Setting a comfortable pace	1	2	3	4	5 _____

Leadership: Generating and channeling energy into creating world-class performance

Being consistent	1	2	3	4	5 _____
Being proactive	1	2	3	4	5 _____
Breaking habits	1	2	3	4	5 _____
Building commitment to a vision	1	2	3	4	5 _____

Concluded

					Team Score
Coaching	1	2	3	4	5 _____
Controlling the ego	1	2	3	4	5 _____
Decision making	1	2	3	4	5 _____
Enabling information flow	1	2	3	4	5 _____
Giving flexible feedback	1	2	3	4	5 _____
Forming relationships	1	2	3	4	5 _____
Setting team process expectations	1	2	3	4	5 _____
Setting challenging goals	1	2	3	4	5 _____
Solving problems	1	2	3	4	5 _____

Organization: Developing the infrastructure that enables joint work

Checking team process	1	2	3	4	5 _____
Creating alignment	1	2	3	4	5 _____
Establishing purpose	1	2	3	4	5 _____
Leveraging resources	1	2	3	4	5 _____
Mapping processes	1	2	3	4	5 _____
Mapping tasks and accountabilities	1	2	3	4	5 _____
Recording decisions, issues, etc.	1	2	3	4	5 _____
Timing	1	2	3	4	5 _____
Tracking progress against milestones	1	2	3	4	5 _____

Priority areas for team improvement:

Actions to be taken (with key dates and responsibilities):

SUMMARY CHECKPOINT

Along with superior financial performance, high levels of customer satisfaction, excellent employee morale, and the power of the company to attract top-notch, globally oriented recruits, productive and innovative collaboration among worldwide units is a sure sign of a healthy global company. Factors affecting this collaboration include global competency development, global context-building, global value clarification, and global skill development.

Organizations with global ambitions need to build their global leadership strengths across at least four bandwidths: individual associate, first-line manager, middle manager, and senior manager. These bands constitute a global leadership spectrum. Specific global roles and responsibilities are associated with each band. Global leader competencies need to be matched against each of the bands.

Context is what people need to know to perform at their best and collaborate with one another. American culture tends to minimize the importance of context and to strip away information to what are considered to be the essentials. That is why we have so many 5- or 10-step programs to success, health, and the like. Global leaders need to understand context in two senses: the global business environment and the organization's business context. The environmental context refers to the world's social, demographic, economic, political, and technological trends. The organization's business context refers to key information regarding the finances of the company, its structure, its market share, growth opportunities, and competitor strategies. Information sharing is critical to the development of global leaders.

Collaborating in an interdependent world also requires a clarification of values. We need to clarify our values at two levels: the macro and the micro. At the macro (world) level, we—and others—need to understand how we do business, what our ethical standards are, and what we consider to be our nonnegotiables. At the micro (team) level, we need to establish a collaborative set of values that promote the building of common working ground.

Values make collaboration possible; skills make it happen. Skills must be built in at least three areas: communication, leadership, and organization. Global team values such as respect, unity, openness, and responsibility, along with a strong set of collaborative skills, provide the ground on which the global talent network can generate breakthrough results.

SOME ACTION IDEAS

Individual

♦ Understand the global leadership competencies needed for your current job and your most likely subsequent jobs (within the same band and the next band). What can you start doing now to make yourself marketable across the organization?

♦ Educate yourself; don't wait for the organization to educate you. It may not happen! Learn as much as you can about the global business environment and your specific company. Subscribe to newspapers and business magazines. Watch international cable TV channels and foreign films. Read foreign literature.

♦ Seek out opportunities to participate in global teams. Put your name forward as someone who is interested in expanding further into the global arena.

Organization

♦ Aggressively communicate the importance of collaboration to the company's global future. Have little tolerance for turf wars or the not-invented-here syndrome.

♦ If you commit to a competency development process, don't let the end product sit on a shelf. Drive the competencies into all company programs and systems.

♦ Support the global education of associates. Circulate information on global subsidiaries and personnel. Circulate readings about international business. Encourage associate study groups in which people build global awareness.

Individual

- Assess your assets and liabilities in terms of collaboration. Talk with those who you trust about your development needs. Clarify your personal values and relate them to the collaborative values listed in this chapter. Are you so strongly individualistic, for example, that deep collaboration is extremely difficult for you? What collaborative skills do you need to build and refine?

Organization

- Conduct a global values audit. What do you as a company say you believe, and what are the perceptions of your practice? What are the business consequences of the gaps between belief and practice?

- Identify global collaboration success stories inside and outside the company. Communicate them to associates, and highlight success factors.

- Have global teams do as much up-front training and miniculture building as possible before starting important projects.

Building the Global Leadership System

I think we're at a point where the quality and customer service people were 5–7 years ago. It took an extraordinary commitment among industrial leaders, and the resources to go with it, to appropriately address the quality and customer service issues. I think it will take that kind of recognition and resource commitment to establish the structure, administration, and support to get the best people moving through the international assignment process.

Ted Westerman, senior vice president, chief administrative officer, Hughes Electronics[1]

Preview

♦ International human resource practices still have a lot of room for improvement. The application of selection, preparation and training, ongoing support, and repatriation strategies and tools is very inconsistent.

♦ The primary options for developing global leadership bench strength in an organization are external recruiting and "growing your own." External recruiting is a relatively simple, quick-fix solution to a complex and long-term problem.

♦ "Growing your own" global leaders requires a comprehensive, systematic approach involving a process of business clarification, program and system development, and integration/alignment.

---

[1]Interview with Ted Westerman, September 25, 1995.

◆ When adopting a systems viewpoint, it is important to take into account the contribution and potential impact on the major components of the organizational system, including inputs from the business environment, global strategy, culture, architecture, and performance systems (such as selection, compensation, education and training, and career development). Global leadership competencies can act as the integrative force in the system.

◆ One way to jump start the change process needed to build global leadership bench strength is a global directions forum. In this forum, key individuals from corporate and the line gather for a few days to develop a compelling vision of the global future, determine global leadership needs in the company, and identify global leadership facilitators and inhibitors in the organization.

OPTIONS

Are you building global leadership bench strength in your company? The research is not very encouraging. In late 1994, NB Selection Ltd., a British international recruitment firm, conducted a survey of international human resource practices in the United Kingdom.[2] The results are similar to, and in some cases better than, those found in American research (see Figure 4–1).

In contrast to the NB Selection findings, language training in the United States is offered by about 33 percent of companies. Forty-three percent of Americans say they would decline to go overseas because they are afraid of not being promoted or even losing rank upon their return.[3] Some human resource experts estimate the failure rate of American managers sent to work overseas is as high as 40 percent.[4] This can rise to 60 percent or more in the Middle East and

---

[2]Elisabeth Marx, *International Human Resource Practices in the U.K.: A Survey on the Selection, Preparation and Support of International Managers*, London: NB Selection Ltd., November 1994, p. 3.

[3]Ronald E. Yates, "U.S. International Executives Corps' Ranks Are Thin," *The Arizona Republic*, March 28, 1994, p. E4.

[4]F. T. Murray and Alice Murray, "Global Managers for Global Business," *Sloan Management Review*, Winter 1986, p. 75.

parts of Asia and Eastern Europe. Virtually all Japanese companies provide language and cultural training and reentry programs aimed at utilizing the expatriate's experience overseas.[5]

What can a company do to build its global leadership bench strength into a strategic asset? In talking with executives and managers with several companies, it became clear that no one has "arrived" at the place where he or she wants to be in terms of developing global leaders. But significant progress is being made. There are at least two major options for building bench strength: external recruiting and "growing your own."

Recruiting experienced global leaders from overseas is becoming increasingly popular, but it is a relatively short-term solution. Many American companies look to Northern Europe, France, Germany, and the United Kingdom to find such leaders. A significant number of companies in Europe have been rotating people on international assignments for years. Mr. Mueller-Maerki, a partner at the Egon Zehnder International executive recruiting firm in New York, suggests that executives from overseas (inpatriates) hold approximately 15 percent of the senior positions in U.S. corporations.[6] Com-

FIGURE 4–1

International Human Resource Practices in the United Kingdom (*n* = 92)

Selection	
Systematic use of international competencies	20.1%
Systematic use of psychological testing	15.2
Interview with spouse at selection stage	4.3
Preparation and training	
Offer of look-see visits	67.0
Offer of language training	85.0
Offer of cultural training	44.4
Ongoing support	
Provided by headquarters or on location	83.9
Mentor system	21.3
Repatriation	
Guaranteed job on return	35.6

Source: Elisabeth Marx, *International Human Resource Practices in the UK*, London, NB Selection Ltd., 1994.

---

[5]Yates, "U.S. International Executives Corps," p. E4.

[6]Lori Ioannou, "Stateless Executives," *International Business*, February 1995, p. 48.

panies most aggressively seeking inpatriates are in the following industries: computer software and hardware, electronics, capital equipment, telecommunications, pharmaceuticals, and chemical and financial services.

The second option, "growing your own" through such methods as expatriation, inpatriation, education and training, and job rotations, is the strategy of choice for an increasing number of companies. Al Zeien, Gillette's CEO, has refocused the company's strategy on being number one in every product and market in which it competes. Zeien recognizes that to do this he needs to grow his global people power. He travels the world meeting with product groups, and he personally conducts 800 performance reviews annually. He also gives personal attention to guiding the careers of scores of managers. Having people with a global perspective is not enough for Zeien: "We could try to hire the best and the brightest, but it's experience with Gillette that we need. About half of our expats are now on their fourth country—that kind of experience. It takes ten years to make the kind of Gillette manager I'm talking about."[7] What Zeien wants is men and women who have an in-depth understanding of the global business context under conditions of rapid change. He gave the following example to Charles Farkas and Philippe De Backer, authors of *Maximum Leadership*.[8] The lowest-cost method—on a specific day—to get razor blade cartridges to the Australian market might begin at a steel plant in Japan, then go to a processing plant in Brazil, a packaging plant in Singapore, and finally to Australia for distribution. But as Zeien says, "that might change tomorrow, so we have to be on top of it. Everyone has to know what everyone else knows; they have to be thinking alike, sharing information, working as one person."[9]

The remainder of this chapter will focus on companies that are strategizing to develop global leaders from within.

---

[7]Charles M. Farkas and Philippe De Backer, "There Are Only Five Ways to Lead," *Fortune*, January 1996, p. 111.

[8]Charles M. Farkas and Philippe De Backer, *Maximum Leadership*, New York: Henry Holt and Co., 1996.

[9]Farkas and De Backer, "There Are Only Five Ways to Lead," p. 111.

ADOPTING A SYSTEMS APPROACH

While there is no one definitive methodology for "growing your own" global leaders, many of our most forward-looking companies point the way. Let's begin with NYNEX, a company that was divested from AT&T in 1984. Many will know NYNEX as the company providing telephone service from New York to Maine. But NYNEX is now a global player with highly profitable ventures in Europe and Asia. It is involved in a joint venture in building a 2.6 million-line Thai telephone system, a system larger than that in Manhattan. It is also a leading sponsor of what is called the FLAG (Fiber-optic Link Around the Globe) Project, a $1.6 billion submarine fiber-optic cable that will expand from the United Kingdom to Japan. It is one of the largest privately funded construction projects ever. How does NYNEX develop the global leaders it needs?

Paul Kurppe, director of strategic work force development, speaks with great energy and passion about the progress NYNEX has made in identifying and developing global leaders:

> In the early 90s, NYNEX embarked on a clarification of its values and guiding principles, such as accountability for results, customer-focused entrepreneurship, and focused and purposeful leadership. They were developed with domestic and global expansion in mind. This period taught us that we needed to give people a common language and clear focus on what we mean as a business, to allow employees to contribute toward company results. Our values and principles are supported and reinforced by our core competencies—there's an integration here, complete alignment with our human resource processes, such as succession planning, staffing, performance management, compensation, and training.
>
> One of the natural outgrowths of the new strategic focus clarification exercise was the development of the NYNEX Global Apprenticeship Program. The program's vision is to develop the skills and experiences required for future leaders of NYNEX to expand our global market share.
>
> Annually we solicit for nominations of high-performing individuals within each of our organizations. We generally get upwards of 100 to 150 nominations for about 10 places. The candidates will be screened against the criteria we have established for the program. We look at the performance appraisal documentation, their education and scholastic background, their languages and special interests. We have a

selection committee to review the information and make the final recommendations.

The Global Apprenticeship Program curriculum lasts for 10 months and was developed in collaboration with Columbia University's Graduate School of Business. It also draws on more than 50 NYNEX managers involved in such areas as international business development, policy, and ethics. Participants also learn directly from employees who have already lived and worked abroad.

Paul Kurppe says,

For two days of each month, participants attend intensive workshops on such topics as the global challenge; global strategy; selecting and entering markets; geopolitical, social, and economic forces; managing international finances; cultural risks; managing customer value internationally; marketing services and products; global branding; governments and international trading; international negotiations; international alliances; living and working abroad; and repatriation.

While the participants are attending the program, they are on domestic assignment lasting one to two years. Following the domestic assignment, the apprentices will be deployed overseas for two or more years. As a communications company, we are looking to take our core capabilities—designing, building, and operating state-of-the-art networks—to the fastest-growing markets in the world. In many cases, what we're looking to do is prepare our most technically proficient managers to do business internationally. Some program participants have become involved in international business development; others have done special cellular assignments. We have also used participants as regional directors on the FLAG project. Those with sales expertise have become branch managers in different parts of the world. We look for a natural fit between the individual and the assignment.

We have a dedicated HR organization focused on our international talent management. There are tremendous complexities involved in such areas as tax, asset transfers, compensation, logistics, performance tracking, etc., and this small, dedicated area is the central support system. We also have in place a mentor support group to ease the transition overseas. They can reach out for consultation and coaching, or just have the ear of someone who has shared similar experiences.

The participants come back to a very clear position in which they build on the skills they have gained overseas. We have a very tight integration with our centralized recruitment and staffing organization. Six months prior to the completion of an assignment, we will begin brokering the in-house placement for their return. When someone returns, first we do a debrief with the officers of the business. They have a vested interest in knowing: *What has been the learning? What can we recycle back into the domestic business?* And then *Where is the best place in the structure to place this individual?* Obviously, this is not the only contact the individual has while away. There is ongoing feedback and dialogue throughout the entire two-year assignment. The formal close is important because at the end you can look back and use hindsight to think about what might have worked better. During that final debrief session, you can reflect on the learning experiences and think about what they mean to us as a business and how we can capitalize on them.

We have also completely integrated with our performance management process. We have a development component to our performance management and compensation process. Participation in the Global Apprenticeship Program qualifies as the development initiative that satisfies the performance management process. In this process, the core competencies are considered very important, and they are rated. The results are tracked and rated, and the combined ratings of the competencies and results determine the compensation payout.

The instrument we use when recruiting externally has been tailored to look for global preparedness. We also have a selection interview guide that has been validated and developed to screen for globally predisposed managers. We don't give this to every employee; if we need a garden-variety manager, we put them through the normal testing and screening process. We use the global tools when we need them.

We didn't come to this model for developing global leaders naturally born. We went through a lot of pain. There were many disconnects in the early stages. I can remember a time five years ago when we were saying, "Where are they going to sit?" Unfortunately, the value of the learning wasn't viewed as something we could recycle and use. Now we really see how important it is! We're now at a place where we are doing some very positive things and some modeling for others.

We are looking to shift the revenue stream for our business from 100 percent of the northeast market to 10 percent of the world market for telecommunications. The Global Apprenticeship Program will play a critical part in our ability to win a sizable percentage of that huge marketplace.

The NYNEX experience points to the need for a comprehensive and systematic approach to developing global leaders. For NYNEX, as for many other companies, it will begin with *clarification*: What business are we in? What role will "global" play in our future success? What should be our core values and principles for operating globally? What are our key capabilities, and how do they rate globally? Who are our key customers now and in the future? What are the strategic markets for our business? How do we organize to best serve our customers and markets most efficiently and effectively? What do our people need to know and do to be successful in leading and supporting a global operation?

From business clarification, the company needs to move into a *development* mode. What kinds of programs and systems do we need to put in place to achieve our global goals? How do we build these programs and systems so that everyone is on board and takes ownership for successful implementation?

From the development stage, the company needs to engage in *system integration and alignment*. How do we make sure that our selection, performance management, career development, education and training, compensation systems, and so on support one another in building global leadership bench strength?

Many of the companies interviewed for this book were engaged in a systematic and strategic effort to develop global leaders to take them into the next century. In discussing their initiatives, it will be useful to consider them in relation to a generic system model such as that in Figure 4–2.

Many organizational system models exist, and I don't want to take up a lot of space reiterating what a reader may already know. Therefore, the following explanation of the key components is relatively brief.

The key *inputs* into the system are numerous. We look to inputs to help us answer questions that will help us develop winning strategies. Five anchor questions are as follows:

- ◆ *Givens*. What are our current internal and external realities (e.g., vision and values, key capabilities, products and services, customers, markets, competitors, organizational structure, cost factors, industry trends, geopolitical forces)?

- *Opportunities.* What are the sources of new opportunity for the firm in the global marketplace?
- *Options.* Given our current realities and opportunities, what options do we have for moving forward most effectively?
- *Drawbacks.* What are the major obstacles we face with each option identified?
- *Strategies.* Given the costs and benefits of the options available to us, what is the best strategic path for us to take?

One drawback of talking about "input" is that it gives the impression that a good organization is simply responsive to information coming in from the outside. The smart organization also tries to be proactive in shaping the environment and transforming its industry.

FIGURE 4–2

A Generic Organizational System

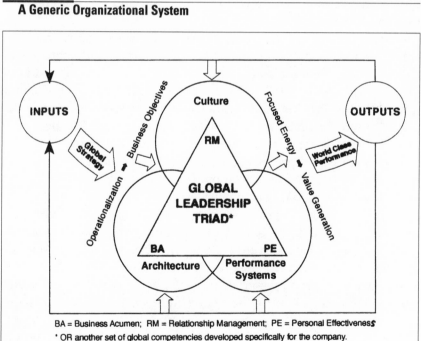

BA = Business Acumen; RM = Relationship Management; PE = Personal Effectiveness
* OR another set of global competencies developed specifically for the company.

Source: © Terence Brake, 1996.

Global strategy is about defining the competitive space in which the company wants to play. It is developed from a mix of information flowing into the system and internally generated information and ideas. In line with the overall business strategy, a global human resource strategy needs to be developed that will put the right people in the right place at the right time doing the right things.

The global strategy is usually *operationalized* by the creation of specific strategies and business objectives for the various operating units, functional areas, and core processes in the company's *architecture*. The key elements of architecture, culture, and performance systems shape, and in turn are shaped by, global competencies (in our model, the Global Leadership Triad). *Culture* refers to the set of shared assumptions, beliefs, values, and norms of behavior expected and accepted in the organization. Performance systems are the tools the organization puts in place to influence the quality and development of its people (e.g., individual development planning, succession planning, compensation and rewards, education and training, recruitment and selection, job rotation).

Architecture, culture, and performance systems are in many ways the organizational equivalents of the Global Leadership Triad. Culture is to the organization what relationship management is to the individual global leader. The organizational culture, formally and informally, defines how individuals relate to one another and to the organization. Architecture is to the organization what business acumen is to the global leader. It is the functional, control-oriented part of the business and provides the framework for operations. Performance systems are the organizational mechanisms for facilitating the drive toward personal effectiveness.

Ideally, the company driven by such a system configuration looks to align strategy, architecture, culture, performance systems, and competencies to focus energy on generating value for stakeholders and producing world-class results. As with any system model, it looks easy enough on paper! The reality, of course, is that creating such an aligned system can be a slow and difficult process. Moving too fast or mandating the changes can destroy the sense of ownership and buy-in needed to make the system work. Such a system is not established in a cultural, structural, and political vacuum.

DIALOGUE BOX

1. Which of the following international human resource practices does your company use?

   Selection
   - Systematic use of international competencies
   - Systematic use of psychological testing
   - Interview with spouse at selection stage

   Preparation and training
   - Offer of look-see visits
   - Offer of language training
   - Offer of cultural training

   Ongoing support
   - From HQ and/or on location
   - Mentor system

   Repatriation
   - Guaranteed job on return

2. What are the most urgent gaps your company needs to fill in its international human resource practices?

3. To what extent is your company taking a systematic approach to developing global leaders? What parts of your system need to receive more attention?

NEWS FROM THE FRONTLINES

To capture the flavor of the triumphs and challenges of developing global leaders, the remainder of the chapter will allow individuals to speak for themselves. Using the system model described in the previous section, the discussion is structured into the following topics: strategy, competencies, culture, architecture, and performance systems.

The predominant voices you will "hear" in this section are those of the following individuals (in alphabetical order):

Mr. Eric Campbell, vice president of human resources, International Flavors and Fragrances (IFF).

Ms. Bettye Hill, director of global education and training, Avon Products, Inc.

Ms. Donna McNamara, director of global education and training, Colgate-Palmolive.

Mr. Michael Michl, vice president of human resources, Avon Products, Inc.

Mr. Pat Morgan, a human resources manager with Bechtel.

Mr. Doug Reid, senior vice president of human resources, Colgate-Palmolive.

Mr. Ted Westerman, senior vice president, chief administrative officer, Hughes Electronics.

Strategy

Every company needs to develop business and human resource strategies that fit its own set of internal and external conditions.

Strategy development at Avon Products, Inc., resides at the level of the Global Business Council (GBC).

Bettye Hill: We have a GBC that is made up of the CEO, the COO, and the heads of the worldwide operating business units. All decisions are made by that team. Centrally, we don't mandate anything. I can't say to an operating unit, for example, that they must use certain training programs. The GBC decides if a training program is needed, what content is appropriate, and who will be trained; i.e., will everyone be trained or just selected areas? If it doesn't go through that group, it doesn't get done. The line managers really manage all decisions. Members of the GBC are responsible for pushing the strategy down through the organization and getting it done. This may be achieved through global or local teams, depending on the issues.

Human resource strategy at Colgate-Palmolive is also developed from a global perspective. In 1989, CEO Reuben Mark expressed the global vision of the company. This vision looks to speed products to market by building close linkage between the human and the business aspects.

Donna McNamara: About four years ago, we put together for the first time a global human resources strategy. In contrast to our product lines, there had not been a tradition of managing our human resources globally. We set out to develop an overall game plan on a global basis, identify key priorities over a five-year span, understand the capabilities needed, and decide what HR systems to put in place on a worldwide basis. Exactly how to apply our HR practices is left to local judgment. It is not a mandated approach. It is an overall game plan that was created collectively. The pacing of what's going to be done, where the particular points of emphasis will be, vary by subsidiary. We assume that no one subsidiary can implement the system at one time. There really has to be some choices made on a local basis.

In creating the strategy, we had the participation of the senior leadership of human resources worldwide and key line managers, e.g., presidents of business units. It was not something done in isolation by human resource people. What was developed on the team was shared at the local level, and input came back to us. It took at least a year, maybe a little more. There's no question that people in the field view this as their own. The very creation of the global education and training function was a direct outcome of the strategy. Up to then, there was no education and training on a global basis.

The global team of about 25 people met in groups to develop global criteria for selection, succession planning, coaching, and performance management. According to Brian Smith, director of global staffing and HR strategy, "This global business strategy requires identifying a certain type of manager who understands not only the particular niches and communities in which we operate locally, but who also has that global perspective and understands the tremendous benefits of a global product line."[10] The company used to roll out one product a year; that number is up to five today, and there are plans

---

[10]Charlene Marmer Solomon, "Staff Selection Impacts Global Success," *Personnel Journal*,
    January 1994.

to double that number.[11]

While a deliberate attempt may be made to develop global strategies, the smart company is flexible enough to make rapid changes. Ask Ted Westerman at Hughes Electronics.

> *Ted Westerman:* We designed what we believed to be a global strategy. The model we have in place today is dramatically different from the one designed three years ago. As we started to implement the original model, we realized it wasn't going to work, even though we had designed it collaboratively. We've got such a difference in the kinds of people that seem to be appropriate for the markets we're operating in that a one-size-fits-all international human resources system is not appropriate. We will probably fix the responsibility on the operating companies to function within some overall umbrella set of expectations and standards in managing their people. This is very different from the way we thought it would happen; we expected more centralization, but that's not realistic for us. You end up sizing everything to the least common denominator.

Competencies

A key component in the framework of many strategies is the development of global competencies. Competencies act as the interlocking mechanism for much of the system integration. "Global competencies are the centerpiece of the HR strategy," says Brian Smith of Colgate-Palmolive. "They're grounded in business needs. Armed with competencies that are tiered through the organization, we can target our efforts and be much more effective in bringing the best talent to Colgate."[12]

> *Doug Reid:* The competency work was a great experience. We went around the world and asked for input: "Does this make sense in your country?" There was great buy-in. Although we've just started, we're making use of the competencies in our selection process, and we're reinforcing the importance of the com-

---

[11]Ibid
[12]Ibid

petencies in our performance appraisal system and individual development planning.

The competencies at Colgate-Palmolive include common needs, but were also built to reflect requirements in three different functional areas.

Donna McNamara: One specific of our strategy was to develop global competencies in key critical areas, for example, manufacturing, finance, sales, marketing, and research. We've also just completed human resources. In these functional areas, competencies and career development principles have been established for leadership, management, and technical skills. These have been developed on a global basis and have been introduced around the world.

Competencies at Avon have been built to reflect global management needs rather than being functionally specific.

Bettye Hill: There was an international task force brought in to work on performance review. We wanted a performance review system that could go everywhere in the world. The team also came up with the competencies. We had different constituencies look at them, and members of the team went back to their home countries for feedback. A Global Education Council also took the competencies and reworked them based on a global needs analysis. We directed attention on the future and not just the present. The resulting set of competencies were then approved by the Global Business Council and communicated all over the world.

These competencies have been influential across Avon. They are the thread that weaves through the entire human resource system.

Michael Michl: These competencies, which are broken down into very specific criteria, are used for all that we do. They are used for the appraisal process, for the executive resource process, for developing and selecting people. And if we create a training program, we will screen it against the competencies.

The development of global competencies at Bechtel is tied into an effort to build leadership throughout the company (Bechtel Leadership 2001).

> *Pat Morgan:* As we move forward in the global economy, we'll need leadership. We've developed the Bechtel Leadership Model, which lists the factors we feel are important to us for succeeding in this environment. [See Figures 4–3 and 4–4.] We're now assessing 600 managers against the model. It's a 360-degree assessment, and managers get a very comprehensive view of where they stand against the model. The model balances both leadership skills and technical skills. We're now threading the competencies through our entire people development process.
>
> Some of us thought that developing the leadership model was a check-off item. But it doesn't stay static; that was a bit of a shock. The world changes, and you need to revisit the model, revalidate it, and recalibrate it.
>
> Defining competencies makes sense intellectually. From a practical point of view, we have to realize that it can be very difficult for managers to sit down and define what they want in a person. It will require much more rigor, discipline, and a change in the culture.
>
> We're trying to move the competencies on to the recruiting end. In the development area, we are using competencies as a framework. The next step we've got to get to is compensation. If we're saying the Leadership Model is the vision, we've got to compensate that way. You can't say over in the development area that this is our vision of life, but your employment process and compensation process don't reflect the vision.

Again, participation throughout the organization is key to developing a set of competencies that are implementable. Upfront participation alone, however, does not guarantee their immediate and sustained use. They impose a rigor and a discipline in thinking through staffing and development issues that may have been absent from an organizational culture. "Thread" is the most common metaphor used by those interviewed to describe how global competencies are used to weave the elements of the human resource system together. This thread, however, does wear out. Conditions change and the competencies must be reviewed periodically for their accuracy.

Culture

It helps the process of developing global leaders if you can draw on a well-established corporate culture that consistently communicates the importance of the international experience.

> *Donna McNamara:* Inside Colgate-Palmolive, people really understand that a path to the top is to have experience in various parts of the world. This is well established in our culture, much better understood than in many companies where people are given a mixed message about leaving the home country. They may be told, "It's a very important assignment—a key part of our strategy." On the other hand, they've probably heard stories about the dangers of being left out of the mainstream, of not getting a passport back. In Colgate-Palmolive, people are,

FIGURE 4–3

Bechtel's Leadership Attributes, Skills, and Process

© Bechtel Corporation, 1994.

FIGURE 4–4

Bechtel's Leadership Behavior and Business Success

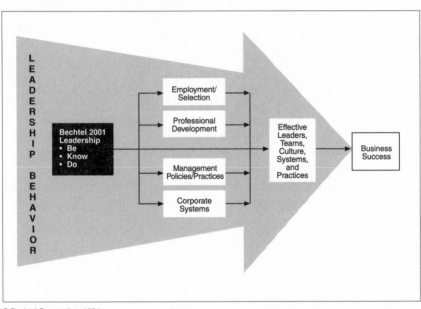

© Bechtel Corporation, 1994.

from a career standpoint, moved from one part of the world to another. This happens continually, and it has happened over the years so that all of our senior people have had international experience. It's a real clear message.

In addition to creating a climate in which international experience is highly valued, a global culture must facilitate the flow of people, information, and resources needed to promote responsiveness and innovation.

Pat Morgan: Our initiative—*Toward 2001*—is part of a broad culture change. We are looking carefully at what we want to retain and what we want to let go. We have vertical silos in our organization, and it's hard crossing those barriers. We're trying to break them down. They get built up over the years, and they really impact how quickly you can form teams and get access to the best people. We need to blow some holes in the walls. Not in a destructive way, but to make those walls more permeable so that people can flow across the organization. You need to do that for at least two reasons. First, you've got to develop individuals and make them more cross-functional, and, second, you need to get the skills spread across the organization.

The person at the top of the silo is being rewarded for its performance. People are reluctant to let people go if it will impact the performance of their silo. We need to change the reward structure to say, "You will be measured on whom you let go out of your silo and whom you let in from the outside." We're trying to work on those measurements. We're tying our rewards and recognition themes to the leadership traits we identified.

What Pat Morgan is highlighting is the paradox of control. Carefully selected controls and measurements can help build a culture of flexibility rather than dig bureaucracy deeper. Eric Campbell (IFF) discusses the value of headcount control in promoting flexibility.

Eric Campbell: Headcount restrictions are part of our culture. We have minimal turnover and a lot of long-service people. We almost operate on a Japanese work ethic. During the course of their career, these folks have ended up moving around the company. They've changed functions, they've moved from country to country, they've moved from the fragrance side to the flavors side and back again.

Because of the restrictive nature of headcount management, a lot of promotions have been done from within. In many ways, it has forced an environment in which people have to learn a variety of different positions. As a result, a lot of traits you identify with successful global management are similar to those you see in a management team that's had to manage with tight resources in a growing business environment over a period of time. Restrictions on headcount really encourage people to work closely together. When you can't build an empire, it's awfully hard to remove yourself from the day-to-day issues.

I noticed when attending the area managers' meeting that there is a very strong multicountry, multicultural team that has been developed over the years. These folks have had the opportunity to be in place long enough to build strong relationships with each other and with customers. You see the give and take that is necessary in a global environment. People have not been moved so quickly that they were not able to build lasting relationships. I've been in organizations where we have rotated managers quickly—with the best of intentions—and culturally it has not been the right thing to do in many parts of the world. It's been to our detriment.

Maintaining tight controls on headcount has saved us from downsizing. This has helped us generate a tremendous amount of organizational trust. A soft item, but very important. Organizational trust is what in many cases allows people to be very frank with one another about options, strategies, and business plans. The strong relationships that have been developed have enabled the company to weather tough times. We have not had to rebuild organizational morale over and over again, or go out there and put people back together because their co-workers have disappeared.

Trust helps build consensus and buy-in, a prominent feature of the culture at Avon.

Michael Michl: It is the culture of this company to look for consensus. In some cases it may take a little longer, but you get commitment. By the time you get something approved and rolled out, you've got people in place who worked on it or who know who worked on it. Rolling out initiatives becomes much less of a problem.

If we're going to be successful on a global basis, it's not going to be through confrontation. It's going to be on learning how to work on multicultural teams, to listen to each other. We must be able to communicate at all levels. Some of this communication can be done via systems, but a lot of it must be done on a personal basis. We are doing a lot to establish networks by having regular contact, setting up meetings, bringing people together. We may be based in New York, but we're not an American company because 60 percent of our business is done outside of the United States. Global success is about mobility, not just physically but mentally.

Building a global culture that facilitates the exchange of information is critical for bottom-line results.

Bettye Hill: If you're going to be a global company, you need efficiencies. You don't want to be reinventing the wheel a hundred times. One of the challenges in a decentralized global structure is to have units accept something from somewhere else. The not-invented-here syndrome is rampant in many companies. Really good global companies say, "OK, we're going into apparel. They did it in such and such a place very successfully. Let's find out what they did." The recognition tends to go to the first one out with something. There is no reward for copying. Our people are getting very smart. We're seeing much more interaction. Someone spends time in Brazil and takes ideas back to Italy. The challenge is not only to move people but ideas.

We do hold global forums on such topics as field fundamentals or marketing fundamentals. People stand up and talk about what they're doing. Other people say, "That's great. I want more information. Those who attended the field fundamentals session were brought back a year later to see how they were progressing. Many people talked about how they had learned from other countries.

One of the critical elements of a company's culture is the way in which it creates what I call a *zone of possibility*. Productive cultures feed into and nurture the aspirations of the people within them.

Bettye Hill: Recognition trips for representatives and zone managers are fantasies. Disney couldn't do a fantasy as wonderful as these trips. Many women have never received such recognition before, especially in the developing countries, but also here in the United States. I remember doing a program in Kentucky with women who had never graduated from high school. We did a recognition/training program for them. They had earned their way to the program by selling at a certain level. At the end of the program, we held a graduation ceremony. You should have heard the weeping. They had never received a diploma or been so pampered with dinners and classes and makeovers. They'd never before been treated that way. We created dreams. It's a whole company built on the dreams and aspirations of these women.

Culture is hard and soft. It is about putting in place the right controls and measurements to reward desired behaviors. It is also about instilling values and beliefs that promote trust, communication, and the exchange of ideas and learning across a complex organization. A global culture also provides a zone of stability and consistency that enables a company to respond to change without fragmenting. Some commentators talk of culture as being the "glue" that holds an organization together. But it is more than just an integrative force. Culture also establishes the zone of possibility for the company and its people; it feeds into and drives aspirations.

Many companies put a lot of faith in the tangible aspects of business, such as production technology. Jeffrey Pfeffer, professor of organizational behavior at Stanford, makes a very telling point about this approach: "During the 1980s, General Motors invested enough money in capital equipment to have purchased on the open market every share of both Honda and Nissan. What it obtained was the highest fixed-cost structure in the automobile industry, and since it did not address its people problems, a very low level of productivity and quality."[13] Technology alone will not compensate for the lack of an organizational culture that inspires and drives people to new levels of achievement.

Architecture

Architecture refers to the structure and processes by which a business operates. This is too big a topic for this book, and the only real observation that can be made is that each company must seek out its own balance of efficiency and effectiveness through varying the degrees of centralization and decentralization. Ideally, the architecture will support the mobility of people and ideas, entrepreneurship at all levels, and the critical linkage between the local and the global without too much redundancy. The most valuable global leaders have extensive knowledge of all the businesses in a company, its worldwide operating units and their environments, and the corporate headquarters.

---

[13]Richard Donkin, "Recruitment: Survival of the Fitters—Policies That Pay Dividends from Investing in People," *Financial Times*, July 12, 1995, p. 11.

Doug Reid: Products with a global potential are identified through operation's reviews with divisional presidents. What's neat about Colgate is that although we are a $8.5 billion company, the management of that is all in this building. The top 15 to 16 people, including division presidents, are all here. We get together once a month to talk about global issues and challenges. In one room, we will have someone who knows what's going on in New Zealand, or Chile, or Norway. It's fantastic! Part of the culture is that people in headquarters are out there in the operating companies, talking to their people, understanding what's going on, learning from them, and bringing that knowledge back to headquarters.

From a strategic point of view, Colgate is fairly centralized, but with heavy input from the operating companies. I think the biggest benefit of having international headquarters here in New York is that it gives the general managers the freedom they need to grow and to let their people grow and develop their business. They can use division staff at headquarters to get help from the center, whether it's technology or HR. If the division staff were in Europe or Asia, they would be spending more time with the general managers and their team, smothering them with overcontrol. With e-mail, planes, and teleconferencing, the interactions that are required can be managed. In my previous company, regional headquarters was forced to be in the region, and as I look back the general managers had to spend so much time keeping their division bosses happy, they weren't spending enough time with their customers. Our business is driven by the general manager, and he or she is better off with the freedom they have.

We do create what we call "global bundles." When introducing global products, the bundle will explain how to manufacture the new product, how to package it, and it will even include some advertising copy. They are developed by people in global business development who will have people from overseas on assignment. Quite often the bundle starts in a particular country where they launch the product and we learn from them. They will take the lead in putting the bundle together. We learn from their experience and take that learning around the world.

Michael Michl (Avon): From an organizational point of view, we are very much a decentralized company. There is very little mandated from corporate, contrary to Coca-Cola, for example, where brand management is the name of the game. Out of perhaps thousands of products, we only have eight that are considered to be global. The companies can decide what they want to market on a local basis, although they cannot tamper with the global brands. With the global brand, they have to go with certain logos and meet specific advertising standards. Other than that, they are pretty much on their own for what they do and how they do it. It's not like many other companies where, for example, if you have a labor problem in one of the companies the skies get dark because corporate flies in. They've had labor problems in the Philippines that were close to a strike, and we didn't know until it was all over. Nobody gets on a plane until he or she is asked. Line is in charge; staff are there for support.

We are organized into nine geographic areas, which are called business units. We have about four or five top management meetings a year to coordinate strategies, talk about new-product introductions, share best or worst practices, discuss market campaigns, and set the scene for leveraging our resources on a worldwide basis.

Europe is very strong in fragrance, and they produce a number of fragrances a year. It is up to the other business units to decide what they will do with these fragrances. There is very little forced direction from the top. The only time that corporate really gets involved is in the October–November time frame, when we look at the profit/operating plans and reach agreement on gross objectives for sales/profit, etc. Once the financial objectives are agreed upon, the units go ahead and do their own thing.

The business unit heads form the Global Business Council (GBC), along with the CEO and COO. Whenever they get together, the focus is on global. They clearly wear two hats: their local geography and the global business. They have to decide where we are going to allocate our resources. For example, they have just decided to open a new plant in China—a major investment for us. They need to look at the long-term strategic impact of closing and opening plants in different parts of the world based on business growth, costs, etc. They have to balance performance for the good of the company overall. They are paid on earnings per share, how the stock price moves, and certain global objectives. They have, therefore, a very high interest to communicate horizontally and vertically. There's a lot of interest in sharing information and leveraging the knowledge we have.

Avon is also looking to set up centers of excellence around the globe.

Michael Michl: You look to a certain region or unit to assume, in addition to their local responsibilities, a global responsibility. We're looking to see where the expertise is located. You centralize either the manufacturing, research, or marketing expertise in one country. That country assumes responsibilities for the region and eventually for the globe.

We have decided to move global marketing, which includes product development, from corporate to the U.S. company, and let them own it. The reason was that the majority of products that have been introduced in the past have been sourced from the United States, and the U.S. de facto has become the supplier for most of the business units. It encourages the United States to be thinking outside of its box. They now have to bring the other business units into the process much earlier. Within the U.S. marketing organization, you now have people assigned to be or become the global experts. They have to understand skin differences and product content preferences worldwide. We're putting information systems for Asia into Australia because they have the best skills in the Avon world and also the most advanced system infrastructure. We will have the expertise, knowledge, and support in one place. Not everyone has to build up their own local expertise. We're all rowing in the same boat.

Performance Systems

Selection

Doug Reid (Colgate): We have a dual intake path: those primarily interested in the United States and those who can't wait to

get overseas. Those who come in on the U.S. side are not pre-
cluded from going overseas at a later time.

Colgate's approach to developing global leaders places a lot
of emphasis on selection, generally right out of college. We look
at language ability, and overseas travel and study. After a relatively brief orientation in the United States ["brief" being defined as a year and a half to two years of planned rotations in
two to three departments, e.g., sales, marketing], we send them
overseas. They might be assigned to work anywhere—Chile,
Greece, the United Kingdom. When they complete that assignment of one to two years, they will be permanently assigned. It
may be in the country in which they are currently working,
somewhere else in the region, or another part of the world.
Ninety percent of their development experience is on the job.

It's called the Global Marketing Development Program [and
some 15,000 people try to enter the program every year[14]]. We
also have the Global Manufacturing Associate Program and the
Global Human Resources Associate Program. What is really
working for us is really zeroing in on the person's interest in
international versus the United States. We probe deeply when a
candidate says they are interested in international. We want to
know "why?" We have found if the person has a language capability, spent summers working overseas, or spent a semester
or two overseas, we're on to a good candidate. We want a tangible expression of interest, not just a thought.

We believe people become leaders in large part when they
have successfully worked in a number of countries. We have a
cadre of about 250 people around the world who have and who
are willing to work anywhere in the world for Colgate. The more
successful ones end up back here in global headquarters in senior line or staff positions. They bring a wealth of overseas experience—20 years or so—with them.

The selection of people becomes increasingly important when
you are not only doing more business in the international arena but
the nature of your business is also undergoing a transformation.

---

[14]Ibid.

Ted Westerman: Until three or four years ago, Hughes was almost exclusively a defense contractor. Virtually all the business we did outside the country was in military markets. About half of it was in foreign military sales, which in effect was selling to the U.S. Defense Department. The department would then sell the hardware. The sorts of people you need to do that are dramatically different from the kinds of people we need now. About 40 to 45 percent of our work is defense, and the rest is commercial. It is also becoming clear that more and more of what we will be doing in our nondefense marketplace is going to be international.

Traditionally, the people who were most suitable to do the business we needed fell into two categories. The first were people who were associated with a particular program, and the skills they brought were mostly technical. The selection and human resource issues were driven more by the program's requirements than the geography. The second group were really professional expatriates who were familiar with the defense marketplace. Many of these were retired military people, and they would take on a marketing role in a particular international market.

The people in Hughes who go and operate in international areas are still those who can deal effectively with the technical aspects of the products. But as Ted Westerman says, "That results—too often—in people going on international assignments for which they and their families are really not prepared. The failure rate for these people—by which I mean returning to the United States before the project is complete—is too high. This is a phenomenon across U.S. industry."

Molex, Inc., an American technology firm based in Lisle, Illinois, searches for foreign national students who are currently living in the United States and have graduated from master's degree programs. Many of these students would like to work for an American company but live in their own countries. These employees have a head start on understanding the target market's culture and its language. Malou Roth, vice president of Human Resources International, says, "We've had more success molding younger people with all the energy and excitement of the company in these entry-level jobs than taking people who've worked for other companies. We've moved up so quickly, and we've done that through demanding extremely long hours and hard work. We want to train people properly from the beginning."[15]

Compensation

> *Doug Reid:* We communicate our needs in a very pragmatic way: through our incentive plans. For example, in Europe we want profit from each individual country; we also want to maximize the opportunities that exist as Europe becomes one market and source products from one or two manufacturing plants versus each country manufacturing their own products. We also want to source raw materials from the low-cost/quality suppliers in one or two countries rather than from everywhere. We have a very simple model that goes something like this: 50 percent of your bonus will depend on how well you do in your individual country, and the other 50 percent will be based on how well Europe does as a division. So, we might say to Italy, for example, "You're not going to manufacture toothpaste anymore, you're going to get it from the U.K." Or we might tell the U.K., "You're not going to manufacture soap anymore, you're going to get it from Italy." We might have to say to the Europeans, "You're not going to buy raw materials from France anymore, but get them from Greece." They'll say, "OK, we'll do that because it's going to maximize the profit of Europe." This is the power of our annual bonus plan to communicate our priorities as a global company. Our operating budget is our primary action document, with reinforcement from the incentive plan.

Sorting out the compensation issues is a major challenge. Molex looks to create compensation packages that treat expats and regular employees equally. Molex distinguishes itself from many other organizations—and illustrates its corporate culture of respect for all of its people—through its expatriate compensation policy. Malou Roth argues, "I think if you really believe all this global palaver that ev-

---

[15]Charlene Marmer Solomon, "Navigating Your Search for Global Talent," *Personnel Journal*, May 1995.

erybody is saying, how can you possibly have different expatriate packages for people you're asking to leave their own country? Lots of companies have two-tiered programs—they treat Americans really well. Why would you pay for one guy's house but not the other's? Every expatriate is eligible for everything the American expatriate is eligible for."[16]

Education and Training

Donna McNamara: The centerpiece of our efforts is the creation of a global curriculum. This curriculum works in conjunction with the competencies and is organized around leadership, management, and technical skill areas. These programs have been created to work on a worldwide basis, but not every part of the world uses the same programs. We have some very basic sales programs for distributors, for example, that we use in Eastern Europe and parts of Asia. In some parts of the world, there has previously been no real sales culture. There are much more advanced programs for use in other parts of the world. It's not as if China or Russia are creating their own programs; they are both working off of something that was built collectively.

The curriculum, like the global competencies, was built with the participation of people from all over the world, including technical experts. A content outline is put together, and the people who are reviewing that outline are the most respected line people in the world. Training helps develop a common vocabulary. We try to balance having a plan with maneuverability. The front-end design really takes into account a lot of perspectives. We build programs that line people can deliver. That way the learning becomes fully integrated into the work setting.

The training people get in the field is also part of our culture-building process. Everybody knows they are going through the same program that Colgate people in Argentina or Malaysia or Italy are going through. We also use training as a direct vehicle for transferring best practices worldwide.

---

[16]Ibid.

One of the programs we've been doing worldwide this year has to do with consumer promotion. This program has probably a good 75 to 80 examples of some of the best consumer promotions, many of which are from within Colgate. The ones from within Colgate are hugely practical as far as giving people really great ideas about what others have done with the same products. We get fabulous ideas passing across product categories and within categories. In terms of driving the culture, sharing information, and continuous improvement, it sets the bar a little higher when everyone is seeing these terrific ideas put to work. It also endorses the need to learn from others and the importance of global cooperation.

Many of our key people need time for reflective thinking away from the immediate demands of making the numbers. We have forums where we bring general managers together on a global basis. These are excellent meetings where people network and share information, but they could be even more effective if we would include more time to consider specific individual and collective business learning: above and beyond whether or not timetables and/or numbers were met, but the "hows" and "whys" of the situation.

Because of it's rapid growth around the world, Colgate has a tremendous need for developing people for general management positions.

Doug Reid: One initiative we have on the drawing boards is to have a seminar for general managers at least once every three years. They would be updated by the functional experts on what's going on in finance, manufacturing, etc. The general managers would update the functional experts on what's working and not working. We would also have those general managers spend a day with the executives talking about what's going on with competitors. There's so much they could learn from each other.

In parallel with that, we need to provide some education and training to our general managers before they go into their first assignment. Often we will take, for example, a director of marketing from Argentina and send him to Tanzania as general manager. He may have worked in sales in Italy, marketing in

Brussels, and now he's a general manager. He's not had any experience in manufacturing, and he may not be sure of what HR is all about.

Ideally, we would have an annual conference for general managers. They could consider, "Here's the plan we had for '96. Here's what worked well and not so well. What have we learned? Here's what we think we should do in '97. What do you think?" This way input from the general managers directly influences the strategy.

Training and education is also a major strategic piece of the globalization effort at Avon.

Bettye Hill: We knew training would be a key element in our building global management bench strength. We put a system in place for identifying high potentials and developing plans for them. We also have a group that looks at attitude surveys and feels the pulse of the organization. We're also getting the message across that it's all right to copy and enhance. I now keep a repository of all training that's done around the world. When someone calls me and says, "Do you have anything on such and such?" I might even be able to give it to them in a language they can use.

We also have two Passport programs in place to develop a cadre of potential general managers and potential sales leaders. People are beginning to see that promotions are coming out of this class. Already six to seven have been promoted, which really gives the class credibility. People are asking, "How do I get into that class?" All the people in the class are chosen by the Global Business Council (GBC).

You have to be very tenacious—stubbing your toe, apologizing, backtracking, and coming back in a very soft way. On staff, we have to be helpful rather than dictatorial. The people in a global corporate function who try to go out and mandate are failing. We've got responsibility without authority. You've got to take the time to persuade by showing how it works for them. You've got to be willing to go back to the line and say, "It won't get done this year in these places." Then it becomes the GBC's job to say, "Yes, you will do this." What difference does it make if it takes two years instead of one year, if in the end they own it? We want these initiatives to make a difference. I would rather something that's almost right and used than something that's technically perfect and unused.

Executive development is also a high priority.

Michael Michl: Our internal program lasts for about six weeks over an 18-month period. It is an action learning program where they get together for a week and go through a program of sales, marketing, etc. There are lots of prerequisites before each course. They need, for example, extensive financial understanding before the finance course because it takes them right into what it takes to manage a business from a financial point of view. In between courses, they have project assignments in addition to their on-the-job assignments.

Participation in the program involves a rigorous selection process. They don't go into the program just for learning; we assess them over the 18-month period. Out of this pool, we select who we believe are the future CFOs, the future HR directors, the future sales leaders, the future general managers. Then we let them run a small country operation.

Career Development

Individual development plans, job rotations, short- and long-term assignments, task force opportunities—these are the primary means by which people are developed into global leaders.

Michael Michl: From a capability and development point of view, all of our operating business unit leaders have expatriate experience. Everyone has exposure to other markets. We have a Chilean running Germany, a Portuguese running France, a Brit running Japan, a Canadian running Asia, an American running Southeast Asia, a Canadian running the United States, a Venezuelan running Argentina. We ask: "Who has the best expertise? Who has the best background? The best understanding? Who can add the most value to the organization?" That's the person who gets the job.

The business unit leaders have a minimum of 5 to 10 years' experience with Avon. We have an executive resource system, one of the few things driven by corporate. This is mainly because of the standards we're trying to achieve. Avon also has career pathing. If you want to be a country leader, a general manager, or a business unit leader, you have to have direct sales experience, experience in at least one other functional area (e.g., finance, human resources, marketing), and international experience. Your international experience doesn't have to be in a completely different language market, although we like it to be because it really broadens the perspective.

How does this work?

Bettye Hill: If you are identified as high potential and that you will be in an international cadre, your home manager "owns" you. This is your career manager. That person is responsible for you during the time when you are on international assignment. That person is also responsible for finding you a meaningful position when you return. The time frame for this assignment will be two to three years. If at some point you decide to make being an expatriate your career, you will be cut free of that career manager and someone else will "own" you in your career expatriate capacity.

In creating an international cadre, one has to balance sensitivity to local cultural practices and the needs and management practices of a Western company. Through their development activities and coaching, people come to understand what it takes to succeed in the company. We are an American company, and there are certain skills and competencies necessary to move ahead. In fairness to all the people, to give people a level playing field, they need to know what the rules are. It is then up to them to choose what adjustments, if any, need to be made. The same holds true as individuals take on roles in other cultures. They need to make adjustments.

A primary objective of the career development process at Colgate-Palmolive is to identify potential leaders.

Doug Reid: We move people around the world quite freely and have people come into global headquarters on assignment from three months to three years and go back out. We believe in task forces, and we will take the best person from wherever he or she is in the world. In this headquarters, there are always people from all over the world working on key projects. We learn from each other. If you look at the backgrounds of our 22 corporate officers, 18 of them have served in one or two countries and some five or six. That sends a real signal about the importance of international experience to people who aspire to the most senior positions.

Donna McNamara's goal at Colgate is to look at the intensive development of those managers a couple of layers down from the top: "I want to look at their values, their perspectives, intelligence, commitment, track record, and experience. Then we can put together very serious development plans for them that also give them the opportunity to experience some of the very best of the world outside of Colgate. If they've developed through Colgate, then they know the things we do very well. It's also them knowing the things we don't do so well that will decide what the future is."

Career development initiatives must also feed into succession planning on a global basis. Candidates need to be identified and assessed against the key success factors of critical positions in the company. They should then be afforded developmental opportunities to acquire the competencies needed to implement the company's global business strategy.

An important approach to thinking about careers is in terms of building organizational capability. When developing people, it is important to think not only of the individual but of the consequences for the organization. Tuomo Peltonen has distinguished different types of career patterns in transnational corporations based on the knowledge base built over successive experiences.[17] Each assignment develops a different type of knowledge, external or internal. External knowledge refers to the environment: local markets, customers, suppliers, and competitors. Managers with external knowledge are called "interface" managers "because the knowledge accumulates through an interface assignment position of a manager between a multinational corporation local subunit and an important environment." Internal knowledge develops through experience in different organizational contexts; it means understanding HQ-subsidiary

---

[17]Tuomo Peltonen, "Managerial Career Patterns in Transnational Corporations," *European Management Journal*, June 1993.

relationships and points of view. A manager with an internal knowledge base is labeled a "corporate career" type. They understand "the mechanisms of strategic control" across the different subunits of the organization. Those managers with both an external and an internal knowledge base are labeled "transnational career" types.

From this categorization, Peltonen identifies six types of career pattern (my adaptations are included in the descriptions):

Interface generalist. Has a comprehensive knowledge base of the dynamics of different businesses and of markets, customers, suppliers, and competitors in different environments. This manager, however, has not developed internal knowledge relating to the inner workings of the company.

Interface specialist. Has a deep knowledge of a local environment. However, he or she has a weak understanding of the internal management of the total company. The external knowledge is also limited because of a narrow focus on one business.

Corporate generalist. Has varied experiences in different business subunits as well as at headquarters. His or her knowledge of corporate management is comprehensive. Such a career is lacking in experiences and knowledge of local environments.

Corporate specialist. Is the most narrow-minded career type. His or her knowledge is concentrated in one business and is focused mostly on the internal functioning of the corporation and its subunits.

Transnational specialist. Has built internal and external knowledge within different organizational contexts, but within one dominant business.

Transnational generalist. Has a very wide and rich external and internal knowledge base. This individual has a great deal of experience in multiple environments critical to the business. He or she has also managed the difficult relationships that can exist between headquarters and subsidiaries.

Peltonen's recommendation for strategic career path management to build organizational capability is to focus on developing high-potential individuals toward becoming transnational generalists.

These individuals will have the most comprehensive knowledge base of businesses, markets, and organizations. This implies frequent mobility, but this must be balanced with the need to maintain and sustain relationships in various parts of the world. It also assumes, of course, a deep commitment on the parts of organizations, individuals, and families to a transnational career.

STEPS TOWARD THE FUTURE

If your company is looking to build its global leadership bench strength and to develop a global leadership culture, it must take a number of major steps. For the sake of brevity, let's imagine the early steps are being taken at a global directions forum consisting of 100 of the top people in the company and conducted over the space of a few days. The advantage of a global forum is that it helps build a critical mass of commitment among senior people. A deeper culture change needs to be driven farther down the organization.

Step 1: Develop a Compelling Vision of the Global Future

What will the company look like when it is recognized as being the best in the world in its selected businesses?

Transformation usually occurs because of a deep crisis or a compelling vision.[18] It is better to work from a compelling vision. This vision may come from the top of the organization or be more broad based. Either way, it must generate and focus energy throughout the organization. The most senior leaders explain to the forum the global competitive challenges and the desire for the company to be the world's very best at what it does. Participants should work in small groups (with facilitators) and visualize the future. Before they go into their groups, they should be challenged to leap and dance outside of the current thinking box. Tracy Goss argues that when most people are asked to look into the future, what they really see is the past and present recycled.[19] Although it might limit radical future thinking, another strategy is to present the group with different sce-

---

[18]Tom Brown, "Re-Invent Yourself," *Industry Week*, November 21, 1994, p. 20.
[19]Ibid.

narios of possible futures and let them explore the probability and desirability of each one. Participants should then be brought back as a large group and given time to analyze the different visualizations. The facilitators should help the group reach consensus on what the future needs to be. While participants are taking a break, facilitators should put the vision into a brief statement that captures the essence of what has been said. This statement should be offered to the group for discussion and refinement until it says what it needs to say.

Step 2: Determine Global Leadership Needs in the Company

What are the core global competencies needed by the men and women who will lead the company into the future? What are the global leadership needs of the company at different levels in the organization?

The next step for the global forum group would be to create a profile of ideal global leaders to make the desired future happen. The Global Leadership Triad described in Chapter 2 could be used as a starting point for profile development. Participants could also be given the global leadership spectrum as a way into thinking about global leadership requirements throughout the organization. Participants should work in small groups to do their analysis. Each small group would then share its analysis with the large group. Facilitators would need to identify commonalties and differences and work with the group toward consensus. Again, while participants are taking a break, the facilitators should try to create a framework that captures the findings of the large group. This framework should be offered to the audience and refined as necessary.

Step 3: Identify Global Leadership Facilitators and Inhibitors in the Organization

What are the key components in our current organizational system, and how do they facilitate or inhibit the growth and development of global leaders?

In this chapter, I have presented a generic model of an organizational system and its key components. Every organization is different. Organizations are shaped over time and, like the rest of reality, can be somewhat messy. They contain a mix of policies, procedures, processes, subsystems, and structures that have evolved to meet the needs of the past. This mixture may be functional to a greater or lesser extent in the present but highly detrimental to the future health of the company.

The next task for the global forum would be to map the current system. They need to produce what Richard Pascale calls "a CAT scan on the organization; in effect they create a real-time case study of themselves."[20] This process helps to create the big picture. The key question for each small group is simply "What does our organizational system look like today?" Some model of the existing organization could be used as a starting point.

One side benefit of taking this step is that it often brings hidden issues to the surface and puts everyone on the same wavelength as far as talking about the whole organization.

The next step for the forum would be look at each piece of the system and determine the extent to which each is contributing to global leadership development in the company (given the profile created earlier). Do our strategies consciously express the need to identify and develop global leaders? Does our culture help break down barriers to mobility, innovation, and responsiveness? Does it also feed the aspirations of people in the organization and create a highly charged zone of possibility that encourages potential leaders to express and develop their talents? Do our performance systems convey the message that global leadership is highly valued in the organization and will be rewarded? Does the architecture of our company support the freedom and empowerment of individuals to develop their leadership potential, or are they overcontrolled and burdened by central mandates and bureaucratic procedures?

It is important to understand that building global leadership bench strength cannot be achieved overnight. While immediate steps can be taken and real results achieved, the most profound benefits may not be felt for 10 to 15 years or more. According to Alfred Zeien, Gillette's CEO, "it takes at least 25 years to build an international management corps that possesses the skills, experience and abilities to take a global organization from one level of success to the next."[21]

Is it time to get started?

---

[20]Ibid

[21]Jennifer J. Laabs, "How Gillette Grooms Global Talent," *Personnel Journal*, August 1993.

DIALOGUE BOX

1. From the interview segments in this chapter, what do you think are the key learning points for your organization? Why?

2. What should be the next steps for your organization in building a global leadership development system?

3. What is the single biggest impact you can make in moving this effort forward?

SUMMARY CHECKPOINT

While the research on developing global leaders is not very encouraging, a number of forward-thinking companies such as Avon, Bechtel, Colgate-Palmolive, Gillette, Hughes Electronics, International Flavors and Fragrances, Molex, and NYNEX are modeling the way for others.

There are two methods for building global leadership bench strength: recruiting from the outside, particularly from Europe, and "growing your own." The former may serve the short-term need, but the latter is of greater strategic value.

The best companies are taking a systematic approach to global leader development. They are paying attention to strategy, competency identification, the corporate culture, the organizational architecture, and performance systems (such as selection, education and training, compensation, and career development).

It is important for the company to be thinking in terms not only of the development of individuals but also of organizational capability. Global companies need to aim toward the development of transnational generalists who have a comprehensive knowledge base of multiple businesses and environments as well as the inner workings of the company.

In moving forward, companies need to work their way through several major steps:

Step 1: Develop a compelling vision of the global future (to create a platform for future developments);

Step 2: Determine global leadership needs in the company (at all levels and locations);

Step 3: Identify global leadership facilitators and inhibitors in the organization (to surface obstacles and put everyone on the same wavelength).

Developing global leaders does not happen overnight. The most significant benefits may not be realized for 10 to 25 years.

SOME ACTION IDEAS

Individual	Organization
◆ Identify those programs and/or systems you would like to see implemented in your company to meet your own and the company's global leadership development needs.	◆ Assess whether or not the organization recognizes the development of global leaders as a strategic asset. If not, who do you know is in the best position to raise the issue to a strategic level?
◆ Determine what impact you or others within your circle of influence can have on the development of such programs/systems. Can you present solutions as well as problems?	◆ Determine if there are international human resource practices that can be instituted immediately to get the organization on the path to building global leadership bench strength.
◆ Identify the best strategy for communicating your needs in the company. Locate the key decision makers and those who influence them.	◆ Analyze the current strategy for developing global leaders in your company. What are its strengths and weaknesses? Does it support the overall business strategy? Will this strategy meet the organization's needs in 5 to 10 years?

Individual	**Organization**
• Use the ideas presented in this chapter to generate debate among your colleagues, influencers, and decision makers. Start building a critical mass that will help generate and sustain change.	• Assess whether or not a piecemeal (rather than systematic) approach to change is more suitable to your organization. If so, what parts of the system should be targeted for near-, medium-, and long-term change?
• Expect resistance and plan to meet it assertively. Keep the global needs of the business rather than personal issues in the foreground.	• Identify the major challenges that can be expected to emerge in development and implementation. Where are the critical risk points?
• Seek opportunities to build energy around the issue by linking it to business plans, including those of competitors.	• Identify critical objectives and measurable results for each system change.
• Identify any inconsistencies between what the organization says it does to develop global leaders and what it actually practices. Challenge the inconsistencies (in a constructive way).	

CHAPTER **5**

Toward a Culture of Possibility

The future is not a gift; it is an achievement.
Gerald Baliles, former governor of Virginia

Preview

- If a global organization is to sustain world-class performance, it needs to be highly responsive to its environment (proactive, whenever possible). To do this, it needs to be capable of continuous transformation. Organizational transformation is dependent on people transformation.
- A leadership culture acts as an enabling force for both organizational and individual transformation.
- Culture consists of psychological and social boundaries we place on what is possible. Leadership cultures aim to redefine our boundaries of what is possible, both individually and collectively.
- As organizations strip down to their core capabilities, everyone is expected to think and act as a professional contributor to the organization. Professionals take actions that consistently add value through their knowledge / expertise, demonstrate high levels of individual responsibility, engage with and take ownership of problems, demonstrate high levels of autonomy and collaboration, engage in lifelong learning, and produce results to the highest worldwide standards.

♦ Personal mind management is the key to self-transformation and the release of leadership capabilities. This process
  attacks leadership inhibitors such as denial, homeostasis,
  and limiting beliefs.

♦ A game plan for self-transformation includes such objectives as: facing reality, committing to growth, adopting
  transformational beliefs, focusing energy, relating to others,
  and engaging with purpose.

♦ In developing a leadership culture, an organization needs
  to engage its people in an ongoing dialogue and change
  cycle. The key points in the cycle are disturbing the present,
  surfacing obstacles, challenging obstacles, constructing new
  expectations, and integrating new expectations.

♦ In maximizing their collective intelligence, organizations
  can not only change themselves but change the world.

THE TRANSFORMATIONAL CHALLENGE

Scores of men and women at the St. Louis World's Fair in 1904 are
said to have been physically overcome by the new technologies on
display.[1] They would drop to the ground in a dizzy faint. How would
those men and women respond to the changes that have taken place
between 1904 and 1996?

Global organizations must be in perpetual motion as they drive
for breakthroughs in speed, service, price, product development,
quality, customization, precision, and so on. In December 1995, *Personnel Journal* reported the results of a survey conducted among human resource professionals in the top 100 revenue-producing
companies in the United States. Each company was asked to identify its most challenging HR issue in 1995. Seventy-eight companies
responded to the question, and 56 (72 percent) identified "managing
change" as one of their major challenges.[2]

In planning a transformation strategy, we must first recognize
that change is both *inside-out* and *outside-in*. Most change experts focus on one or the other.

The inside-out approach puts the emphasis on personal charac-

---

[1]Gillian Flynn, "HR's Year in Review," *Personnel Journal*, December 1995, p. 64.
[2]Ibid., pp. 65–76.

ter and individual readiness for change, that is, self-transformation. There can be no sustainable organizational change without individual growth and development.

The second approach views change as being driven from the outside-in, and it stresses the influence of the organizational environment. It charges us all with creating the conditions for personal and organizational success. Such a view is captured by Robert L. Crandell, chairman and president of American Airlines: "I think the ideal leader for the 21st century will be one who creates an environment that encourages everyone in the organization to stretch their capabilities and achieve a shared vision, who gives people the confidence to run farther and faster than they ever have before, and who establishes the conditions for people to be more productive, more innovative, more creative and feel more in charge of their own lives than they ever dreamed possible."[3]

One of the characteristics we have associated with global leaders is an ability to enrich the pool of ideas by refusing to accept either/or dichotomies. In that spirit, we will not opt for one side of the debate or the other. Engaging in such a debate would be fruitless and time consuming.

In creating the changes needed to develop global leadership talents and skills, we must look to both sets of actors in the situation: individuals and the organization. Together they must determine what the expectations are, what accountabilities exist, what new behaviors are critical to the change, and what each can do to influence the outcomes. The process can be described as a dialogue loop (see Figure 5–1).

The accountability for setting world-class expectations and challenging people to succeed in this new environment lies with the organization, at least initially. The organization must also work with individuals and groups in the company to generate the tools and systems needed to facilitate the desired results.

The individual must recognize his or her responsibility for actual results and be responsible for the personal growth and development needed for success. The individual must also be willing and able to push back on the organization when the tools and systems

---

[3]Lynne Joy McFarland et al., *21st Century Leadership: Dialogues with 100 Top Leaders,* New York: The Leadership Press, 1994, p. 195.

FIGURE 5–1

The Transformational Dialogue Loop

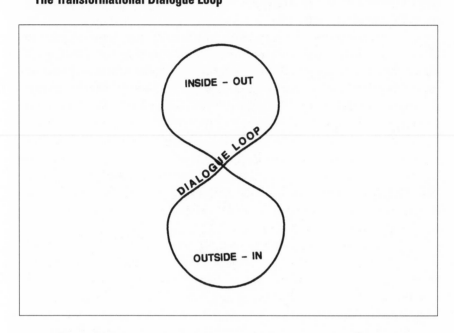

are not what is needed. The relationship between the individual and the organization must be one of continuous dialogue and mutual investment.

A leadership culture is the enabling force for both individual and organizational transformation. It is the psychological and social space we create for exploring possibility.

LEADERSHIP CULTURES

A culture is the learned way of life of a group. It is the pattern of typical assumptions, values, and behaviors that distinguish one set of people from another. An organizational culture defines the characteristic way of *being* and *doing* in a company.

That is one way to look at organizational culture. It stresses the familiar, the habitual, the "way things are." In this view, culture is what we can call a *zone of familiarity*. Within this frame of reference, we also refer to culture as the "glue" that holds our organizations together. As an integrative force, culture offers us needed stability, a sense of safety. With culture, we know what to expect—*expect* being the key word.

But we are not prisoners of our cultures; culture is not destiny. By adopting another frame of reference, we can think of culture as a *zone of possibility* rather than the familiar. Culture is a psychological and social boundary we place on what is possible. Along with others in our group, we reconstruct (and sometimes disturb) this boundary every day in our thoughts, feelings, and behaviors. As soon as we recognize our personal involvement in creating culture, we can take responsibility for its ongoing construction and / or change. As a group we should be asking, "Does the zone of possibility we have created for ourselves fit with our needs? If we are to lead enriched and fulfilling lives in today's world, do we need to redefine our boundaries of what is possible?" Leadership cultures aim to set new boundaries for the possible.

A global leadership culture is an organizational culture in which everyone is expected to (1) take personal ownership of the challenges posed by global competition, (2) develop and expand his or her circles of influence to generate the organizational energy needed to beat those challenges, and (3) collaborate with others to drive the transformation of those energies into world-class performance. In other words, a leadership culture expects everyone to think and act as a professional contributor to the organization.

Early industrial organizations tended to rely on punishment cultures. The emphasis was on coercive control, and the typical worker response was one of alienation and hostility. (See Figure 5–2, "Organizational Power Shifting".) Middle and late industrial organizations shifted toward remunerative cultures. The worker's involvement with the organization was based on a transactional, cost / benefit calculation. Personal engagement with the organization was and is fairly minimal. Today organizations are shifting to the power of normative culture, that is, the power of symbols, values, and beliefs. The aim is to personally engage the associate and generate active commitment and engagement. Rather than simply being the site in which individuals produce work for the achievement of economic ends, the organization also becomes the vehicle for personal and professional growth, the source of meaning and purpose. The key shifts to remember are

FIGURE 5–2

Organizational Power Shifting

	Power	Associate Orientation	
High Control ↓	Coercive (punishment)	Alienation Intense negative involvement	**Industrial**
	Remunerative (reward)	Calculative involvement Low positive/negative involvement	
↓ **High Commitment**	Normative (symbolic rewards, meaning)	Moral involvement Personal engagement Intense positive involvement	↓ **Professional**

Source: Inspired by discussion of the work of A. Etzioni in Peter Anthony, *Managing Culture*, Buckingham, U.K.: Open University Press, 1994, pp. 22–23.

- ◆ *High control* to *high commitment*.
- ◆ *Industrial mindset* to *professional mindset*.

Under pressure to generate higher levels of competitiveness in a global economy, many companies have been reengineering, restructuring, and the like. A large number of observers are saying that the corporate world will never be the same again. The loyalty-security paradigm has been shattered. The old paternalistic model of "I do what you tell me in exchange for a relatively safe guarantee of employment" is a thing of the past. Charles Heckscher, a Rutgers University sociologist and author of *White-Collar Blues: Management Loyalties in an Age of Corporate Restructuring*, argues that a shift is needed in our understanding of employment contracts. The shift is one from a loyalty to a professional paradigm. In the latter, managers need to model their careers on professionals such as doctors and lawyers. These professionals understand the need for continuous learning to maintain and build knowledge and skills, and they establish wide networks outside of a particular company or institution. The new employment contract would be framed around "coming together for a common purpose, say, developing a new technology, rather than a life long expectation of loyalty and security."[4] Other writers echo similar sentiments. Sumantra Ghoshal and Christopher Bartlett call for a new "moral contract." The essence of this new contract would be that "each employee takes responsibility for putting in a best-in-class performance. In exchange, top management undertakes to ensure not the dependence of employment security but the freedom of the individual's employability."[5] The employer would do this by presenting opportunities for continuous learning and enhancing skills. In this scenario, security comes from performance in the marketplace rather than paternalistic management.

Whether or not we see a new "moral contract," we can be assured that organizational cultures in the global economy will stress professionalism at all levels. With organizations stripping themselves down to their core capabilities, there is little room for people who don't contribute value to those capabilities. It sounds harsh, but it's reality. Demonstrating leadership will soon no longer be a choice but a necessity for employability.

What do I mean by *professionalism?* First, I don't mean that everyone should rush off to become a doctor or a lawyer. A professional associate in a company is one who *takes actions* that consistently *add value* to the outputs of the business through *knowledge* or some other kind of *expertise;* he or she demonstrates a high level of *individual responsibility* and engages with and takes *ownership of problems.* The professional has a high level of *autonomy* but can also *collaborate* with other professionals to tackle problems that require a broad range of expertise. The professional seeks to develop contributory value through *lifelong learning* and by increasing his or her personal capacity to produce results that are consistently recognized as being of the *highest standards* in the world.

Do most of our organizations expect and support these kinds of attitudes and behaviors? In my experience, no.

A leadership culture expects everyone to demonstrate the professional characteristics mentioned above. For many, this will require

---

[4]Barbara Presky Noble, "If Loyalty Is Out, Then What's In," *The New York Times,* January 29, 1995, p. F21.

[5]Sumantra Ghoshal and Christopher A. Bartlett, "A New Moral Contract," *The World in 1996,* London: The Economist Publications, 1995, p. 115.

- Heightened levels of self-awareness.
- A radically new readiness to explore and adapt to change.
- A more intense engagement with work and the world.
- Ongoing investments in personal and professional learning.

As global organizations reduce their reliance on command and control structures, individuals will be forced to take on greater command and control of their own lives and careers. In short, it will take a great deal more personal mind management than we are used to or, even more broadly, a commitment to developing a Transformational Self.

DIALOGUE BOX

1. How would you describe the *dominant* culture of your organization?

   Coercive (punishment based)
   Remunerative (monetary reward based)
   Normative (symbolic reward based)

   Is any kind of shift taking place in the organization's culture? If so what kind? Why?

2. How would you categorize your own professional assets and liabilities?

	Asset	Liability
Takes actions that consistently add value to core capabilities		
Demonstrates knowledge/expertise		
Demonstrates high level of individual responsibility		
Engages with and takes ownership of problems		
Demonstrates high levels of autonomy and collaboration		
Engages in lifelong learning		
Produces results to the highest worldwide standards		

THE TRANSFORMATIONAL SELF

We would rather be ruined than change.

W. H. Auden[6]

In Chapter 2, the idea of the Transformational Self was placed at the center of the Global Leadership Triad. It was described as a philosophy of possibility and personal engagement with the world, that is, a drive toward meaning and purpose through activity strengthened by reflection, personal mind management, and openness to change.

Human beings are creatures of the familiar. Tom Rusk, MD, a noted professor of clinical psychology at the University of California, notes that "Resistance to change is the most powerful force in human psychology."[7] But we are not prisoners of our past selves, unless we choose to be.

Viktor Frankl, one of the most important contributors to 20th-century psychiatry, describes human beings as having a "will-to-meaning."[8] His experiences in Nazi concentration camps brought home to him the importance of a person's ability to choose his or her response under a given set of circumstances. He was very fond of quoting Nietzsche, who said, "He who has a *why* to live can bear with almost any *how*."

Thankfully, this viewpoint is gaining more of a foothold in the social sciences. For too many years, we have been brainwashed into thinking of ourselves as having little control over our lives. I call this the "human puppet syndrome." Psychology in particular has tended to promote a view of human beings determined by unconscious forces shaped by early childhood experiences or by learned patterns of stimulus-response. Behaviorism, with its simplistic portrayal of human beings shaped by rewards and punishments, has done untold damage to our collective psyche.

According to Ernest Becker, author of *The Birth and Death of Meaning,* "The development of mind . . . is a progressive freedom of reactivity. The reactive process which is inherent in the organism not

---

[6]Richard Gillet, *Change Your Mind, Change Your World,* New York: Simon & Schuster, 1992.

[7]Tom Rusk, *Instead of Therapy,* Carson, CA: Hay House, 1991, p. 61.

[8]Viktor E. Frankl, *Man's Search for Meaning: An Introduction to Logotherapy,* New York: Simon & Schuster, 1959, p. x.

only gradually arrives at freedom from the intrinsic properties of things but also proceeds from there to assign *its own stimulus meanings*. Mind culminates in the organism's ability to *choose* what it will react to."[9] In the same vein, William Glasser, MD, urges us to substitute the word *information* for stimulus and *choice* for response. This helps us to take accountability for our behaviors. It also helps us focus on how we interpret the world, for it is our interpretations (mental models) that drive our behaviors.

To develop a transformational self that will increase our own personal leadership capabilities in the global economy, we need to increase our powers of personal mind management and reflection. This can be difficult, but it is critical to success. Remember, the objective here is not to psychoanalyze yourself or reach a higher spiritual plane but to release your leadership capabilities. We all have these capabilities, but we do need to make investments in them. The mind management process is as follows:

Step 1: Commit to personal exploration.

Step 2: Detach from who you think you are.

Step 3: Observe yourself in action.

Step 4: Keep a trash can in your head.

Step 5: Play with possibilities.

Step 6: Act by design.

Step 1: Commit to Personal Exploration

Unfortunately, the process of personal exploration usually begins with a crisis, such as loss of a job or a death in the family. Through crisis, we often discover resources and potential we never knew we had. Although it is difficult for our minds to wrap around the issue, we do have a competitive crisis on our hands. It is not only our organizations that are competing with the best in the world; we are also competing for our jobs with the best in the world. Talent is no longer constrained by borders. To succeed, we must continually expand the envelope of our own performance.

---

[9] Ernest Becker, *The Birth and Death of Meaning: An Interdisciplinary Perspective on the Problem of Man*, 2d ed., Harmondsworth, Middlesex: Penguin Education, 1972, p. 19.

Step 2: Detach from Who You Think You Are

Who you think you are is one possibility in a world of possibilities. Just think if you had been born and raised several thousand miles from where you were. You would now very likely be speaking a different language, observing different customs, perhaps worshipping a different god, be eating different foods, thinking different thoughts, and experiencing different feelings. You are nothing but possibility. We inherit a genetic foundation from our parents, but the house built on that foundation is largely a product of chance and choice.

Unfortunately, most of us spend our lives thinking we are who we are, and that's that! We become frozen into a "thing" rather than an ongoing "possibility." Once we detach from any fixed notions about who we are, we can open up to new possibilities that can be more fulfilling and rewarding and that better equip us for succeeding in our new world.

Step 3: Observe Yourself in Action

Many years ago, I was a songwriter (it was the late 1960s, and perhaps everyone was a songwriter). I have never been so alive as I was at that time. I carried a small notebook with me, and I would take notes as I observed myself and others. The world was always puzzling and engaging.

Observe yourself in different environments—at work, home, play—and see what thoughts, feelings, and behaviors are typical of each environment, what events trigger which thoughts, and so on. At home or on the tennis court, you might be energized, sociable, passionate, full of ideas about the future, a leader. At work, you may be resentful, alienated, bitter, withdrawn, passive. Why? What factors are at work? Have you always related to work this way, or just at this job? Does your boss trigger something in you that needs to be dealt with? Did your parents have resentful attitudes toward work? Did you have a bad experience in a previous job that now colors your attitude toward all work?

As you observe yourself, you will begin to recognize patterns emerging. Patterns indicate frozen bits of yourself; they need to be put under the warm light of examination and thawed until they lose their inhibiting power.

Start by observing yourself for a day and then for a week. You might want to think of yourself in the third person; it helps the process of detachment. Soon will you get into the habit of saying, "Why is this person behaving this way in this place at this time? Is this behavior working for or against him or her?" You might want to do this by keeping a log. Imagine this was your log for a week:

	Thoughts	Feelings	Behaviors
Work	"Somebody else can do this."	Angry	Avoid making decisions
	"If I keep quiet, I'll be OK."	Bored	Don't share ideas in meetings
	"Whatever I do doesn't make	Exploited	Avoid more challenging
	a difference."	Vulnerable	assignments
		Helpless	Keep to myself
			Avoid conflict
Home	"I'll take care of things."	Worthwhile	Fix things around the house
	"My family means the	Supportive	Pay bills, balance the checkbook
	world to me."	Secure	Take kids to the game
		Happy	
Play	"I play to win."	Confident	Arrange games for the league
	"Work and play don't mix."	Excited	Organize the club's annual dinner

It's quite obvious that this person (you) is leading a double life. A great deal of positive energy is directed toward home and play and a lot of negative energy toward work. At home and play, this person characterizes himself as being active, while at work he is basically passive and looking to avoid. Why? "Work and play don't mix"—where did he learn that thought? Doesn't he realize that his behaviors at work are increasing his feelings of vulnerability? Doesn't he also realize that he may damage his life at home and play if he doesn't pay attention to his life at work? You get the idea.

The philosopher Friedrich Nietzsche developed the idea of Eternal Recurrence. What has this got to do with observing yourself? As you look at your log, ask yourself, "If I had to live my life over and over again for all eternity, is this the life I would choose to live?" A deep and disturbing question. What would you change, and why? What can you do *now* to make those changes?

Step 4: Keep a Trash Can in Your Head

Some cultures refer to the mind as the "mad monkey." One thing it does is try to freeze who we are. The mind is always seeking to impose limitations: "You've never done that before." "What if something goes wrong? "That's going to make you feel terrible." "Who are you to be doing that?" If you've ever used a Macintosh computer, you know they have a small trash can icon on the screen where you can get rid of files you don't want. Imagine you have a Trash Can in your head. Don't hesitate to dump limiting thoughts and beliefs into your mental Trash Can. Put them out of harm's way. By doing this, you refuse to let your self-imposed and habitual fears define you. Under times of stress, these dysfunctional thoughts may come back with a vengeance. Just keep returning them to the Trash Can. Don't let them settle. Remember, you are a possibility, not a thing.

Step 5: Play with Possibilities

In writing this book, I created a file I called "Holding Tank." It was for those passages I had written that were promising but didn't yet have a place in the book. The "Tank," as I came to refer to it, was a place where I could play with ideas and test them out before they became either an integral part of the evolving book design or history (perhaps to be used in a later book).

Just as we all need a Trash Can in our heads, we also need a Tank. The Tank is a place for mental experimentation and rehearsal. Here we can visualize those thoughts, feelings, and behaviors that we feel will serve us better. We can place ourselves in work, home, and play situations and imagine experiencing different outcomes.

Step 6: Act by Design

Most of the time we don't think about the way we act. We just act. We're often afraid that if we choose to act in a certain way, we'll lose our spontaneity. Unfortunately, what we think of as spontaneity is usually a rehash of old patterns made to look like new.

When you act by design, you are stepping into your chosen future. It may feel uncomfortable at first. The thoughts, feelings, and behaviors may not sit easily with one another. You may begin asserting yourself as an influence leader in a situation where you have always taken a passive role. Your confident exterior and your self-doubting interior may be at odds with each other. Your self-doubt may be increased by the discomfort of your colleagues who are not quite sure how to respond. In time, the confident feeling will follow the confident behavior. You will be perceived differently by others, and you will perceive yourself differently.

DIALOGUE BOX

1. Record your major thoughts, feelings, and behaviors for a week (at work, home, and play).
2. What patterns emerge?
3. Which patterns inhibit your growth as a leader in your organization?
4. What new behaviors do you need to adopt to resist the force of the old patterns?

Is this process easy? No. It takes time, persistence, courage, endurance, and most of all patience. Patience with ourselves.

In creating our Transformational Self, it is best to have a game plan. Fundamentally, we want to attack those forces within ourselves—and our cultures—that inhibit professional engagement and global leadership. We also need to set new objectives for ourselves, objectives that energize us and open up new leadership possibilities (see Figure 5–3).

Face Reality

Denial is the defense mechanism we all share, to a greater or lesser degree, that causes us to avoid anxiety-causing information. We might say to ourselves, "This globalization fad will soon be over," or we might just withdraw from thinking about its consequences, that is, assume it's business as usual. After all, "I've been pretty successful so far."

Recognize the Impact of Global Competition on You and the Organization

◆ Don't take for granted the old assumption that loyalty equals security. Restructuring, outsourcing, joint ventures, and alliances will continue to reshape our corporations as the reality of global competition hits home.

◆ Take control of your destiny. Paternalism is dying, and the entitlement culture is under attack. You can fight back, but that's a lost cause. You can mentally withdraw, but that is a sure-fire way to find yourself without a place at the global table.

◆ Recognize that jobs are changing. There is a push for higher skill levels as technology drives deeper into our corporations.

◆ Recognize the reality of multiple realities. Skills related to working with people from other cultures will be at a premium as our global organizations seek to utilize talent from anywhere in the world.

◆ Don't just occupy space, add value. As companies strip down to their core capabilities, they look to everyone to contribute increased professionalism and leadership. There is no room for passivity or professional stagnation.

Honestly Assess Your Capabilities

◆ Build on strengths and target weaknesses. One way to do this is to rate yourself, and have others rate you, on the competencies listed in the Global Leadership Triad (see Chapter 2). What are your primary assets and liabilities? If you're having problems with communication in particular, get some help. You won't go anywhere in a global environment without an ability to get your point across— sometimes under very difficult circumstances.

◆ Seek out cross-cultural training, and go not to just one session but to as many as you can attend. You can't develop cross-cultural competence overnight or simply check it off a to-do list. It's a lifelong process and requires constant attention.

◆ Continually look to identify and create opportunities to demonstrate leadership and add tangible value. This means taking risks. Failure, like success, is often soon forgotten. No one has the monopoly

---

FIGURE 5–3

Targets and Objectives

Targets (Leadership Inhibitors)	Objectives (Leadership Facilitators)
Denial	Face Reality
Homeostasis	Commit to Growth
Limiting Beliefs	Adopt Transformational Beliefs
Scattered Energy	Focus Energy
Manipulation	Relate to Others
Alienation	Engage with Purpose

on global expertise; we're all feeling our way forward. What counts is how you handle failure, not the failure itself.

◆ Don't stand still. The knowledge base is changing continually, and you need to stay in touch with the changes. Practice personal *kaizen*, that is, continuous improvement.

◆ Also, look to your bosses and your organization. What are their capabilities? Are your bosses globally oriented? What can you learn from them? To what extent are they willing and able to develop your skills, open doors, nominate you for global assignments? If they aren't, you should be looking elsewhere. And what about your organization? Is it aggressively pursuing global leadership in its industries and creating opportunities for long-term development on the global stage? If not, this may not be the right organization for your future.

Commit to Growth

Homeostasis is our tendency to settle into an equilibrium position. Some might call it a "comfort zone"—a place of habit and familiarity. This tendency can inhibit our growth and sabotage our success.

Take Charge of Your Career

◆ Get used to a higher degree of self-directed career management. Peter Drucker was once asked what questions he would ask if he were just starting out on his career, and his response was: "First question, where can I get a job that is willing to pay for whatever skills I have? Second, am I learning something? Third, and a question—that to be frank—I didn't ask until I was in my forties, what are my strengths, where do I belong? The one difference, and the one thing I hope young people will learn, is that they have to take responsibility for placing themselves."[10]

◆ Think to yourself, "I'm only as good as my last performance." One writer compares this new working environment to Hollywood. Making a film involves numerous players: actors, agents, producers, directors, stunt people, extras, and technicians of all kinds. Each

---

[10]Mike Johnson, *Managing in the Next Millennium*, Oxford: Butterworth-Heinemann, 1995, p. 144.

player adds value to the team, and each is rewarded according to his or her abilities. When the project is finished, the team is wound up, "And if we are part of a team that produces a product the customer likes, we might be asked back to try and do it again."[11]

+ Think of your knowledge and skills as an investment portfolio. You cannot rest on expertise that will be obsolete in 3 to 5 years. Our focus must not simply be on knowing but on learning. While knowing can add value at a certain point in time, it is a static concept. When we *know*, we also tend to leap to the obvious, the tried and true, the quick fix regardless of context and change. Learning is active, open, generative, and transformational. Learning sparks a creative tension between what we think we know and the actual conditions we face. Staying sharp and valuable may mean investing in ourselves, our ongoing education, training, and personal development. We want to make sure we are employable outside of our existing organizations as well as inside. In taking charge of our careers, we need to communicate to others —particularly supervisors—who we are, where our interests lie, and the direction we want to take. Organizational needs do not always fit with individual needs, but the chance for a win/win is greater when there is dialogue. As the old saying goes, "Luck is when preparation meets opportunity."

+ Demonstrate commitment at all times. Taking ownership of our careers does not mean that we psychologically disconnect from our organization(s). While there may be no guarantees of lifelong employment, we need to commit to delivering peak performance for the duration of our stay. With fewer levels of management, decentralized decision making that is close to the customer, and an emphasis on entrepreneurial activity at all levels, companies look for an engagement with the business, a sense of being in business for oneself.

Adopt Transformational Beliefs

One of the most critical but underemployed insights of psychology is that we are what we believe; our outer lives are reflections of our inner lives. Much of our inner life is governed by limiting beliefs that we have learned from numerous sources: culture, country, parents,

---

[11]Ibid., p. 136.

friends, race, class, media, schools, and so on. From these limiting beliefs, we determine what probabilities are likely in our lives. But *we can just as easily relate to possibilities as to probabilities.*

Put the Past in Its Place

♦ Start to recognize the limiting beliefs that influence your everyday actions. Pay attention to those times when you say, "I can't . . . " or some variation ("I can't speak my mind here": "I have no influence over these people"; "I can't take that assignment in Eastern Europe. I've never been out of the country"; "I'm not qualified to negotiate with the Japanese delegation"; "I don't think it's possible for me to learn a foreign language"). Unfortunately, such beliefs become self-fulfilling prophecies.

♦ Don't struggle too hard trying to find the source of your limiting beliefs. It may take years or even be a fruitless search. Remember, you always have your internal Trash Can. Use it. Limiting beliefs are just a drain on power and energy, and in today's economy you can't afford to lose either one.

Put the Future in Its Place

♦ It's what you want in the future that should define how you act now. Continually ask yourself, "Am I acting in my future or my past?" The present is simply a reflection of the past or the future. You choose.

♦ Don't delude yourself into thinking that by playing it safe and not taking risks you'll be more secure. All you are doing is rationalizing your inaction. The world is changing around you whether you want it to or not. As Helen Keller said, "Security is mostly a superstition. It does not exist in nature . . . Life is either a daring adventure or nothing."

Focus Energy

When energy is scattered, it loses its ability to drive momentum and change. Stay on target and be purposeful. (See "Engage with Purpose," p. 185.) If succeeding in the global economy is your focus, design your life toward that end. Consciously develop the skills, behaviors, and lifestyle that will promote that success.

Create a Plan

◆ Think ahead. Career planning is useful not because it presents a blueprint for the future but because it pulls, pushes, and twists the imagination. A plan helps to release and channel power and energy. Your plan needs to address the gaps in your global capabilities as well as determine a possible career path. Study your current organization. What global career paths are visible at the present time? What are the company's global plans for the future? What kind of people will the company need to fulfill those plans? Although it is important to plan, it is also important to be flexible. Opportunities arise that can never be foreseen.

◆ Ask yourself how you can get the broadest possible experience. Chapter 4 outlined six global career patterns. Those with primarily external knowledge were called "interface managers"; those with internal knowledge were described as "corporate managers"; and those with both internal and external knowledge were labeled "transnational managers." Transnational generalists have comprehensive knowledge of a number of businesses in the organization and many local environments and markets, as well as a deep understanding of how the organization works at global and local levels. Transnational generalists are going to be the leaders in greatest demand.

◆ In your plan, take into consideration your family, education, health and fitness, and social/cultural activities. How supportive will your family be if you need to switch continents, cultures, climates, schools, houses, and neighborhoods? Do they share your sense of adventure and curiosity about the world?

◆ Examine the deficits in your education. To what extent do you need to overcome parochial schooling by learning foreign languages, world geography and history, or international economics and politics? Do you need to go back to school? If you do, you might want to check out Insead in Fontainebleau, France; IMD in Lausanne, Switzerland; or the American Graduate School of International Management (Thunderbird) in Glendale, Arizona. The ad pages in *The Economist* are increasingly advertising schools offering courses in international business.

◆ What new social and cultural horizons can you explore in your home country before you ever leave its shores (e.g., making friends from different cultures, watching foreign films, eating a variety of foreign foods, listening to music from different regions of the world, going to foreign art exhibitions, reading world literature)? Are there people from foreign cultures at your workplace? If so, talk with them about their cultures and the differences they are having to cope with in your country. Most people love to talk about where they came from and the challenges they are facing in making adjustments.

Seek Global Experiences

◆ All the training, education, and book learning in the world are no substitute for real-life work experience in other countries. If you can, get international experience early and often. Tourism doesn't count. A tourist confronts only the surface aspects of culture: food, dress, gestures, language, and the like. Only in lengthy working encounters do cultural issues begin to break down habitual frames of reference and cause the discomfort necessary for learning and enrichment.

◆ Learn from the people who have reached the tops of their organizations. Their backgrounds speak volumes. (See Figure 5–4.)

◆ Expect change to be uncomfortable. Typically, an individual will go through several stages of adaptation. The *Honeymoon* phase occurs at the beginning of the encounter. There can be a feeling of euphoria and excitement about entering the new culture. This tends to be followed by the *Creeping Shock* phase. Here the individual confronts differences as annoyances. The *Full-Blown Shock* may occur later when the individual feels he or she can't cope with the differences. There is usually a tremendous feeling of loss (the comfort zone of the home culture). The *This Might Not Be So Bad* phase evolves as the person confronts and deals with situations on a daily basis. A feeling of being somewhat in control develops out of small successes. During this phase, the individual is adapting and finding new functional attitudes and behaviors. Gradually, progress is made toward the *I Feel At Home Here* phase. The same cycle is likely to recur on returning to the original culture. The return may be even more difficult because where the individual believed she or he belonged and was really understood has changed. Try to find a mentor who has experienced the reentry process and can offer guidance to you and your family on what to expect.

FIGURE 5–4

Taking on the World

Individual	Latest Post	International Experience
Samir F. Gibara	President and CEO, Goodyear Tire and Rubber	Worked abroad (France, Belgium, Morocco, Canada) for 27 of his 30 years there
Raymond G. Viault	Vice chairman, General Mills	Previously was president and CEO of Kraft Jacobs Suchard in Switzerland
Michael Hawley	President and COO, Gillette	Spent 20 of his 35 years there outside the U.S. (U.K., Hong Kong, Canada, Colombia, Australia)
Harry Bowman	Chairman, president, and CEO, Outboard Marine	Ran Whirlpool's European business for 2 years as part of his 24-year career there
Lucio A. Noto	Chairman and CEO, Mobil	Worked abroad (Italy, Japan, Saudi Arabia) for 17 of his 34 years there

Source: Joann S. Lublin, "An Overseas Stint Can Be A Ticket to the Top," *The Wall Street Journal*, January 29, 1996.

◆ If mobility is a necessary evil for you and your family, you may want to rethink your vision and your career. There are at least two reasons for this. First, the traditional reasons companies send people overseas—to transfer skills and technology, set up businesses, work on global teams, and so on—will not disappear in the foreseeable future. Second, technology will eliminate some travel, but mostly at the operational level. Collaboration requires commitment; commitment is founded on relationships; and relationships need to be formed and nurtured with some level of face-to-face interaction.

Relate to Others

As discussed in Chapter 1, one of the core capabilities needed by global organizations is relationships. Relationships facilitate the flow of resources, ideas, and so on among the scattered locations of the enterprise. Your ability to build relationships quickly will be a definite advantage.

Build Strong, Authentic Networks

♦ Build global networks so that you can see and be seen. But relate honestly and directly. Too many relationships in the workplace can be described as *manipulationships* rather than relationships. We have all come across would-be leaders who use insidious means to serve their own purposes. Manipulative people change in an instant to promote their advantage. The price of manipulation is build-up of resentment and a lack of trust. If global networks are to be successful, they need to be fueled by trust and integrity. You can use your influence to its greatest effect only when you have formed solid relationships based on interconnected needs and interests; clean, undistorted communication with no hidden agendas; honesty; respect; and understanding, caring, and fairness. Without those ingredients, your influence will self-destruct.

Find Multiple Mentors

♦ Look inside and outside your company for people who can give you direction. Having one mentor is good; having several is better. Dale Winston of Battalia Winston International told *Fortune*, "Old-style mentoring is being replaced by the need to build constituencies. Just as you have to manage your own career and be your own CEO, so you have to create your own board of advisers."[12] Outsiders—from noncompeting companies and/or professional associations—can provide a wide-angle portrait of your company and industry and challenge your habitual frame of reference. Many companies (or parts of companies) are driven by internal agendas, such as the smooth functioning of existing systems and procedures. They can lose sight of the external realities of customers and markets. An outside mentor can often put you back in touch with these realities.

♦ Learn the basics of getting ahead in your company. Mentors inside the company from different levels, functions, and cultural groups can offer a variety of perspectives on the organization, its politics, and it's culture. Explorations into the organization culture, especially for non-home-country managers, offer insights into the "game rules" for getting ahead in the dominant culture. Mentors

---

[12]Marshall Loeb, "The New Mentoring," *Fortune*, November 27, 1995, p. 213.

can feed back information on how you are perceived elsewhere in the organization and make suggestions on priority development areas. These mentors might include

1. Someone of higher rank (although not your immediate manager or your manager's manager). This person should have his or her finger on the pulse of the organization, understand its global strategies in depth, and be aware of what opportunities might be opening up for someone with global ambitions. The person may also be able to clue you in on global versus local issues in the company and other challenges.
2. Local academics who specialize in global business and specific countries.
3. Colleagues who have more experience working on the global playing field and know the inner workings of the total organization.

Engage with Purpose

Purpose, which is connected to our deeply held values, is the core energizing force of life. Purpose drives out the alienation that is so pervasive in our places of work. There are many talented people in the world, but far fewer who enrich their lives with that talent. Without purpose and persistence, talent is often—to paraphrase Shakespeare—full of sound and fury, but signifying nothing. Together vision and values activate, guide, and sustain the leadership process.

Create a Vision

♦ Create a personal global vision that provides the energy for your career development. It is the source from which you can refresh yourself when the going gets tough. A personal vision provides meaning and purpose in conditions of great uncertainty and ambiguity. It is our proactive gesture toward the world. It is the essence of personal leadership.

♦ Create your vision out of your most deeply held values. My own personal global vision (which is part of a broader vision for my life) is: *Work through the medium of business to promote cross-cultural understanding and facilitate the creation of shared wealth.* Nothing is more fulfilling to me than helping people become more culturally aware of themselves and others and supporting the process of building common working ground. This personal vision feeds into the vision for my business: *Provide business professionals with the capabilities needed to lead and support competitive organizations in the global business environment.* To a large degree, my personal global vision is aligned with the global vision of my business. There is no disconnect here that could cause emotional havoc in my life and negatively affect my performance. This can be somewhat more difficult when working in a global corporation, but is by no means impossible. Avon's corporate vision is one with which many of its associates can engage at a personal level: "To be the company that best understands and satisfies the product, service, and self-fulfillment needs of women—globally." When personal and business needs are aligned, huge productive sources of energy are released. If your company doesn't have a globally inspiring vision, write one. Make yourself heard. Send out signals that you are committed to thinking and acting on the global stage.

Clarify Your Values

◆ Communicate respect, fairness, and all the other collaborative values we identified in Chapter 3. Succeeding in global leadership will take a commitment to fundamental human values that promote the building of common ground. Technique will not cover a black hole where values should be.

◆ Identify your nonnegotiables, that is, lines you won't cross. Global leaders need to have confidence in who they are and the integrity to stay their course. Global leadership is as much about character as competence.

◆ Pay attention to the heroic in yourself. When I talk about "heroes" with people (using the term in a gender-neutral way), the reactions vary. "That's a guy thing" is a common one. "Aren't we past all that?" is another. We talk more of dysfunction and victimization than we do of accomplishment and character. No sooner do we elevate someone than we want to tear the person down, to show his or her feet of clay. Some may consider this to be the democratic thing to do. I say that when carried too far, it becomes a perversion of the democratic ideal. In a democracy, we need to be aware of human imperfection and constraints while encouraging ourselves and others to reach beyond what appear to be the limits of the possible. Global leaders at all levels need to recognize and nurture the heroic in themselves and others.

THE TRANSFORMATIONAL ORGANIZATION

We have considered the inside-out part of the change equation. Now we must look at the outside-in component.

Before going on to discuss a culture transformation process in organizations, let's consider some of the things we know about change.

+ Change is an experience of difference to varying degrees. It may be a radical difference or relatively inconsequential, a positive experience or a negative one. All change involves gain and loss and can trigger intense emotions such as anger, confusion, fear, discomfort, helplessness, isolation, or betrayal. Resistance is a given.

+ The change process is iterative, and messy. It doesn't flow in an unwavering straight line from beginning to end.

+ A managed change process requires agreement on the purpose of the change, clear goals and objectives, credible leadership, clarity of roles and responsibilities, a well-understood methodology, excellent communication, wide involvement in the process, education and training, suitable performance systems, an organizational architecture

DIALOGUE BOX

1. Review the targets (leadership inhibitors) mentioned earlier: denial, homeostasis, and so on. Which ones do you think cause you the most personal and professional damage?

2. Consider each of the objectives (leadership facilitators): face reality, commit to growth, etc. Starting today, what investments can you start making in each one of them (an investment could include a new attitude, a training program, or anything that you do consciously to move toward an objective).

that works with the change and not against it, and follow-through.

♦ Managing change is not a one-time event but a continuous process. It needs to be a core competency in our organizations. Change and learning are two sides of the same coin.

♦ Change happens when the emotions are engaged. Rational arguments and power may help persuade, but they don't work on their own.

♦ Change is helped along by seeking the help of objective outsiders.

How do we make a transition toward a leadership culture that will maximize the collective intelligence of the organization and drive us toward higher levels of global performance? There are at least five generic steps in the process (see Figure 5–5).

It is a process in which new expectations are identified, clarified, and brought alive. From our previous discussions, some of those expectations might be the following:

You will be treated as a global professional in what you do.

You will be expected to make timely actions that consistently add value to the business through your knowledge and expertise.

FIGURE 5–5
A Culture Change Cycle

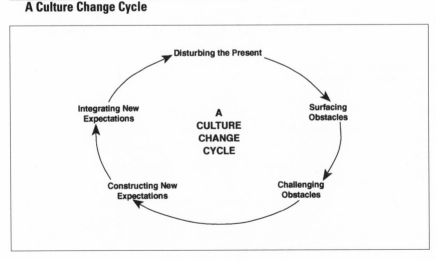

You will be expected to demonstrate a high level of individual responsibility for the success of the business and to treat its challenges and opportunities as your own.

You will be expected to work autonomously to get things done within agreed-upon time frames and other constraints.

You will be expected to work collaboratively with others to maximize the collective intelligence of the group.

You will be expected to use and expand your circles of influence to initiate actions that enhance the competitive advantage of the company; that is, you will be expected to actively create rather than passively wait.

You will be expected to increase your value to the organization through lifelong learning and competency development.

You will be expected to produce results that are not only good but consistently recognized as being of the highest standards in the world.

Disturbing the Present

Guiding Principle: Energize Hearts, Minds, and Spirits

Primary Objectives:

- ◆ Articulating the company's (business unit's) global challenges and opportunities.
- ◆ Providing an energizing vision of how to reach new levels of competitiveness through cultural transformation.
- ◆ Communicating a participatory methodology for accomplishing the cultural change.

The competitive environment in which a business operates undergoes continuous change. Senior leaders must monitor this environment, assess the organization's vulnerability and opportunity points, and formulate business strategies and objectives. Ideally, they will do this with significant participation from within the organization so that there is already a broad understanding of the challenges and opportunities and a feeling of ownership of the way forward.

At this stage in the process, the change is driven primarily from the top. The key role of these change leaders is to educate others on the challenges the business faces. The challenges must be defined as precisely as possible, without falling back into rationalizations or denial. Tell people the consequences of not changing. Send some people to Japan, Korea, China, or Germany if you have to, and have them report back to company associates on the competitive challenges. Illusion is no foundation on which to build a future. Speaking in positive statements only (a practice of many companies) is self-deceptive and ultimately self-destructive. Information on the challenges must be shared and trust built from the very beginning.

The existing culture—zone of familiarity—of the organization needs to be defined as part of the problem and not part of the solution, and the goal of creating a leadership culture in the organization needs to be articulated. (The type of global directions forum described in the last chapter could provide a great deal of preliminary information about the current state of the business culture and the issues that need to be addressed. Input from customers should also be used.) One word of caution: In many successful companies, core values have remained the same for a considerable period of time. Change and adaptation do not mean that fundamental values have to be compromised.[13]

Once the challenges and opportunities have been articulated, it is important that they be communicated and discussed throughout the organization. This can be done in cascade meetings, for example, where senior managers communicate the message to middle managers and so on down through the organization. Large meetings of associates can also be held in hotels and via satellite. (These methods ensure that a critical mass of people hear the same message at the same time.) Senior leaders should not be afraid to dramatize their important message (remember how Eckhard Pfeiffer disappeared through the auditorium ceiling after announcing his new company stretch goals).

It is important that in this Disturbing the Present phase, senior leaders convey not only the challenges but also an overall vision of

---

[13]James C. Collins and Jerry I. Porras, *Built to Last: Successful Habits of Visionary Companies,* New York: HarperCollins, 1994, p. 8.

the future and a methodology for bringing the culture into line with new realities.

It is also important to convey the message that everyone in the organization is a stakeholder in this culture change. It will be an organizational dialogue lasting for an extended period of time (although there should be a time frame). It is not another fad.

Very senior managers (a change transition team) with excellent people and communication skills need to be assigned to coordinating the culture change process at the companywide level and down into the business units. Make sure this team understands its specific roles and responsibilities.

Finally, time this phase so that the next phase begins immediately. Maintain the momentum.

Surfacing Obstacles

Guiding Principle: Open the Windows and Let the Air in

Primary Objectives:

◆ Gathering data about the factors that facilitate and inhibit leadership behaviors in the organization.

◆ Broadening the scope of participation to build ownership in the problems to be addressed and accountability for successful change.

◆ Building deeper and interwoven relationships through mutual understanding.

People up, down, and across the organization now need to be heavily engaged in the culture change.

The process now moves into making the present *zone of familiarity* explicit. In *Culture Challenge Groups,* members of the organization need to be able to express and explore their thoughts and feelings about the obstacles that will get in the way of creating a global leadership culture. One technique is to form groups that are cross-functional and multileveled. Formal positions would not be announced or discussed; everyone is given an equal voice. The goal is authentic communication. These groups need time to explore such questions as

- What assumptions, values, and behaviors define how we in this organization see the world? (You might try to get at this information by asking groups to profile an ideal customer or a hypothetical successful manager and associate in the organization. You can then work back to assumptions, values, and behaviors.)
- What stories are told here about the organization (official stories and unofficial stories)?
- When people talk about the organization, what kinds of metaphors do they use?
- What kinds of symbols, rituals, and ceremonies do we have, and what do they tell us about ourselves?
- Is there a gap between our stated values and the ones actually in existence on a daily basis?
- Are there conflicts among the values held in the organization? What are the consequences of these conflicts?
- What are our primary mental models about our worldwide stakeholders (customers, suppliers, distributors, etc.)?
- Do we breed passivity in the organization? How?
- Are we prone to denial of critical issues affecting our competitive success?
- Where are the communication blockages?
- Do associates and lower-level managers have enough information to take on leadership roles?
- Do we lack openness and trust?
- Do we overcontrol or undercontrol?
- Are existing power relationships counterproductive?
- Are there specific rules and regulations that cause more trouble than they are worth?
- Do we lack persistence in implementing change? What is our change history?
- Are we seduced by fads? Why?
- Do we have a not-invented-here mentality in the organization?
- Are we trapped in traditional mindsets about "leadership"?
- Are we clear enough about what a *leadership culture* would look like in our organization?

One exercise to do in Culture Challenge Groups is to have the group think about the following question:

If we had an organizational culture in which everyone was expected to demonstrate leadership in their day-to-day activities, what would it feel like for

> *Our customers?*
> *Our other stakeholders?*
> *Our associates?*

After answering this question, the group can work back to surfacing the facilitating and inhibiting forces at work in the organization's culture. One challenge will be to keep the groups from rushing into solutions. Findings from the groups should be collated and analyzed for common themes.

As Charles Hampden-Turner points out in his excellent book *Creating Corporate Culture: From Discord to Harmony*, many of our corporate cultures are low-context (work with little information). High-context cultures, on the other hand, "are rich with the feelings, beliefs, ideas, and experiences of their members, and these are intensively and meaningfully woven into their shared culture."[14] One technique described by Hampden-Turner is to set up an interviewing process in which senior managers interview their subordinates. This process has been used with success at Anheuser-Busch. Interviews are ongoing and held on a monthly basis; the goal is simply to learn more about one another and to weave relationships together. Interviewers look to engage with the whole person, not just the person's role at work. One way interviewers learn about the culture is to ask about the associate's entry into the culture. This discussion draws out how aspirations may have collided with realities.

Trust is critical at this stage. People should never be punished for speaking openly and honestly. The emergence of conflicting perspectives and values needs to be recognized as a source of potential breakthroughs and richer solutions. Resistance is to be expected, and feelings should be respected. Responses to change will vary between active and passive, for and against.[15] This level of authentic sharing

---

[14]Charles Hampden-Turner, *Creating Corporate Culture: From Discord to Harmony*, Reading, MA: Addison-Wesley (The Economist Books), 1990, p. 55.

will feel unusual for many, and some will choose not to engage. They will feel protective of themselves, their jobs, and their reputations. A set of guidelines for the meetings will be useful; these guidelines can be derived from the set of collaborative values presented in Chapter 3: caring, confidentiality, fairness, honesty, openness, participation, respect, responsibility, results, sharing, unity, and understanding. If the groups don't feel "safe," nothing of value will emerge.

A skilled facilitator will be needed to help distinguish between specifically personal issues that individuals have with other individuals or company systems and issues that are embedded in the culture as a whole.

Surveys could supplement the Culture Challenge Group process, if necessary.

Challenging Obstacles

Guiding Principle: Focus on Possibilities, Not Probabilities

Primary Objectives:

◆ Feeding back information to the Culture Challenge Groups for review.

◆ Brainstorming possible interventions for the Culture Initiatives Package.

◆ Identifying priorities for specific change projects.

◆ Emphasizing individual responsibility for challenging obstacles on an ongoing basis.

The goal of this stage in the process is to produce a prioritized package of organizational initiatives that will disempower the old cultural expectations and behaviors and promote professional growth and development. Some changes may be implemented almost immediately, while others will take longer to develop and absorb.

---

[15]Michael Ward, *Why Your Corporate Culture Change Isn't Working . . . and What to Do about It,* Aldershot, U.K.: Gower, 1994, p. 142.

Facilitators will present the results of the first round of meetings and ask for responses and additional input. After the initial meeting, associates may have become more attuned to observing assumptions, values, and behaviors at work. They will have had time to reflect. New information may simply confirm issues that were raised earlier, or it may add new insights.

Some participants will have had time to think of new reasons for resistance. Those who resist most will most likely be those with the most power to lose. William Hudson, chief executive of AMP, an electronic connectors company, gives his people some nonnegotiables: Decisions must be made close to where the action is, or *I* and *my* cannot be used to refer to departments. Another of his strategies is to form task forces of executives and scatter the resisters among them to diffuse their negativity.[16]

One key responsibility of the facilitator is to help individuals recognize their own accountability for challenging the cultural status quo on an ongoing basis. Although the next stage will aim at producing formal organizational initiatives, the real challenges will be at the personal level.

Constructing New Expectations

Guiding Principle: Keep Returning to the Vision and the Customer

Primary Objectives:

◆ Establishing project teams to develop initiatives arising out of the Culture Challenge Groups.

◆ Coordinating the efforts of the project teams to ensure alignment of efforts and synergy.

◆ Developing appropriate time frames and measurements to evaluate progress.

◆ Informing associates of progress being made on the formal initiatives.

At this stage, initiatives (e.g., new performance and behavioral expectations, the removal of unnecessary hierarchical barriers, a com-

---

[16]Thomas A. Stewart, "How to Lead a Revolution," *Fortune*, November 28, 1994, p. 57.

munications audit, global leadership training programs, new selection and hiring requirements, a new reward system) are explored by dedicated teams with heavy input from line managers and associates who have become recognized as culture change leaders. The emphasis of each initiative needs to be on behavioral change rather than attitudinal change. Attitude changes will follow behavior changes.

It is important to keep in mind that sophisticated programs may not be the answer to creating a culture of leadership. The answer may lie more in simple things such as opening up the possibility of authentic relationships and letting them grow over time.

Education and training programs are almost inevitable when instituting a cultural change, but they should be at the tip of the iceberg. They tend to become propaganda machines for change. Peter Senge is reported to have said, "Don't push growth: remove the factors limiting growth."[17] This is an important principle as the change makers begin to institutionalize their products. Pushing just creates push-back.

It would be very easy at this point to lose sight of the vision and drown in program details. Drowning in the details will probably result in some form of return to the past, the known. It's not unusual during the transition for many to experience doubt. The vision must be kept in the foreground at all times as an inspiration for expanding the realm of the possible.

The Change Transition Team needs to ensure that all the initiatives fit with the overall objectives of the culture change and the business strategy. Intensive coordination and project management are critical at this stage.

There is a danger during this period that things will go quiet. Teams will be working on their specific assignments, and many associates may well become confused about the seeming lack of change. The Change Transition Team should take accountability for measuring and communicating progress and keeping the energy flowing throughout the organization.

---

[17]Frank Hoffman and Bill Withers, "Shared Values: Nutrients for Learning," *Learning Organizations: Developing Cultures for Tomorrow's Workplace*, ed. Sarita Chawla and John Renesch, Portland, OR: Productivity Press, 1995, p. 464.

Integrating New Expectations

Guiding Principle: Don't Tolerate the Old

Primary Objectives:

◆ Implementing new policies, procedures, programs, systems, and so on to encourage new behaviors.

◆ Maintaining Culture Challenge Groups to gauge the impact of specific changes.

◆ Continuing to build and interweave relationships that are respectful but challenging.

Leaders in formal positions must model the expected behaviors continuously and create the conditions for others to do the same. Old behaviors and expectations should be given no place in the new environment.

Culture Challenge Groups should continue to meet to assess the impact of the changes taking place and to make additional recommendations.

One of the dangers in this process is that the implementation of company programs may seem to excuse individuals from taking accountability for their own change. The outside-in efforts must complement and not distract individuals from their own inside-out growth programs.

Critical to the integration process is the issue of accountability. Morris Shechtman is very clear on this point: "Without it [accountability], growth doesn't take place. Accountability provides the structure for growth and development . . . when managers don't hold their people accountable, they're abandoning them, and nothing could be more cruel than that action."[18] He lists seven important prerequisites to foster accountability:

1. Accountability is to individuals, not to groups, committees, or organizations.

2. Clarify the areas in which one will be held accountable.

3. Expectations must be stated in a specific and clearly differentiating manner.

---

[18]Morris Shechtman, *Working without a Net*, Englewood Cliffs, NJ: Prentice Hall, 1994, p. 168.

4. Measurement of expectations must delineate quantity and time frame.

5. Consequences for meeting or failing to meet established expectations must be stated in detail.

6. Consequences must be enacted with immediacy, objectivity, and clarity.

7. Accountability must be consistently modeled by top management.[19]

The change cycle, of course, continues on. People learn and generate new questions and new ideas; the environment changes; and the organization settles down into another zone of familiarity and loses sight of possibilities.

A key to both self- and organizational transformation is deep reflection. Several years ago, someone said that feedback is the breakfast of champions. If so, reflection is dinner! Increasingly, global leaders have to act in situations where there are poorly structured tasks, complex relationships to sort through, and unclear objectives. No one is quite sure what the problem is or its scope. There is often no time for lengthy, up-front analysis. Reflection is the learning equivalent of the sports action replay. We can analyze what worked and what didn't work. We can analyze our motivations and responses and look for self-defeating thoughts, feelings, beliefs, and behaviors. We can loosen our grip on habitual ways of doing things and create perspective.

Effective reflection breaks our compulsion with activity for its own sake and helps put us in touch with our capabilities. It creates new horizons of possibility. It disturbs the present, helps us surface and challenge mental models, and help us construct and integrate new models. Analyzing backward can help us move forward with a clearer vision.

As organizations build their leadership resources, they release the collective intelligence of their people. Hopefully, this intelligence permeates beyond the boundaries of the organization and into the world at large. The world also needs reminding that it is a possibility and not a thing.

---

[19]Ibid., pp. 157–66.

Doubt is one of the great enemies of change. But remember what Margaret Mead said to us (I paraphrase): "Never doubt for an instant that a small group of committed individuals can change the world. Indeed, it is the only thing that ever has."

SUMMARY CHECKPOINT

Global organizations must be in perpetual motion as they drive for breakthrough performance in speed, service, price, product development, quality, customization, precision, and other factors. Change is omnipresent and unceasing.

The type of change required is both personal (inside-out) and organizational (outside-in). No organizational transformation can occur without self-transformation. Organizations are charged with setting world-class expectations. Individuals are charged with recognizing their own responsibility for results and undertaking the personal and professional development needed for success.

A leadership culture is the enabling force for both individual and organizational transformation. Leadership cultures set new boundaries for the possible.

As organizations strip themselves down to their core capabilities, there is little room for individuals who don't add value to those capabilities. Every associate will be expected to contribute to the organization as a mature professional, that is, take actions that consistently add value to the outputs of the company through knowledge and expertise; demonstrate a high level of individual responsibility and engage with and take ownership of problems; demonstrate high levels of autonomy as well as collaboration; develop contributory value through lifelong learning and personal development; and produce results that are consistently at world-class standards.

As global organizations reduce their reliance on command and control structures, individuals are forced to take on greater command and control of their own lives and careers. This means taking on a commitment to ongoing self-transformation. To do this requires increased capabilities of personal mind management and reflection. The personal mind management process involves six steps: (1) Commit to personal exploration; (2) detach from who you think you are; (3) observe yourself in action; (4) keep a Trash Can in your head;

(5) play with possibilities; (6) act by design. This process is difficult and requires persistence, courage, and patience.

In creating our Transformational Self, we need to target those factors that inhibit our leadership potential: denial, homeostasis (the pull toward a comfort zone), limiting beliefs, scattered energy, manipulation, and alienation. Our objective should be to aim toward those factors that increase our leadership potential: facing reality, committing to growth, adopting transformational beliefs, focusing energy, relating to others, and engaging with purpose.

The Transformational Self agenda deals with the inside-out part of the equation. The organization must complement this with a drive toward building and sustaining a global leadership culture that aims to release the collective intelligence of its members.

There are five generic steps in a culture change process: disturbing the present; surfacing obstacles; challenging obstacles; constructing new expectations; and integrating new expectations.

Central to both self- and organizational transformation is deep reflection. Reflection creates new horizons of possibility in a world constantly pulling us back to the zone of familiarity.

SOME ACTION IDEAS

Individual

- Examine your personal readiness and capacity for change. Do you tend to be fairly closed and skeptical about change, cautious, somewhat cautious, or very eager?
- Think about your ability to sustain change in the past. Have you always reverted back to old behaviors? Why?

Organization

- Assess what kinds of changes have been implemented in the past. What is the legacy of those changes? Did they make a significant and lasting impact, or did they increase the level of cynicism? What can you learn from those previous initiatives as you move forward?

Individual	Organization
♦ Reflect on those experiences in your life that you think have shaped your response to change. Should you disempower those experiences and move on to more productive responses? Or do you think your current responses will serve you well?	♦ Analyze your own organizational culture. To what extent does it resemble a leadership culture? What factors in the organization do you think inhibit the development of leadership resources? What factors are working for you?
♦ Spend time thinking about the idea of self-transformation and what it would mean to you in terms of life changes.	♦ Gather a group of influential individuals in your organization and discuss the idea of a leadership culture. Share your analysis of the organization's culture. Test the waters and see what feedback you get. Is the company ready to explore new possibilities?
♦ Think about what you can do immediately to promote your personal growth and development. Identify resources inside and outside the organization that can support your efforts (e.g., courses, mentors). Commit to creating your life and not coping with it.	♦ Prepare for any intended change by understanding the forces that stand in your way. Organizations are political through and through. The more you can identify barriers, the better able you will be able to take a proactive approach in diffusing their negativity.

The Culture Prism

1. You ask, "Do we have a deal?" Your counterpart says, *"Inshallha."* In what part of the world are you likely to be? And what is your counterpart telling you?

2. What are *neibu* rules?

3. What is *guanxi,* and where does it have an impact on doing business?

4. What is *malu*?

5. What is a *chaebol,* and where would you find one?

You will find answers at the end of the appendix.

In an era of global business, contact among cultures is of more than anthropological interest. A clash of cultures affects the bottom line directly and can destroy a potentially rewarding joint venture or strategic alliance. The business press is full of stories in which highly successful companies have suddenly become grounded on the hidden sand banks of international cultural differences.

On paper, Corning's joint venture with the Mexican glass manufacturer Vitro seemed made in heaven. Twenty-five months after it began, the marriage was over. Cultural clashes had eroded the potentially lucrative relationship.

What happened? American managers were continually frustrated by what they saw as the slowness of Mexican decision making. Compared to the United States, Mexico is a hierarchical culture and only top managers make important decisions. Loyalty to these managers is a very high priority in Mexico, and to try to work around them is definitely taboo. The less urgent Mexican approach to time made scheduling very difficult. The Mexicans thought the Americans wanted to move too fast, and vice versa. Communication was also difficult, and not simply because of language. American directness clashed with the indirectness of the Mexicans. The Americans often thought Mexican politeness was an attempt to hide problems and faults. Corning also thought Vitro's sales style was unaggressive. Over time, the differences were felt to be unbridgeable.

Corning's experience is by no means unique. Disney's experience in France is another high-visibility example. I remember seeing EuroDisney referred to in British and French newspapers as America's cultural Vietnam or Chernobyl. Procter & Gamble had a rocky start in Japan. Its aggressive style of TV advertising (which knocked the competition) offended the Japanese taste for surface harmony, or *wa*, and damaged P&G's initial credibility. David Ussery, an Amway executive in South Korea, also knows about the impact of cultural differences. He was led from his office with his ankles and wrists bound, interrogated for 48 hours, and then locked in a jail cell for eight days. His "offense" was to bring American-style direct marketing to Korea. Prosecutors believed Korea's family-based culture was particularly vulnerable to this sales approach, relying as it does on recruiting family and friends to be distributors. "How could family members refuse to become involved?" argued the Koreans. David Li, an executive with Sunrider, a California-based company selling herbal food supplements, was also jailed for 12 days by Korean prosecutors for relying on the same sales technique.

Doug Reid, senior vice president of human resources at Colgate-Palmolive, sees cultural sensitivity as perhaps *the* major issue to be addressed in global leadership:

> If you don't know how to manage relationships, you'll fail in most environments outside of the United States. The challenge is cultural sensitivity and understanding how things get done elsewhere. In some countries, government relationships are key. In others, sensitivity to the importance of the family is important. How you communicate by constructive suggestions rather than direct orders can make or break you. The business issues are very much the same around the world. We're good at making sure the person knows enough about the business to go overseas and that they have a track record of making things happen. When our people do trip up overseas, it's over a cultural sensitivity issue most of the time.

Eric Campbell, vice president of human resources at International Flavors and Fragrances, seconds the view held by Doug Reid:

> I remember taking part in a think tank here in New York in which we had expatriate assignment managers from about 30 of the top companies—Citibank, IBM, Sony, Siemens—and I remember asking, "How

many of you have seen an assignment fail because the individual didn't possess the technical skills?" No one among these major companies could think of an instance where the issue was technical capability. Unfortunately, many of our business schools haven't heard the message. With very few exceptions, many still drive the hard stuff—economics, finance, marketing, and accounting. The foreign schools seem to balance the hard curriculum with language and leadership training, etc., attempting to address some of the soft skills. These are critical issues, and they must be addressed if U.S. companies are going to be successful in a global marketplace.

How does the individual who is pulled and pushed into working in unfamiliar cultures do business against the odds? The tapestry of world cultures is extremely complex and always in an unstable state. While it is impossible to always be prepared for every cultural difference, it is possible for a manager to commit to a cycle of cultural learning that builds competence and confidence (see Figure A1–1).

The cycle is a continuous learning process in which we expand and deepen our home-culture mental perspectives and social skills.

The first step in the process is *recognizing*. This is much more difficult than it sounds. Many people have a surface or intellectual understanding of differences, but have not experienced the emotional stresses and strains that can accompany a cross-cultural encounter. Deep recognition begins with the emotions, not the intellect.

FIGURE A1–1
The Cultural Learning Cycle

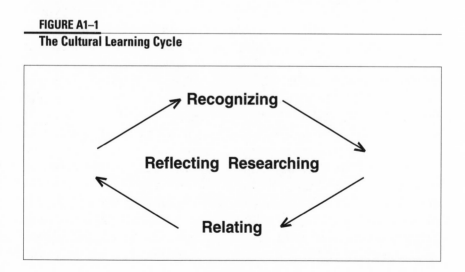

Too often, we begin with unconscious denial or an attitude of "Underneath we're really all the same." This is particularly dangerous when the cultures are said to share a common cultural heritage. I came to live in the United States from England 13 years ago. The first six of those years were spent trying to adjust to American culture. The first difference that caused problems was language. I remember a job interview where I was proudly telling the interviewer that I had served on a working party of the Schools Council in the United Kingdom. At the mention of "working party," the interviewer bristled and said, "Are you telling me you're a communist?" "Working party" in the United Kingdom is basically equivalent to the American "task force."

After coping with many instances of linguistic misunderstanding, other incompatibilities started to emerge. There was my infuriating—to Americans—indirect communication style. My slower, quieter speech, laden with pauses for reflection, prompted Americans to fill in the silences at every opportunity. My greater deference to hierarchy and formality frustrated my managers, who wanted me to be more confrontational and assertive. There was also my reluctance to conduct projects in the American "do it, and we'll make course corrections as we go along" approach. I tended to plan in a more ponderous, methodical manner, looking to cover all possible contingencies.

My writing style was also a bone of contention. One day a manager called me into her office. She said, "You're English aren't you? I can tell by your writing. I've been to England. Lots of small houses crowded together. You write the same way." What she wanted was big words (by which she meant buzzwords and hyperbole that would sell the argument) and lots of white space on the page so that it was very easy to read. There were other issues. In writing memos, I would first lay out the evidence and then write my conclusions. That was too European. I needed to write my conclusions first and then give a brief explanation of how I had reached them.

If we have only a surface understanding of differences, we sometimes fall into the trap of thinking that the differences themselves are relatively superficial and can easily be bridged. We assume our personal qualities and good intentions will quickly close the gaps. The apparent superficiality between peoples often arises because we *project* our deep cultural preferences onto others. I remember giving

my wife some cultural tips before she went to Japan. She was skeptical. My wife is lovely and charming and thrives on meeting new
people and developing friendships. She had met with Japanese
people in the States and hadn't come across any major difficulties. A
few days after arriving in Tokyo, she called and said, "Thank God
you gave me those tips. I can't believe it! This really is a *different
world.*" To paraphrase the Zen masters, "We must unlearn what we
think we know and learn how to pay attention to *what is.*"

In explaining how the experience of cultural difference *feels*, I
often use a lithograph created by Maurits Cornelis Escher (1898–1972)
called *Relativity* (see Figure A1–2). Escher is a popular artist, perhaps
too popular. His magical and complex images are consumed through
T-shirts, calendars, posters, and the like. His popularity can interfere
with our appreciation of his relevance to understanding our times.
When we see images too often, they become part of the visual muzak
of our culture: visible but not seen, accessible but with little impact.

Created in 1953, *Relativity* is a lithograph containing three different worlds or three different states of being-in-the-world. While
the worlds are distinct from one another, they coexist in a complex
harmony. Bruno Ernst, author of *The Magic Mirror of M. C. Escher*, is
an excellent guide through the labyrinth of Escher's work. Ernst di-
vides the 16 figures in the print into three communities and gives
them the names the Uprighters (their heads point upward, e.g., the
figure walking up the stairs at the bottom of the picture), the Left-
leaners (their heads point to the left), and the Right-leaners. All three
worlds inhabit the universe of the print, but their perspectives will
be very different. As Ernst says, "What is a ceiling to one group is a
wall to another; that which is a door to one community is regarded
by the other as a trapdoor in the floor."[1]

The print contains three gardens, one for each of the three
worlds. The Uprighters' garden is in the lower center of the picture
(we can see the tops of a couple of trees). The Left-leaners' garden is
top left, and the Right-leaners' garden is bottom right. When
Uprighters, Lefties, and Righties meet one another, their relative
positions will look exceedingly strange. Imagine the Upright person
at bottom center walking up the center set of stairs and then turning

---

[1]Bruno Ernst, *The Magic Mirror of M. C. Escher*, New York: Barnes & Noble, 1994, pp. 47–49.

FIGURE A1–2

Escher's *Relativity*

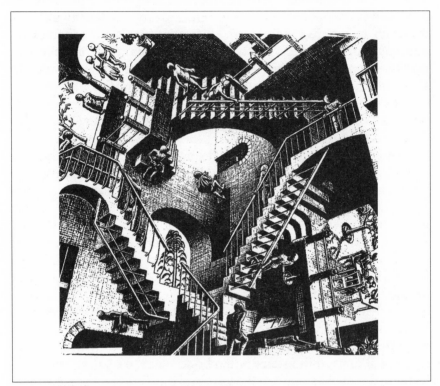

left. The Right-leaner sitting and reading will see someone walking along horizontally. It isn't that the position of the Uprighter or Right-leaner is wrong; rather, each one is living on a different plane. The perspective we identify with depends on our angle of vision. Imagine more than three worlds!

Americans I meet in global management seminars are, at least on the surface, willing to learn and adapt to other cultures. In practice, the commitment to diversity may fall far short of intent. In a multicultural seminar I co-taught for a global financial company headquartered in the United States, the participants were asked to review a short case in which an American manager is having problems dealing with the management style differences in Asia. They were asked to decide what might be the best strategy or combination of strategies for managing the conflict. The American managers in the audience chose a combination of initial avoidance followed by increasing collaboration. All the Americans in the audience nodded in agreement. The sweetness and light in the room then began to dissolve. First, a gentleman from Singapore quietly asked me to get a response from a certain American manager sitting in another row. At first, the American was reluctant to speak, but was persuaded to do so. His response was that while collaboration was ideal, the reality was that the company was committed to speed. A young Japanese man then stood up and, in a very un-Japanese-like fashion, commented that Americans go to Asia and talk collaboration when what they really mean is "Do it our way."

I then told the story of the young Zen Buddhist monk visiting his master. The novice said to the master, "Please teach me about Zen." The master said nothing, but started pouring tea into the novice's cup. He poured and poured, and the tea overflowed across the table. The novice grew increasingly nervous. "Please, just teach me about Zen!" cried the novice. "How can I teach you?" said the master. "Your cup is already full." Across to my left, I saw a group of Asians nodding and smiling. Americans, they felt, were full cups. They came to Asia saying they wanted to learn, but in fact they clung to their own ways of doing things and showed little capacity for learning something different. The frustration of the non-Americans in the room only bubbled under the surface, but caused enough ripples to get noticed.

America prides itself on being multicultural and diverse, and I have often heard that this should serve the United States well in the global marketplace. To some extent, these commentators are right. But—and it is a big but—how real is the diversity in the United States? Benjamin Schwarz argues that there is a diversity myth in America. In his view, "Variants of the cry, 'Why can't they be more like us?' have long served as a staple of American tourists and foreign policy mandarins alike. We have made ourselves at home in the world, characteristically, by regarding it as America in the making. Thus imbued with ourselves, we often get the world wrong." And, he continues, "We get the world wrong because we get ourselves wrong."[2]

---

[2]Benjamin Schwarz, "The Diversity Myth," *The Atlantic Monthly*, May 1995, p. 57.

We like to believe America is founded on liberal notions of pluralism and tolerance, whereas in fact it is founded on ethnic dominance. Schwarz sees this dominance as being English in nature. The American character has been formed not from a blending of cultures but by pressure to conform, to assimilate to an Anglo ideal. According to a world values survey conducted in the 1980s, the United States ranks 11th in the world in tolerance of people whose ideas, beliefs, and values differ. More than 40 percent said they had some reservations about (and almost a quarter of them said they dislike "quite a lot" or "very much") being with people with different ideas and values.[3] Recognizing differences, therefore, may not be as easy as we think. As one retired senior vice president from a major U.S. corporation put it, "We have the technology and we know the business, but we are not prepared as a country to deal with cultural differences . . . I have seen relatively little progress over the past 30 years."[4]

Researching is the second step in the cycle. As the French philosopher-mathematician Blaise Pascal once said, "There are truths on this side of the Pyrenees that are falsehoods on the other." You can leap into the ocean of cultural differences unprepared, but it helps if you have some devices for staying afloat and some navigational know-how. There are countless books and an increasing number of videos on "doing business in Japan" (or China, Russia, Brazil, etc.), and you should study the appropriate ones well in advance of your trip, not just on the plane. Unfortunately, such books tend to focus only on the outward expressions of culture, such as gestures, food and drink, clothing, greetings, and so on. It is more important that you become comfortable with recognizing and adapting to the more important and subtle differences among cultures.

What do I mean by "subtle differences"? Let me remind you of the differences that destroyed the relationship between Corning and Vitro. Those consisted of differences in orientation toward power and authority, time, communication style, and formality. Culture is not simply about outward gestures, do's, and taboos of gift giving. It

[3]Andrew L. Shapiro, *We're Number One! Where America Stands—and Falls—in the New World Order*, New York: Vintage Books, 1992, p. 108.

[4]Gary Bonvillian and William A. Nowlin, "Cultural Awareness: An Essential Element of Doing Business Abroad," *Business Horizons*, November 1994, p. 44.

is about the embedded psychological reality of a group and how it affects thoughts, feelings, and behaviors. It is a group reality that has evolved over many years. The novelist V. S. Naipaul says it very eloquently: "Most of us know the parents or grandparents we come from. But we go back and back, forever; we go back all of us to the very beginning; in our blood and bone and brain we carry the memories of thousands of beings . . . We cannot understand all the traits we have inherited. Sometimes we can be strangers to ourselves."[5]

Let me give you an example of a relatively subtle difference in communication style. In Asia, the need to avoid "losing face" is an important social and psychological reality, connected to the fact that the group takes precedence over the individual. To cause another person to lose face can disrupt social harmony and is considered dishonorable. Therefore, an indirect communication style is the norm in many parts of Asia. A participant in one of my cross-cultural seminars told me of her experience with indirectness in China as an exchange student. She would sometimes ask her "Chinese family" if she could go to town. If the family wanted to say *no*, they would say something like "The bus may be broken today." If the answer was *yes*, they would say something like "Today should be a sunny day." The directness of American speech in such cultures can appear to be very hostile. The "say what you mean, and mean what you say" cultural style works in a direct, individualistic culture such as America, but causes embarrassment in a collectivistic and indirect culture such as Japan.

Often you have to pay very close attention to the other person's body language to recognize that you are confronting an invisible cultural barrier. What often happens in Asia is that the person is saying "Yes, yes, yes," but his or her body language is saying "No, no, no." Here's a tip: Always pay more attention to the body language.

Having a model to help you make sense of many of the subtle differences is useful. A number of models exist. Geert Hofstede and Alfons Trompenaars have well-known and useful models. In a previous book I co-authored with Danielle and Tim Walker (*Doing Business Internationally: The Guide to Cross-Cultural Success*, Irwin

---

[5]V. S. Naipaul, *A Way in the World*, New York: Alfred A. Knopf, 1994, p. 11.

Professional Publishing, 1995), we presented a 10-variable model of cultural differences. There are many ways to categorize cultural differences, and readers should choose a model with which they feel comfortable (a list of useful books is given at the end of the appendix).

My latest approach is to look at culture as a social and psychological prism (see Figure A1–3). We think we perceive the world around us *as it is.* In fact, the world is mediated through our dominant assumptions, values, and beliefs. Our cultural prism determines how we understand and know ourselves, others, and the world. Each of our cultural prisms is built out of the history of our group, our religions and other belief systems, economies, educational and legal systems, aesthetics, language, and to some extent our geography (although two countries may be physically very close but culturally very distant, e.g., the United States and Mexico).

FIGURE A1–3
The Culture Prism

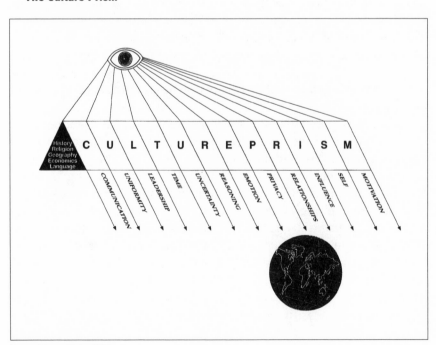

Source: Terence Brake, 1996.

Each major category in the culture prism can be broken down into different pairs or triads of cultural preferences. The descriptions that follow are high-level generalizations and are written without value judgment. The description of each element in the prism is necessarily brief.

Communication: How Individuals in the Group Exchange Meaning

Implied   We stress shared understandings and empathy. We don't need to explain everything because we assume others will understand even before we finish speaking. This type of communication is common in cultures that stress the importance of group harmony and homogeneity over the individual and difference (e.g, Japan). Indirection helps preserve surface harmony and avoid embarrassment.

Stated   We do not assume you know what we want to say. We express everything. Such a communication style is common in cultures that emphasize individuality over the group. When common experience cannot be assumed, misunderstanding can be avoided only if meaning is expressed precisely and explicitly. Americans usually like to be explicit and not assume there is shared understanding.

Circular   When you ask us a question, we will need to give you the complete background to the problem so that you understand the context. Without the context, you will not be able to understand how we arrived at our conclusions. When we finish, you will have a complete picture. Such an approach is typical of many southern European countries, Latin America, and Japan.

Straight   When you ask us a question, we will point directly to an answer. We may lead you through series of short, logical steps, but they will be concise. You don't need to understand all of the background to make sense of our conclusions. When we finish, you will have questions, and we will fill in the background as needed. An American presentation or proposal often starts with the bottom line and provides relatively little context.

Ordered   Each social situation has certain protocols that need to be followed; otherwise there will be confusion and misunderstanding. We feel comfortable when others conduct themselves in the manner appropriate to the situation. Japan and many other Asian nations maintain relatively strict protocols.

Casual   Every situation is much like any other. Protocols get in the way of individual expression and real, honest communication. We feel comfortable when we can just be ourselves. Australians and Americans try to sidestep protocols whenever possible. The English are thought to be more formal than they actually are.

Uniformity: The Importance the Group Places on Commonality

Standard   When we create rules, we expect them to apply to everyone in the same way. We don't expect certain individuals or groups to be favored over others, regardless of any personal relationship we may have with them. In creating products and services, we look for standardization and mass consumption. American culture is famous for creating standardized goods (e.g., McDonald's burgers) and for creating policies and procedures to be applied to any place at any time. (I have heard many European managers complain that when American companies acquire a foreign company, they rush in with their own policies and procedures manuals and try to create a mini-U.S., regardless of local circumstances.)

Unique   Things get done because of specific relationships, not abstract rules. We create rules, but they will be applied according to who you are—your status, my friendship with you, and so on. We stress uniqueness rather than standardization. Circumstances change, and we flow with them. The French create countless rules and regulations, but are constantly seeking ways to work around them—a process they know as *systeme'D* (*D* stands for *debrouillard*, which is beating the system or overcoming obstacles).

Leadership: Who the Group Expects to Wield Power and How

Vertical   Good organization depends on a clear understanding of who is in charge. We expect leaders to lead and exercise power, and we don't feel comfortable in situations where the hierarchy is fuzzy. Everyone should know his or her place, and obedience is valued. Decision making is autocratic. Many parts of the Middle East, Latin America, and Asia have well-defined, vertical power structures.

Horizontal   While there may be a chain of command, it is fairly flat. Leadership may shift depending on who has the expertise in a particular area. We all have something to contribute, so the less hierarchy, the better. While American organizations have levels of power, the movement is toward flatter structures with few levels of management and an increased flow of information toward empowered employees.

Achieved   Leadership and status must be earned through personal effort. We don't accept the belief that certain people are expected to lead because of the circumstances of their birth. Our leaders emerge through the competitive process. In this way, power will be exercised by those most qualified to handle it. The achievement orientation is characteristic of Western cultures to different degrees.

Attributed   Leadership and status are tied to who you are, not necessarily to what you do or have accomplished. We may attribute leadership to those with seniority, those with charisma, or those whose birthright places them in a position of authority. This orientation is common in the Middle East, Asia, and Latin America.

Time: How Members of the Group Define the Nature of Time and Its Appropriate Use

Event   Time is relatively abundant. The strict scheduling of events cannot be controlled. We take whatever time it takes in a meeting to do the business at hand. Others may need to wait until we have finished. This is sometimes called an "agricultural" or "seasonal" view of time. A preference for event time is common in the Middle East, southern Europe, and Latin America.

Clock   Time is a scarce resource and needs to be used efficiently. We value time management and relatively strict deadlines. Fast decisions are imperative. We break up time into small chunks and construct precise schedules. This is sometimes called an "industrial" view of time. Many others know it as "American Time."

Plural   We prefer to do a number of things at any one time—conduct several conversations, listen to another, sign letters, answer the telephone. Life is not linear. You must pay attention to all of those things that are in front of you. Anyone who has done business in the Middle East, Latin America, or France will recognize this style.

Singular   We feel it is best to do one thing at a time and give it our full attention before moving on to something else. Whenever possible, there should be no interruptions. Although Americans juggle many projects, their preferred approach to time tends toward the singular rather than the plural.

Then   We look at whether a proposal fits into the existing plan and established patterns of doing things. France often looks to place initiatives in the context of the past, although it also looks to the future (witness the striking postmodern architecture in Paris).

Now   We value the short-term payoff. We look for where we can be most profitable in the here and now. The United Kingdom and the United States tend to look for immediate results, and plans are created for only two to three years into the future at most.

Long Term   We are building for the future. We may accept short-term losses to establish a stronger base for the years ahead. Japan tends toward long-term plans, as do many European cultures such as Sweden and Finland.

Uncertainty: How the Group Relates to Change

Inelastic   We don't value change for its own sake. Change does not always equal progress. The status quo exists for a good reason. Tradition, custom, tried and true policies, procedures, and methodologies help reduce the uncertainty of life. Some European countries (e.g., Greece, Portugal, and Belgium) and many Latin American countries avoid the risks of uncertainty.

Elastic   We pride ourselves on being flexible. Life gets better all the time as long as we are open to change. New is good. There is always a new and better way to do something. If it isn't broken, break it! America, to a relatively high degree, thrives on trial and error, pushing the envelope, and breaking through to new possibilities.

Reasoning: The Typical Problem-Solving Processes Used in the Group

Conceptual Driven   We believe there is nothing as practical as a good theory to make sense of the world. We work from the general to the specific. Many European countries place a high value on conceptual frameworks to bring meaning and order to existence. The French in particular respect theory.

Data Driven   We place value on the gathering and analysis of statistical evidence. We work from the specific to the general. The gathering of data is a preoccupation in the United States. Apart from business and science, Americans spend a great deal of time collecting sports data. The commentary of every sports game on TV is built on statistics: yardage, the percentage of free throws, runs batted in, and so on. When the World Cup was hosted in the United States, the Americans created new statistics to make soccer more palatable to an American audience.

Absolute   We believe there are absolute truths that do not change with the circumstances. Something is either true or false. This is a common view in much of the Western hemisphere and in cultures that are monotheistic (have one god).

Relative   Truth is relative to circumstances, personal obligations, and maintaining harmony. This view will be found in many cultures of the East and those that are polytheistic (have many gods).

Parts   We analyze the parts and then try to put the whole together. Any problem or system can be broken down into its key elements. The predominant metaphor we use in thinking about the world is the *machine*. Americans are "predominantly analytical, spending more energy deconstructing than constructing."[6]

Wholes   We like to look at the big picture (the system) and the relationships among the parts. We do not believe you can understand the whole by focusing just on the individual pieces. The predominant metaphor we use in thinking about the world is the *organism*. Japan, France, and Germany have been identified as being more holistic in their thinking patterns.[7]

Emotion: The Degree to Which Emotion Is an Expected and Accepted Part of Daily Interaction in the Group

Expressed   We consider it perfectly natural to exhibit anger, joy, or any other emotion openly and honestly. Many countries in southern Europe and in Latin America are highly expressive, verbally and nonverbally.

---

[6]Charles Hampden-Turner and Alfons Trompenaars, *The Seven Cultures of Capitalism,* New York: Doubleday, 1993, p. 31.

[7]Ibid., p. 31.

Checked   We believe that expressing emotion has no place in maintaining normal relationships with others. We are reserved and expect others to be the same. The open expression of emotion leads to embarrassment. Japan and the United Kingdom are well known for the degree to which they suppress emotion.

Privacy: The Degree to Which Individuals in the Group Are Expected to Cross over into Another's Psychological and Physical Space

Open   We readily share personal information about ourselves. We appear extroverted, informal, and easy to get to know. We do have a private life closed to others, but it is relatively small. Because of our openness, our relationships may appear to be superficial and lacking in commitment. The mobility of American society drives the need to create fast but relatively short-lived relationships. Americans, on the whole, develop many acquaintances rather than deep friendships, particularly as they get older and become involved in their careers.

Closed   We do not divulge a great deal of information about ourselves. We come across as being introverted, formal, and difficult to get to know. If others try to get too close too fast we can be evasive. Over time, we may develop strong, intimate relationships. Many European cultures fall into this category; becoming a friend may also mean becoming part of a wider family.

Close   We stand close to one another and touch a great deal. Arabs, Africans, and Latin Americans maintain a close conversational distance that often disturbs the American "space bubble," which is about an arm's length in all directions.

Distant   We prefer to stand some distance apart from one another and avoid unnecessary touching. In addition to most Anglo and Germanic cultures, the Japanese also like to maintain a conversational distance of about three feet.

Relationships: What Factors the Group Believes Are Important for Effective Social Interaction

Trust   We need to feel there is a chemistry among us. How can we do business unless we spend time developing a relationship and building trust with one another? We tend to look at building long-term relationships. Most of the Middle East, Latin America, Africa, and Asia lean toward this orientation.

Task Our focus is on getting the job done. Business is and should be relatively impersonal. Rather than focus on trust building, we aim to persuade you to do business with us by demonstrating our knowledge and expertise. Americans are well known for their dedication to task.

Harmonious Our relationships are built on cooperation and achieving consensus. This style is common among group-oriented cultures such as those in Asia. England also leans toward a consensual approach to decision making (although anyone who has seen a televised debate in the British Parliament may find this hard to believe).

Adversarial Good, solid relationships are built on getting conflict out in the open and dealing with it constructively. The best decisions arise out of the competition among ideas. In the United States, conflict is an expected and accepted part of healthy relationships.

Influence: Where the Group Places the Locus of Control in the World

Internal We are in control of our own lives. Our destiny is governed by our own choices, not by forces outside of ourselves. Luck is what happens when preparation meets opportunity (a saying in the United States). One of the largest shelves you will find in American bookstores will be devoted to self-help/personal improvement. We shape our life and world to our own ends.

External We do not believe we govern our own fate. Any other view is naive or even blasphemous. It doesn't pay attention to the forces of history, to the circumstances of birth, to the environments in which we find ourselves, or to God. We do what we can under the constraints we face. Islamic cultures look to God as the ultimate controlling force; *Islam* literally means "submission."

Self: The Degree of Importance Placed on the Individual versus the Group

Individual We value the uniqueness of each person. Personal responsibility, self-reliance, and the expression of individual talent and potential are paramount. The group is loosely structured, often relying on individual guilt for social control.

Group   Our personal identities are intimately linked to our social groups (e.g., family, class, clan, caste). Loyalty and duty are prized, and decision making tends to be autocratic or consensual depending on the group. Sharp distinctions are usually made between the in-group and the out-group. Social control is based largely on the fear of shame. Cultures in Asia, Latin America, the Middle East, and southern Europe lean toward a predominantly group orientation.

Motivation: The Primary Drivers for Actions Taken by Members of the Group

Productivity   We place a high value on performance and acquisition, on getting things done in the least amount of time. Work is central to life. It allows us to build material wealth and status. America is perhaps *the* productivity culture, although many Asian cultures are making a dramatic shift to this orientation.

Quality   We do not live to work. There are many other things in life besides money and things. It is important to enjoy life, to maintain a healthy separation between work and personal life. This orientation is not uncommon in Europe, the Middle East, and Latin America.

Calculation   The commitments we make are tied to potential rewards rather than relationships. We place great emphasis on cost/benefit considerations in making decisions. When people follow their self-interests, they ultimately benefit the group. Such a motivational drive is common in individualistic and competitive cultures where security is dependent on personal achievement (e.g., the United States).

Affiliation   The commitments we make are based on loyalties. In our culture, personal security is strongly linked to group membership. Our emotional and financial well-being is derived from the collective. Following our own private self-interests may not be good for the group. In Japan, the interests of the national group may take precedence over others. George Lodge reports that an executive of Mitsui, one of Japan's giant trading companies, placed the purposes of his company in the following order:

1. To contribute to Japanese society to serve the greater glory of Japan.

2. To realize profit for the company to promote the welfare and happiness of its employees.

3. To foster and strengthen the spirit of Mitsui for the future as that spirit is set forth in the company motto, *"Ten, Chi, Jen"* (heaven, earth, and human beings).[8]

Taking care of shareholders was a means to these ends. In this example, you can see the priority given to specific groups, particularly national and internal company groups.

In researching another culture, you can use the different elements described in the Prism (leadership, etc.) to help you gather and classify information. Rather than using books, you may talk to other people with experience in a specific culture. In this case, you can frame questions around the model elements (e.g., "How are business leaders selected in your culture?"). The model will also help you to organize your real-time experiences with others.

The influence of culture on leadership style is evident in Figure A1–4, "Leadership Priorities across Cultures."

It is interesting to look at the priorities in this chart in relation to underlying cultural differences. It should be no surprise that the United States, with its very dominant preferences for *task* and *productivity*, is the only country that rates "get results—manage strategy to action" as the number one priority.

Some other cultural observations of interest are as follows:

♦ Having a global mindset is a high priority for leaders in Japan and Korea. While making dramatic leaps into global markets, both Japan and Korea have historically been isolated in terms of playing a global role. Some Japan commentators believe Japan is at least a decade behind other countries in developing a global mindset. In the May–June 1995 issue of the *Harvard Business Review*, Kenichi Ohmae writes, "in 1995, no industrialized nation can be an economic island, yet Japan continues to behave like one."[9]

♦ Flexibility and adaptability are high priorities in Italy and Spain. Although their cultures are undergoing change, both Italy and

---

[8]George C. Lodge, *Managing Globalization in the Age of Interdependence*, San Diego: Pfeiffer & Company, 1995, p. 80.

[9]Kenichi Ohmae, "Letter from Japan," *Harvard Business Review*, May–June 1995, p. 154.

FIGURE A1–4

Leadership Priorities across Cultures

Description	Australia/ New Zealand	France	Germany	Italy	Japan	Korea	Spain	United Kingdom	United States
Be a catalyst/manager of strategic change	3	5	2		5	1			4
Be a catalyst/manager of cultural change		2		1				4	
Be flexible and adaptive				2			4		
Have a "global" mindset		1	1		4	4			
Articulate a tangible vision	1				2	2		1	2
Communicate effectively on a day-to-day basis		3	3	4					
Influence others without authority							3		
Manage internal and external resources		4							
Think integratively about the total business					3	5	5		
Have integrity and trust						3	2		
Take risks/initiative									
Exhibit a strong customer orientation	5		5	5				2	5
Manage quality improvement								5	
Empower others to do their best	4		4		1		1		3
Get results—manage strategy to action	2			3				3	1

Note: Numbers in cells represent the top five capabilities selected by nationality.

Source: *Champions of Change: A Global Report on Leading Business Transformation*, by Dr. Douglas Ready, Executive Director, International Consortium for Executive Development and Research, Lexington, MA: Gemini Consulting/ICEDR, 1994.

Spain tend to function on event time rather than clock time. They also tend toward a plural rather than singular use of time. An event view of the flow of time is looser than the strict demarcation of clock time into seconds, minutes, and hours. Events demand their own time, and things will happen in "their own good time" regardless of the strict timetables placed on events by those watching the clock. In event-driven cultures, things tend to get done because of the importance of relationships rather than imposed schedules.

In cultures with a plural view of time (e.g., Italy and Spain), many things will happen at once (several meetings may coexist at the same time and place, and a manager will find it normal to be in a meeting, answer the telephone, and sign letters all at once).

No matter how much you research another culture or cultures in general, there is no substitute for direct experience. There comes a time for *relating*, for demonstrating that you have taken the trouble to learn about the other culture. This is important for at least three reasons.

First, it shows respect. You are acknowledging the existence of the other culture—of which its members may be extremely proud—and not simply trying to impose your own. Don't forget, many cultures in the global marketplace have experienced Western imperialism firsthand. If you treat the other culture as an irrelevancy in the pursuit of your business, you may well be perceived as yet another exploiter. And don't be afraid of making mistakes. Other cultures can be very forgiving as long as you demonstrate an openness to learning.

Second, showing your learning about the other culture helps build all-important relationships. Showing a sincere interest in the other culture, especially through intelligent and informed questions, can take you miles down the road to a successful business relationship. As a culture, America tends toward a reverence for the task at hand. We assume that if we "get down to business," "cut to the chase," "go straight to the bottom line," and so on, all will be well. We don't need a significant relationship to do business. Just the opposite is true in many parts of the world.

Third, demonstrating what you know about the other culture communicates something about you as a person. Unfortunately, because of their narrow focus on the business at hand, American managers can appear to others to be one-dimensional or lacking in worldly sophistication. Businesspeople in Europe and Latin America often pride themselves on their eloquence and erudition. Discussions of philosophy, literature, art, and history can be interwoven with business talk. Be prepared to step outside of your usual conversational domain. Displaying some knowledge of local history, writers, and artists communicates a breadth of character as well as that all important *respect*.

The last stage in the cycle is perhaps the most important: *reflection*. You can have all the direct experience you want, but if you don't reflect on and learn from your experience, it counts for next to nothing. Reflection begins with asking questions: What was I expecting? What actually happened? Why did it happen this way? What would I do differently next time? The value of this kind of reflection is amplified if we have a partner who shared the same experience. We need time to process what we learned, but too often we quickly move on to the next item on the checklist.

What is the goal of this reflection? As a vice president of an international hotel chain once said to me, "We should at least try to move from unconscious incompetence to conscious incompetence." Becoming conscious of why we do what we do and why they do what they do is very empowering. It opens our minds to new possibilities and ways of seeing, which is why cross-cultural contact is so exciting and challenging. It helps us identify opportunities to build common ground and, perhaps most important, it enables us to see many differences as being nonpersonal. One concern of the hotel chain vice president was that his American managers overseas would be too quick to jump to the conclusion that a local employee had an

DIALOGUE BOX

1. Use the culture prism to identify your own cultural preferences.
2. Would you say your own cultural preferences are typical for your home country? Are there regional differences?
3. Use the culture prism to map out the preferences you have encountered in people from other cultures. How might the differences between you and them affect your working together and your leadership styles?

"attitude" when in fact a cultural difference was at work. Operating on the assumption of cultural rather than individual differences allows us to depersonalize our conflicts.

What personal qualities should you nurture as you work through the cultural learning cycle? Here are 10 of the most important.

1. Authenticity. Learn to relate to the flesh-and-blood individuals in front of you and not abstract conceptions of their culture. While it helps to prepare yourself for expected cultural differences, be receptive to individuals. Don't rush into a quick explanation of the behavior you see in front of you, but remain open to information the person is giving you about himself or herself. Quick explanations usually derive from stereotypes, and stereotypes close off authentic communication. The best international managers form impressions and develop tentative explanations; they modify their explanations and approaches as information accumulates and events unfold.[10] Observe your own mind as you meet with someone from another culture. Does it leap to a theory about why the person is behaving the way she or he is, or does it hold back and let the impressions form over time?

2. A sense of humor. I don't mean that it helps to tell jokes. Jokes rarely translate well. A sense of humor, however, brings a sense of perspective and lightness to what can be a stressful cross-cultural situation. It helps to laugh at one's own difficulties in an unfamiliar environment rather than become overly embarrassed and defensive. Humor guards against arrogance and helps us recover from mistakes. But make sure you laugh *with* others and not *at* them. While jokes are local, a sense of humor is universal and appealing. What about your own sense of humor? Can you laugh at your own ignorance and cross-cultural blunders?

3. A sense of wonder. The human race is a miracle and deserves respect for what it is and not what you would like it to be. If all you see when you look around are people who want to be like you, you are not looking hard enough. A sense of wonder about human diversity helps to keep us curious and energized. Curiosity may

---

[10]David J. Hickson and Derek S. Pugh, *Management Worldwide: The Impact of Societal Culture on Organizations around the Globe*, Harmondsworth, U.K.: Penguin Books, 1995, pp. 261–63.

have killed the cat, but it is the driving force of the global leader. If you become overwhelmed or jaded by difference, find another line of work. If you don't get excited by encountering new ways of being-in-the-world, stay at home. Do you have a sense of wonder about the world around you, or do you wish others would just shape up and get with the program?

4. Courage. Let's face it, we all feel comfortable with the familiar. The unfamiliar can generate fear as well as excitement. Working globally is a real challenge. There is nothing easy about doing business with people who see the world through different culture prisms. Although it gets easier with time, the courage to face worlds that are strange to us is a *must-have* quality. It also takes mental and moral courage to stand our ground, when necessary, to recognize and hold onto lines we cannot cross. How do you rate your own ability to recognize the fear and do it anyway?

5. Resilience. Yes, working globally can be exhausting, both emotionally and physically. On a recent trip, I circled the globe in a few days. ("If it's Tuesday at 1 AM, this must be New Delhi. But is it Tuesday? And is it really 1 AM? Was New Delhi yesterday? Perhaps this is Bangkok?) Resilience is the ability to adjust quickly to change and to withstand shock. It is the firm determination to carry on through the seeming chaos to achieve one's goals. It is not moving ahead by brute force but what I refer to as *quiet tenacity*. It does help to have anchor points in your life, such as people with whom you have long-term relationships or activities such as reading, writing, or photography, that give you a sense of consistency as well as a space to rejuvenate.

6. Realism. Men and women who have been very successful in their domestic organizations are sometimes very hard on themselves when they find they cannot achieve the same results globally. At the very least, it may take them longer. Successful people don't like to be thrown back into more childlike, dependent modes of learning, which is often the case when working across cultures. It pays to recognize the difficulties up front, to set realistic goals with longer time frames. Beating up on yourself because things are not going as planned is a quick path to burnout and increased failure.

7. Patience. Yes, you will have to reach down into yourself and discover hidden reserves of patience. If you reach down and they are not there, you're in trouble. You will need the patience to be tolerate of yourself and others.

8. Discernment. This is not a commonly used term today, but it is important. Discernment is the ability to recognize and comprehend what is not self-evident. It is about accurate perception and an ability to distinguish what is significant. Working across cultures requires the refined listening and observational skills of a detective, along with good intuition. Discernment can be developed over time, but it takes a conscious effort.

9. Self-confidence. All global leaders need to be chameleonlike and adapt to their surroundings. They do not, however, lose their sense of identity. They have a strong sense of self, a clear set of personal values, and high self-esteem. These characteristics allow them to integrate new attitudes and behaviors. They see difference not as a threat but as a source of possible enrichment. Those with a weaker sense of self or low self-esteem may be more inclined to put up defenses. It should be added that self-confidence does not equal arrogance. Self-confidence has to do with strength of character, not self-aggrandizement.

10. Detached engagement. It sounds like a paradox, and it is. You won't learn about others and how to work with them effectively if you don't engage and get involved. If you don't try to see the world through their eyes, you will never understand their motivations and reasoning. If you don't develop empathy, you will always feel at a loss to understand and a crippling sense of confusion. But that doesn't mean that you "go native" and see the world only through their eyes. As a global leader, you need to enrich your capabilities by seeing the value of multiple perspectives. No one perspective has the monopoly on truth or the lock on adding value. Part of your function as a global leader is to enrich others with new ways of seeing and doing.

Is it possible to develop these qualities? Absolutely! Is it easy? Absolutely not! How can you change? The process is identical to the self-transformation process outlined in Chapter 5:

1. Commit to personal exploration.
2. Observe yourself in action. Pay attention to how your mind works in cross-cultural situations. What thoughts

come into your head (e.g., "I don't think I can do this" [a self-confidence or courage issue]; "I can't believe I'm so stupid" [a realism issue]; "They are what they are and there's no changing them" [an authenticity issue])? What typical behaviors of yours become exaggerated or downplayed (e.g., some people yawn or play with their hair when they get nervous)? What feelings are aroused in cross-cultural situations (e.g., superiority, anger, frustration)? Such thoughts, behaviors, and feelings point to underlying issues that need to be addressed.

3. Distance yourself from any dysfunctional thoughts, behaviors, or feelings. Refuse to let them define who you are. Remember the Trash Can in your head, and mentally throw them in. When they return, throw them in again. Don't let them settle and get comfortable. Keep them busy and out of harm's way.

4. Mentally rehearse the thoughts, feelings, and behaviors you believe are more functional for your well-being in a cross-cultural world. Conduct little thought experiments in which your new behaviors and so on come into play. Visualize their effectiveness.

5. Act out from your new level of conscious understanding. Under stress, the old dysfunctional thoughts will come back to distract you. Just keep on putting them back in the Trash Can.

If you find it is too difficult to distance yourself from your thoughts and feelings, concentrate on your behaviors. The thoughts and feelings will follow. For example, concentrate on behaving in a patient manner and patience will follow.

DIALOGUE BOX

1. How would you rate yourself on the 10 qualities needed for cross-cultural effectiveness?

   Use the following scale:

   5 = Excellent; 4 = Very Good; 3 = Good; 2 = Fair; 1 = Poor

Authenticity	_____
Sense of humor	_____
Sense of wonder	_____
Courage	_____
Resilience	_____
Realism	_____
Patience	_____
Discernment	_____
Self-confidence	_____
Detached engagement	_____

2. Which personal qualities pose the great challenges for you to develop?

3. Think of a recent cross-cultural encounter. What thoughts, feelings, and behaviors of yours do you think were dysfunctional? What are the underlying issues you believe need to be addressed?

SOME USEFUL BOOKS

Culture Clash: Managing in a Multicultural World.
H. Ned Seelye and Alan Seelye-James, Chicago: NTC Business
Books, 1995.

Cultures Consequences: International Differences in Work-Related Values.
Geert Hofstede, Beverly Hills, CA: Sage Publishing, 1980.

Doing Business Internationally: The Guide to Cross-Cultural Success.
Terence Brake, Danielle Medina Walker, and Thomas (Tim) Walker,
Burr Ridge, IL: Irwin Professional Publishing, 1995.

GlobalWork: Bridging Distance, Culture & Time.
Mary O'Hara-Devereaux and Robert Johansen, San Francisco:
Jossey-Bass, 1994.

*Internationally Yours: Writing and Communicating Successfully in
Today's Global Marketplace.*
Mary A. De Vries, Boston: Houghton Mifflin, 1994.

*Management Worldwide: The Impact of Societal Culture on Organizations
around the Globe.*
David J. Hickson and Derek S. Pugh, Harmondsworth, U.K.:
Penguin Books, 1995.

Managing Cultures: Making Strategic Relationships Work.
Wendy Hall, Chichester, U.K.: John Wiley & Sons, 1995.

Multicultural Management: New Skills for Global Success.
Farid Elashmawi and Philip R. Harris, Houston: Gulf Publishing,
1993.

*Riding the Waves of Culture: Understanding Diversity in Global Busi-
ness.*
Alfons Trompenaars, Burr Ridge, IL: Irwin Professional Publishing,
1994.

The Seven Cultures of Capitalism.
Charles Hampden-Turner and Alfons Trompenaars, New York:
Currency Doubleday, 1993.

*Understanding Global Cultures: Metaphorical Journeys Through 17
Countries.*
Martin J. Gannon and associates, Thousand Oaks, CA: Sage Publica-
tions, 1994.

QUIZ ANSWERS

1. Your counterpart is telling you that you have a deal if God wills it to be so (Muslim Middle East).
2. The unwritten rules of doing business in Asia, particularly China (usually unpublished administrative rules and procedures).
3. Powerful connections. (China)
4. Causing someone to lose face and status. (Indonesia)
5. An industrial conglomerate. (Korea)

The Global Leader and the Internet

The "Net" is becoming one of the most productive ways for global leaders to access current international business information. Whether you need country data, advice on traveling, international business statistics, news on international trade shows, or insights into international finance, taxes, or the law, it can be found in cyberspace.

Following is a list of some of the most useful Internet addresses for the global leader.

CIA World Factbook

http://www.odci.gov/cia/publications/95fact/index.html
Developed by the CIA, this site offers key information on multiple countries around the world. The information for each country includes a map and sections on geography, people, government, the economy, transportation, communications, and defense forces.

Economics

gopher://nysernet.org
From within the Business and Economic Development Special Collection, you can access such resources as Export Trade Leads–U.S. Department of Commerce, the International Business Practices Guide (UM–St. Louis), and the National Trade Data Bank.

Economics WPA

http://econwpa.wustl.edu/
This service is provided by the Economics Department of Washington University and offers free distribution of working papers in economics. There are 22 subject areas, including international trade and international finance.

The Global Network Navigator/Koblas Currency Converter

http://bin.gnn.com/cgi-bin/gnn/currency
Click on the desired currency and the value of all other currencies on the listing will be calculated relative to the one you selected.

International Business Directory

http://www.et.byu.edu/~eliasone/main.html
Maintained by Brigham Young University, this site offers access to resources including currency exchange, foreign languages/dictionaries, international finance, government sources on international trade, international law, markets, international news and magazines, and international stock market information.

Internet Cultural Center

http://204.250.87.42/emporium/C/CAPNET/shrine.htm
This site is quite an experience. Visit Cultural Center Townhalls grouped by continents and countries, and learn about cultural differences.

MSU-CIBER—International Business Resources on the WWW

http://ciber.bus.msu.edu/busres.htm
This directory is maintained by Michigan State University, Center for International Business Education and Research (CIBER). Links are provided to such areas as international news/periodicals, regional- or country-specific information, international trade information, international trade leads, and international trade shows/seminars/business events.

Nijenrode Business Webserve

http://www.nijenrode.nl/nbr/
Maintained by the Netherlands Business School, Nijenrode University, this site offers economic data, statistical data, trends per country, international business, international law, and much more.

Resources for Economists on the Internet

http://econwpa.wustl.edu/EconFAQ/ECONFAQ.html
Maintained by Bill Goffe at the Department of Economics and International Business, University of Southern Mississippi, this guide lists many resources for those interested in economics. Contents include U.S. macro and regional data, world, and non-U.S. data.

Trade Zone

http://www.tradezone.com/tz/trdzone.htm
This site provides a comprehensive source of information on international trade, including business opportunities, chambers of commerce, embassies/consulates, global travel, trade directories, trade law, trade statistics, transportation, and shipping.

WebEc International Economics

http://www.helsinki.fi/WebEc/webecf.html
This site provides excellent access to materials on such topics as international affairs, international trade, international trade data, international trade news, international trade journals and working papers, international trade mailing lists, international migration, international finance, international organizations, and international treaties.

Staying in Touch: The Printed Word

The amount of international business-related news available in printed form has exploded over the last few years. Following is a list of sources I find particularly useful. Review them in your local library to see which ones meet your needs at this time.

Newspapers

As well as looking at *The Wall Street Journal* and London's *Financial Times*, you might want to review the *International Herald Tribune* ("The World's Daily Newspaper"). Subscription number in the United States is 1-800-882-2884.

Magazines and Periodicals

The Brookings Review Published quarterly by The Brookings Institution, 1775 Massachusetts Avenue, N.W., Washington, DC 20036. General articles on domestic and international affairs by respected thinkers.

Business Ethics: The Magazine of Socially Responsible Business Published bimonthly by Mavis Publications, Inc., 52 S. 10th Street, #110, Minneapolis, MN 55403-2001. A driving force in promoting the Caux Round Table Principles for Business.

Business Week Published weekly by McGraw-Hill. Subscriber Services: 1-800-635-1200. An increasingly global magazine with many articles related to global business.

The Economist Published weekly in the United States by The Economist Newspaper, NA, Inc., 111 West 57th Street, New York, NY 10019-2211. Perhaps the most comprehensive source of international business news available.

Foreign Affairs Published six times a year by the Council on Foreign Relations, Inc. Contact address is 58 East 68th Street, New York, NY

10021. Articles on international affairs by some of the most respected internationalists.

Foreign Trade   Published 10 times a year by FT, Inc., 6849 Old Dominion Drive, Suite 200, McLean, VA 22101. Up-to-date articles on a wide range of trade topics, including leads and contacts.

Fortune   Published weekly by Fortune, Time & Life Building, Rockefeller Center, New York, NY 10020. Customer Service: 1-800-621-8000. General business articles, many with a global slant.

The Futurist   Published bimonthly by the World Future Society, 7910 Woodmont Avenue, Suite 450, Bethesda, MD 20814. A fascinating way to keep up with trends (actual and imagined).

Harvard Business Review   Published bimonthly by Harvard Business School Publishing Corporation, 60 Harvard Way, Boston, MA 02163. Domestic and global business articles written by the most influential business thinkers.

Harvard International Review   Published quarterly by the Harvard International Relations Council, Inc., P.O. Box 401, Cambridge, MA 02238. Insightful articles on international affairs by leading thinkers and practitioners.

International Business   Published 12 times a year by IB Communications, Inc., 9 East 40th Street, 10th floor, New York, NY 10016. General articles on global business issues, including management, logistics, and site location.

International Studies Quarterly   Published quarterly with a biannual supplement by Blackwell Publishers, 238 Main Street, Cambridge, MA 02142. Scholarly papers on the varied political, economic, social, and cultural factors affecting societies.

The National Times   Published bimonthly by Krebs Media Corporation, 318 East 84th Street, New York, NY 10028. Presents interesting articles from American and international media.

NPQ (New Perspectives Quarterly)   Published quarterly by the Center for the Study of Democratic Institutions, 10951 West Pico Boulevard, 2nd floor, Los Angeles, CA 90064. Many articles dealing with international affairs by leading thinkers and practitioners.

Trade & Culture   Published bimonthly by Trade & Culture, Inc., 7127 Harford Road, Baltimore, MD 21234-7731. General articles as well as specialist pieces relating to over 20 trade zones around the world.

World Affairs: A Quarterly Review of International Problems   Published by the American Peace Society, 1319 18th Street, N.W., Washington, DC 20036-1802. Publishes articles illuminating issues of international conflict.

World Business Review   Published bimonthly by the World Business Research Center, Inc., P.O. Box 9401, North Little Rock, AR 72114. General articles on the world and U.S. economies.

World Press Review   Published monthly by the Stanley Foundation, 200 Madison Avenue, New York, NY 10016. Excerpts material from the press outside of the United States.

World Trade   Published monthly by Freedom Magazines, Inc., 17702 Cowan, Suite 100, Irvine, CA 92714-6035. General information on global economic topics, including technology, global transportation, and finance.

An International Code of Business Ethics*

Developed in 1994 by the Caux Round Table in Switzerland, these Principles for Business are believed to be the first international ethics code created from a collaboration of business leaders in Europe, Japan, and the United States.

These principles are rooted in two basic ethical ideals: *kyosei* and human dignity. The Japanese concept of *kyosei* means living and working together for the common good—enabling cooperation and mutual prosperity to coexist with healthy and fair competition. *Human dignity* refers to the sacredness or value of each person as an end, not simply a means, to the fulfillment of others' purposes or even the majority prescription.

The General Principles in Section 2 seek to clarify the spirit of *kyosei* and human dignity, while the specific Stakeholder Principles in Section 3 deals with their practical application.

Section 1. Preamble

The mobility of employment, capital, products, and technology is making business increasingly global in its transactions and its effects.

Laws and market forces are necessary but insufficient guides for conduct.

Responsibility for the policies and actions of business and respect for the dignity and interests of its stakeholders are fundamental.

Shared values, including a commitment to shared prosperity, are as important for a global community as for communities of smaller scale.

For these reasons, and because business can be a powerful agent of positive social change, we offer the following principles as a foundation for dialogue and action by business leaders in search of business responsibility. In so doing, we affirm the necessity for moral

---

*Source: *Business Ethics: The Magazine of Socially Responsible Business,* Vol. 10, no. 1, January–February 1996.

values in business decision making. Without them, stable business relationships and a sustainable world community are impossible.

Section 2: General Principles

Principle 1: The Responsibilities of Business: Beyond Shareholders Toward Stakeholders

The value of a business to society is the wealth and employment it creates and the marketable products and services it provides to consumers at a reasonable price commensurate with quality. To create such value, a business must maintain its own economic health and viability, but survival is not a sufficient goal.

Businesses have a role to play in improving the lives of all their customers, employees, and shareholders by sharing with them the wealth they have created. Suppliers and competitors as well should expect businesses to honor their obligations in a spirit of honesty and fairness. As responsible citizens of the local, national, regional, and global communities in which they operate, businesses share a part in shaping the future of those communities.

Principle 2: The Economic and Social Impact of Business: Toward Innovation, Justice, and World Community

Businesses established in foreign countries to develop, produce, or sell should also contribute to the social advancement of those countries by creating productive employment and helping to raise the purchasing power of their citizens. Businesses also should contribute to human rights, education, welfare, and vitalization of the countries in which they operate.

Businesses should contribute to economic and social development not only in the countries in which they operate, but also in the world community at large, through the effective and prudent use of resources, free and fair competition, and emphasis upon innovation in technology, production methods, marketing, and communications.

Principle 3: Business Behavior: Beyond the Letter of the Law Toward a Spirit of Trust

While accepting the legitimacy of trade secrets, businesses should recognize that sincerity, candor, truthfulness, the keeping of promises, and transparency contribute not only to their own credibility and stability but also to the smoothness and efficiency of business transactions, particularly on the international level.

Principle 4: Respect for Rules

To avoid trade frictions and to promote freer trade, equal conditions for competition, and fair equitable treatment for all participants, businesses should respect international and domestic rules. In addition, they should recognize that some behavior, although legal, may still have adverse consequences.

Principle 5: Support for Multilateral Trade

Businesses should support the multilateral trade systems of the GATT/World Trade Organization and similar international agreements. They should cooperate in efforts to promote the progressive and judicious liberalization of trade, and to relax those domestic measures that unreasonably hinder global commerce, while giving due respect to national policy objectives.

Principle 6: Respect for the Environment

A business should protect and, where possible, improve the environment, promote sustainable development, and prevent the wasteful use of natural resources.

Principle 7: Avoidance of Illicit Operations

A business should not participate in or condone bribery, money laundering or other corrupt practices: indeed, it should seek cooperation with others to eliminate them. It should not trade in arms, or other materials used for terrorist activities, drug traffic, or other organized crime.

Section 3: Stakeholder Principles

Customers

We believe in treating all customers with dignity, irrespective of whether they purchase our products and services directly from us or otherwise acquire them in the market. We therefore have a responsibility to:

- Provide our customers with the highest quality products and services consistent with their requirements;
- Treat our customers fairly in all aspects of our business transactions, including a high level of service and remedies for their dissatisfaction;
- Make every effort to ensure that the health and safety of our customers, as well as the quality of their environment, will be sustained or enhanced by our products and services;
- Assure respect for human dignity in products offered, marketing, and advertising; and
- Respect the integrity of the culture of our customers.

Employees

We believe in the dignity of every employee and in taking employee interests seriously. We therefore have a responsibility to:

- Provide jobs and compensation that improve workers' living conditions;
- Provide working conditions that respect each employee's health and dignity;
- Be honest in communications with employees and open in sharing information, limited only by legal and competitive restraints;
- Listen to and, where possible, act on employee suggestions, ideas, requests, and complaints;
- Engage in good faith negotiations when conflict arises;
- Avoid discriminatory practices and guarantee equal treatment and opportunity in areas such as gender, age, race, and religion;
- Promote in the business itself the employment of differently abled people in places of work where they can be genuinely useful;
- Protect employees from avoidable injury and illness in the workplace;
- Encourage and assist employees in developing relevant and transferable skills and knowledge; and
- Be sensitive to serious unemployment problems frequently associated with business decisions, and work with govern-

ments, employee groups, other agencies, and each other in addressing these dislocations.

Owners/Investors

We believe in honoring the trust our investors place in us. We therefore have a responsibility to:

+ Apply professional and diligent management in order to secure a fair and competitive return on our owners' investment;
+ Disclose relevant information to owners/investors subject only to legal requirements and competitive constraints;
+ Conserve, protect, and increase the owners/investors' assets; and
+ Respect owners/investors' requests, suggestions, complaints, and formal resolutions.

Suppliers

Our relationship with suppliers and subcontractors must be based on mutual respect. We therefore have a responsibility to:

+ Seek fairness and truthfulness in all of our activities, including pricing, licensing, and rights to sell;
+ Ensure that our business activities are free from coercion and unnecessary litigation;
+ Foster long-term stability in the supplier relationship in return for value, quality, competitiveness, and reliability;
+ Share information with suppliers and integrate them into our planning processes;
+ Pay suppliers on time and in accordance with agreed terms of trade;
+ Seek, encourage, and prefer suppliers and subcontractors whose employment practices respect human dignity.

Competitors

We believe that fair economic competition is one of the basic requirements for increasing the wealth of nations and, ultimately, for making possible the just distribution of goods and services. We therefore have a responsibility to:

- ◆ Foster open markets for trade and investment;
- ◆ Promote competitive behavior that is socially and environ-mentally beneficial and demonstrates mutual respect among competitors;
- ◆ Refrain from either seeking or participating in questionable payments or favors to secure competitive advantages;
- ◆ Respect both tangible and intellectual property rights; and
- ◆ Refuse to acquire commercial information by dishonest or unethical means, such as industrial espionage.

Communities

We believe that as global corporate citizens, we can contribute to such forces of reform and human rights as are at work in the com-munities in which we operate. We therefore have a responsibility in those communities to:

- ◆ Respect human rights and democratic institutions, and promote them wherever practicable;
- ◆ Recognize government's legitimate obligation to the society at large and support public policies and practices that promote human development through harmonious rela-tions between business and other segments of society;
- ◆ Collaborate with those forces in the community dedicated to raising the standards of health, education, workplace safety, and economic well-being;
- ◆ Promote and stimulate sustainable development and play a leading role in preserving and enhancing the physical environment and conserving the earth's resources;
- ◆ Support peace, security, diversity, and social integration;
- ◆ Respect the integrity of local cultures; and
- ◆ Be a good corporate citizen through charitable donations, educational and cultural contributions, and employee participation in community and civic affairs.

INDEX

A

Absolute truths, 217
Accountability, 52
  cases, 61–62, 67
  mapping, 114
  prerequisites for fostering, 197–198
Achieved leadership, 215
Acting by design, 175
Acting out, 24
Adaptability, 62–63
Adaptation, 60–61
  to other cultures, 208–209
Adler, Nancy J., 71–72, 74
Adventures of Working Abroad (Osland), 65
Adversarial relationships, 219
Affiliation, 220–221
Age of Paradox (Handy), 33
Age of the Network (Lipnack and Stamps), 28
Agility, 11–12
Alignment, 113
Allard, Leigh Ann Collins, 63n
Allen, Robert, 91
American Graduate School of International Management, 181
Amway, 204
Anheuser-Busch, 193
Anthony, Peter, 168
Armstrong, Larry, 58n
Arthur Andersen Company Global Practices Initiative, 23
Asea Brown Boveri, 5
Ashkenas, Ron, 3n, 6n, 29n
Asset and resource configuration, 90
Asset efficiencies, 16
Assumption clarification, 109
Attributed leadership, 215
Auden, W. H., 171
Authenticity, 225
Autonomy, 169
Avon Products, Inc., 5–6, 15–16, 55–56, 67, 68, 132, 135, 140–141, 144–145, 151–153, 186

B

Baliles, Gerald, 163
Bartlett, Christopher A., 88–90, 91–92, 169
Bechtel Corporation, 12, 62, 68
  Leadership Model, 136–138
  Toward 2000 initiative, 138
Becker, Ernest, 171–172
Beckhard, Richard, 79n, 86n
Beedham, Brian, 99–100
Behaviorism, 171
Bell Labs, 63
Benchmarking, 20
Bennis, Warren, 29
Best practices, 20
Birth and Death of Meaning (Becker), 171
Bonvillian, Gary, 210n
Boundaryless organization, 6–7
Bowman, Harry, 183
Brake, Terence, 5, 44
British Airways, 24
Brown, Tim, 156n
Browning, E. S., 65n
Burns, Greg, 61n
Business acumen
  cases, 57–59
  depth of field, 45–46
  entrepreneurial spirit, 46
  need for, 43
  over- or under-emphasis on, 69–70
  professional expertise, 46–47
  stakeholder orientation, 47
  total organizational astuteness, 47–48
Business clarification, 128
Business context, 103
Business environment analysis, 85–85
Business ethics, 241–246
Business units, 144–145
Business Week, 68

C

Calculation, 220

Other books of interest to you from Irwin Professional Publishing . . .

A MANAGER'S GUIDE TO GLOBALIZATION: SIX SKILLS FOR SUCCESS IN A CHANGING WORLD, REVISED EDITION

Dr. Stephen H. Rhinesmith

ISBN# 0-7863-0545-2

Have you joined perceptive managers, preparing now for the 21st century? Begin adapting yourself and your company for 2001 and beyond by reading the second edition of Stephen H. Rhinesmith's best-seller, *A Manager's Guide to Globaliza- tion.* You will learn skills needed to lead multicultural teams of diverse nationalities and acquire the international mindset necessary to move successfully beyond our borders.

GLOBAL IMPACT: AWARD WINNING PERFORMANCE PROGRAMS FROM AROUND THE WORLD

Sylvia B. Odenwald and William G. Matheny

ISBN# 0-7863-0958-X

American managers and trainers, long accustomed to searching within U.S. borders for solutions to complex performance challenges, are quite often finding the best answers across the globe. *Global Impact* serves as an "idea bank" for any professional looking for fresh perspectives and approaches to both new and age-old problems.

RIDING THE WAVES OF CULTURE: UNDERSTANDING DIVERSITY IN GLOBAL BUSINESS

Alfons Trompenaars

ISBN# 0-7863-0290-9

World-renowned consultant Trompenaars shows you how to build the skills, sensitivity, and cultural awareness needed to establish and sustain management effectiveness across cultural borders.